The Reflexive Novel

The Reflexive Novel

Fiction as Critique

Michael Boyd

Lewisburg
Bucknell University Press
London and Toronto: Associated University Presses

Associated University Presses, Inc.
4 Cornwall Drive
East Brunswick, NJ 08816

Associated University Presses Ltd
27 Chancery Lane
London WC2A 1NF, England

Associated University Presses
2133 Royal Windsor Drive
Unit 1
Mississauga, Ontario L5J 1K5, Canada

Library of Congress Cataloging in Publication Data

Boyd, Michael, 1943–
  The reflexive novel.

  Bibliography: p.
  Includes index.
  1. Fiction—20th century—History and criticism.
2. Fiction—Technique. I. Title.
PN3503.B65   1983   809.3'04   81-72029
ISBN 0-8387-5029-X

Printed in the United States of America

Contents

To Kay
Less than kin, more than kind

Preface

The modern novel defines itself in terms of its rejection of the conventions of formal realism. Recognizing that the relationship between reality and its representation in fictional discourse is problematic, the reflexive novel seeks to examine the act of writing itself, to turn away from the project of representing an imaginary world and to turn inward to examine its own mechanisms. Although the strategies for negotiating this inward turn will vary from novel to novel, all novels written in the reflexive mode seem to use similar techniques of alienation to disrupt their readers' willing suspension of disbelief. These readers soon learn that the story told counts for less than the telling; that language, which would attempt to efface itself in the traditional realistic novel, can have the power to overshadow what it purports to denote; and finally, that authors can become the major characters in the stories they tell and their writing the central action.

A central contention of this study is that the fiction of Conrad, Joyce, Woolf, Faulkner, Nabokov, Beckett, and others working in the reflexive mode offers the most sustained interrogation of the novel as an art form to be found in the writings of the present century. Such an interrogation should be seen as a species of critical activity that subverts the "normal" disjunction between creative and critical discourse or between literary and nonliterary uses of language. That novelists can give us fictional presentations of theories of fiction would seem to call into question distinctions that have long been considered among the givens of critical theory. Ours becomes the Age of Criticism not, fundamentally, because our major writers are critics but because they are novelists who have turned the novel itself into an instrument of critical inquiry.

This is not to deny that modern critical theory, especially that emanating from France, has influenced the substance if not the form of the readings that follow. If reflexive fiction may be said to imitate the form of the novel while it invades the realm of critical discourse, poststructuralist literary criticism may be said to imitate the form of critical discourse even while it seeks to expose its continuity with the fictional texts it examines. Such criticism, now called "deconstructive," although it

7

moves in the opposite direction, lends its support to reflexive fiction by seeking to cross that boundary between literary and nonliterary uses of language.

Nevertheless, one need only observe the privileged place occupied by Proust in so much recent French critical theory to recognize the historical priority of fiction as critique over what might now be called critique as fiction, as practiced by Barthes, Derrida, and the Yale deconstructionists. While I would not wish to regress to the notion that criticism is but a servant to literature—indeed, the major lesson taught by the reflexive novel is the primacy of theory, and, indeed, much postmodern fiction needs to catch up with postmodern criticism—I should like once again to celebrate the enormous achievement of the modern masters of the novel, to say that they have made possible current modes of seeing and writing.

The labor of reflexive fiction is a fait accompli, while the work of deconstructive criticism is only beginning. Although I read with great interest the experiments of Barthes, Derrida, de Man, Hartman, and Miller, I do not think that they have, as yet, developed a method as flexible, as subtle, as demanding as that of those novelists who transformed themselves into theoreticians of the novel. Still, I admire their audacity, their commitment to the reflexive project, and I feel obligated to explain my own relative methodological timidity in the readings that follow. I have tried—too successfully, no doubt—to supress in my own text those questions of the indeterminacy of self and language which constitute the reflexivity of the texts that I examine. The motive for these elisions is not hard to find: I wanted to finish this book. I felt that what I had to say could not wait for a way of saying it. J. Hillis Miller is no doubt correct in viewing the deconstructivist enterprise as a form of entrapment: "Rather than surveying the text with sovereign command from the outside, it remains caught within the activity in the text it traces."[1] If I seem to impersonate, in the familiar, old, new-critical fashion, the sovereign command of one who seeks artificial closure, or if I too abruptly and arbitrarily cut the chain of signifiers, it is simply because I wished to escape that labyrinth which is the text of the reflexive novel and return to tell, in the language we understand without believing, what I found there.

Through their shared recourse to the reflexive mode, such seemingly dissimilar novelists as Joseph Conrad and William Faulkner offer sustained interrogations of the realistic novel and find it unsuited to the task of representing the multiplicity of reality. In *Chance* and *Absalom, Absalom!* the past, which was to have provided the subject matter for these novels, is all but submerged by the conjectures and manipulations of narrators posing as historians. Author-surrogates, Marlow and Quentin Compson become the centers of the stories they tell. In spite of their common obsession with the past, that past remains hidden, or rather, becomes a fiction of the story-telling present.

By reading creatively and writing critically, Virginia Woolf constructs what is probably the most intense critique of realism to find expression within the reflexive mode. Through a process of reduction, *The Waves* dissolves each of the traditional aspects of fiction—plot, setting, and, most thoroughly, character—until what is left is simply "the completely expressive androgynous mind," not a mind external to the text but one whose thinking is a writing. A close reading of Woolf's *A Writer's Diary* reveals that *The Waves* should be viewed as a dramatization of the author's acts of composition.

In the writings of James Joyce, Samuel Beckett, and Vladimir Nabokov, reflexivity takes the form of a linguistic playfulness that is unable to conceal a sense of the demise of the mimetic tradition and its faith in language. In the works of these novelists, parody becomes an instrument of demystification, an elegiac echo that confirms the exhaustion of the past. If the reflexive tradition is founded on the notion that art is the only subject worthy of the artist, Joyce, Beckett, and Nabokov carry their researches one step farther and begin to examine their own myths of creation.

Because they do not seek to tell yet another story but to examine the story-telling process itself, reflexive novels must be seen as works of literary theory and criticism. The sharp distinctions we have devised between critical and creative modes of discourse are no longer valid in an age in which the writer's self-confidence—in relation to both self and craft—excludes the possibility of innocent or "natural" writing. Once the artificiality of fiction is asserted, once its devices are laid bare, our reading of all fiction—even that firmly rooted in realism—must change, as must our attitudes toward nonliterary language. In asserting the primacy of language as a mediator between "reality" and consciousness, the reflexive novel teaches us new ways to look at our fictions and our lives.

Some special note of gratitude and affection should be extended to Professor Robert Ackerman, who, in the early stages of my work, supplied me with an example of the kind of enthusiasm for literature and philosophy that would be necessary if I were to carry it through; to Professor Gary Davis, who told me what books to read; to Professor

Vincent Louthan, who read the manuscript of a friend when it was still unreadable; to Professor Annis Pratt, who was generous with ideas and strategies; to Professor John O. Lyons, who was always willing to talk about writers we both admired; to Professor Marja Wareheim, who reminded me that we write in order to be read; to the late Professor Paul L. Wiley, who directed my research and encouraged me when encouragement was needed, which was more often that I now care to remember; and finally, to Kay C. Tipsord, who read the work, talked it, edited it, and typed it, and whose presence on these pages is small recompense for her absence in my life.

NOTE

1. J. Hillis Miller, "The Critic as Host," in *Deconstruction and Criticism* (New York: The Seabury Press, 1979), p. 251.

Acknowledgments

Permission to quote from the following works is gratefully acknowledged:

From *Dubliners* by James Joyce. Copyright © 1967 by the Estate of James Joyce.

From *A Portrait of the Artist as a Young Man* by James Joyce. Copyright © 1916 by B. W. Huebsch, Inc.; renewed 1944 by Nora Joyce. Copyright © 1964 by the Estate of James Joyce. Reprinted by permission of Viking Penguin Inc.

From *More Pricks Than Kicks* by Samuel Beckett. Copyright 1934. ALL RIGHTS RESERVED. Reprinted by permission of Grove Press, Inc.

From *Murphy* by Samuel Beckett. First published 1938. ALL RIGHTS RESERVED. Reprinted by permission of Grove Press, Inc.

From *Watt* by Samuel Beckett. First published 1953. ALL RIGHTS RESERVED. Reprinted by permission of Grove Press, Inc.

From *The Aleph and Other Stories, 1933–1969* by Jorge Luis Borges, edited and translated by Norman Thomas di Giovanni in collaboration with the author. English translation copyright © 1968, 1969, 1970 by Emece Editores, S.A., and Norman Thomas di Giovanni. Reprinted by permission of the publisher, E. P. Dutton.

From *The Real Life of Sebastian Knight* by Vladimir Nabokov. Copyright © 1941, 1959 by New Directions Publishing Corporation. Reprinted by permission of New Directions.

From *Tyrants Destroyed and Other Stories* by Vladimir Nabokov. Copyright © 1975 by McGraw-Hill International, Inc. Used with the permission of McGraw-Hill Book Company.

From *Look at the Harlequins!* by Vladimir Nabokov. Copyright © by McGraw-Hill International, Inc. Used with the permission of McGraw-Hill Book Company.

From *Absalom, Absalom!* by William Faulkner. Copyright © 1936 © 1951 by Random House. Used by permission of Random House, Inc.

From *The Order of Things: An Archaeology of the Human Sciences* by Michel Foucault, translated by Alan Sheridan-Smith. Copyright © 1970 by Random House. Used by permission of Pantheon Books, a division of Random House, Inc.

The Reflexive Novel

1

The Reflexive Novel

If artists wish to speak of the process of artistic creation or of the relationship between art and life, they may express their ideas discursively, as Wallace Stevens does in *The Necessary Angel*. Or they may express these ideas directly in their creative work, dissolving the distinction between critical and imaginative modes of discourse, as Stevens does in his poetry. For modern artists the latter approach has often seemed more desirable, in part because it allows them the freedom of expressing their critical consciousness in the medium most available to them—the language of their art—and in part because it allows them to affirm in a most direct way the unique cognitive value of imaginative discourse.

For modern novelists, however, this desire to look closely, within a fictive context, at the theoretical foundations of their art comes into sharp conflict with the equally modern imperative to remove the teller from the tale. No longer permitting themselves periodical asides to the reader, interweaving critical comments about their art with fictional presentations, they often choose instead to make their self-consciousness an integral part of the fiction itself.

When a novel pauses to look at itself, to consider itself as a novel, it strikes what Albert Cook calls a reflexive attitude.[1] Occasionally, this attitude becomes so pronounced that it forms the theme of the novel, as in *The Life and Opinions of Tristram Shandy*, *Les Faux-Monnayeurs*, or *The Waves*. Part of an impressive tradition in the history of the novel, these works share an interest in several conflicting demands, demands that can generally be subsumed under the conflict between life and art. Of course this conflict is implicit in the work of any novelist who wishes both to show the complexity of life and to structure that complexity into a work of art. The reflexive novel is distinguished by its practice of exposing the conflict, of allowing the process of making a novel out of a given fictive situation to overshadow the situation itself.[2]

15

I propose to clarify the nature of this tradition by describing some of its defining characteristics. Such a description would provide the most meaningful definition of reflexivity and perhaps enable us to see particular works in new ways. Since E. D. Hirsh, Jr., has shown that "an interpreter's preliminary generic conception of the text is constitutive of everything that he subsequently understands, and that this remains the case until the generic conception is altered,"[3] such a description can actually distort our perception of particular works if it fails to avoid the pigeonholing techniques that nullify much genre-criticism. The defining criteria, therefore, will be described in terms of problems dealt with rather than in terms of solutions offered, in the hope that such a formulation will provide a broad basis from which to examine particular works.

Reflexivity can be used to describe an element in a work or to describe the controlling compositional idea behind the entire work. In this respect it resembles satire, which can be used to classify a work generically or to describe an attitude found in a part of a work. It may be the case that all novels are at least partially reflexive,[4] but in the readings that follow this introductory chapter I shall be dealing exclusively with novels that I feel can be most completely understood as belonging to a specific type of novel by virtue of the centrality of the defining characteristics described below. It is, however, the double nature of the reflexive—as *element* and as *type*—that makes this kind of novel an important commentary on all novels.

I should also not wish the notion of genre or type to be confused with a classification of works of literature based on subject matter—the novel of the artist, the college novel, the American divorce novel, and the like. I hope that the defining criteria I use may be viewed as both formal and thematic. This should follow from the fact that these novels themselves attempt to deal with the form/content problem as it confronts both the novelist and the critic.

REAL FICTIONS AND FICTITIOUS REALISM

i

That *reductio ad absurdum* of the novel form, *The Life and Opinions of Tristram Shandy*, achieves its objectives—the questioning and parodying of the new literary form devised by Defoe, Richardson, and Fielding—not so much by rejecting the fundamental rules of literary realism as by following those rules up to and beyond the point at which they seem to claim that literature can capture life in all its fullness. "So assured, indeed, is this mastery of realistic presentation that, had it been applied to the usual purposes of the novel, Sterne would probably have been the supreme figure among eighteenth-century novelists. But, of course, *Tristram Shandy* is not so much a novel as a parody of a novel. . . ."[5] By defining the novel in terms of its "formal realism" and by acknowledging Sterne as a master of the techniques of realism, Ian Watt would seem to be forced to conclude that the author of *Tristram Shandy* was a great novelist. In fact, only a few pages of *The Rise of the Novel* are devoted to Sterne, whose epistemological skepticism, expressed through parody, is used as grounds for excluding him from serious consideration as a novelist.

The book Sterne mentions most often, *Don Quixote*, is generally considered to be the first novel. And yet few readers have failed to notice that the book could just as easily have been called an antinovel, *if* we could forget chronology for a moment and see Cervantes's work as a critique of those realistic novels yet to appear. *Don Quixote* parodies not only those romances that it replaces but also those novels which will follow it, follow it without questioning, as *Quixote* questions, their status with regard to the reality they purport to represent.

What is realism in fiction that it must ultimately reject works central to its tradition because they look too closely at the aesthetic and epistemological foundations of that tradition? What are the goals of literary realism and what is the point at which the pursuit of those goals can transform a novel into a parody of a novel?

ii

The contradiction implied by Watt's rejection of *Tristram Shandy* points to a central characteristic of realism: Realists wish to "capture reality and bring it back alive,"[6] but they also want to place it, once caught, in a cage; they want to present it under ideal conditions. As J. P. Stern points out, even the most naive realist seldom confuses representation with reduplication.[7] Realists will select "the best perspective, which will get all the relevant details into the picture."[8] It is curious that the earliest critics of realism attacked it on platonic grounds, insisting that it did not do justice to the essence of things, "that it sacrificed a higher and more permanent for a lower, more mundane reality."[9] What is the belief in a "best perspective" but another way of distinguishing, platonically, between appearance and reality, of reasserting the essential, the absolute?

Although they often pretend to deny the contributions of the self in the act of perception, realists usually recognize the impossibility of "perception in a vacuum"[10] and its formal equivalent, a literature without style. Even Watt recognizes and catalogues the properties of a "formal realism" that may or may not distort "reality"—whatever that is.

Nevertheless, in spite of some falling away from the goal of presenting life as it is, realists do aspire to establish a finer correspondence between life and literature than do artists who see their art more in terms of its conventions or as a making rather than a matching, to use a distinction formulated by E. H. Gombrich.[11] The progression toward the objectives of verisimilitude in all the arts is not an illusion but a progression toward the idea that the unbroken illusion is the aim of art.

For Stern, no contradiction is implied by the desire to capture and to cage reality. Realism is seen as a compromise between matching and making, subject and object, fantasy and journalism—the achievement of a middle distance.[12]

And yet, in spite of the general agreement as to the limitations of realism in presenting life as it is, practicing realists often continue to pretend that their art is not a compromise but a slice of life—not the whole of life, perhaps, but a selection that reveals a one-to-one relationship with the experience to which it refers. Realism pretends to be what it is not. Realism is a form of bad faith.[13]

iii

Another contradiction implied by the aesthetics of realism is its failure to be concerned about the nature of reality. Although their characters may be uncertain about what is really real, realistic novelists never are: reality is simply the given. According to Stern, "realism doesn't ask whether the world is real, but it occasionally asks what happens to persons who think that it isn't."[14] Realism is seen to be "philosophically incurious and epistemologically naive," denying that "in this world there is more than one reality, and that this denial is in need of proof."[15] This attitude must create problems for modern antirealists when they read a realistic novel. Do they find themselves taking sides *against* the novelist with certain fictional madmen who dare to wonder if the world is real? Or dare to wonder what "real" means?

If the realist pretends that fiction is life, the antirealist *knows* that life is a fiction. (Antirealists are themselves involved in a contradiction here: How can they disavow all claim to reality and at the same time claim knowledge of that reality? Their one defense—which is at the same time their *raison d'être*—is that they know that they cannot know.) For the antirealist, reality is protean, a mental construct bereft of the certitude given by the belief in any universal laws of the mind. Everyone is a novelist.

For the antirealist, the realist's epistemological complacency is enough to account for both the achievements and the failures of realism. Like the man of faith, realists are freed of the necessity of beginning at the beginning. They may travel more freely in fictional worlds because they have no doubts about origins and ends. Persons who doubt are more careful, less productive. Small truths are their domain. And yet they cannot envy the man of faith, even if he is correct as well as carefree. Like the unearned success of Plato's blind man who takes the right road by accident, the realist's success is a fluke and always a surprise to those who wish to know what they know.

All writers reacting against realism are essentially concerned with the question of the nature of reality. Therefore, there is some justice in their claim to the title of neorealists.[16] By their refusal to say more than they know, by their insistence that *reality* is a problematic concept, they come far closer to the methods and conclusions of that contemporary arbiter of truth, modern science, than do the proponents of realism.[17] The problem of terminology here arises from the double use of the concept of reality to describe both literature and life. This confusion has always been encouraged by the realists, since it obviously works to their advantage. Perhaps their opponents would do well to refuse to contribute to this confusion by restricting their use of the term to literature and accepting the title of antirealist.

iv

There are as many different varieties of antirealism as there are of realism—perhaps more. All that they have in common is their rejection of the basic tenets of mimesis in art, tenets that have to a large degree dominated both the production and reception of art since the Renaissance. And yet the violence of this rejection, the fact that antirealism is almost single-mindedly concerned with attacking and questioning a powerful literary tradition, makes it even more strongly tied to that tradition. As Gabriel Josipovici has observed, antirealism is perhaps more conscious of its relation to tradition than any other artistic revolution in history.[18] It is possible, then, to distinguish between different forms of antirealism by noting their different attitudes toward realism. Such distinctions, once made, should isolate the specific mode of antirealism that I call the reflexive.

If we recognize that the principal feature of literary realism is its desire to create worlds like the one in which we live, we can recognize that works often seen as rejections of realism are, in fact, simply presenting different versions of where we live. Both Mr. Bennett and Virginia Woolf want us to believe in Mrs. Brown. To the extent that some modern novelists wish to portray the life of the mind as the true reality, they too belong to the tradition of realism. Impressionism and expressionism are disguised forms of mimesis. They differ from the tradition only in terms of their choice of object to be represented. It is only when the search for a new language in which to portray the life of the mind leads to an awareness of the artificiality of all invented languages that the various forms of psychological fiction prepare the way for a rejection of verisimilitude as a norm. By freeing the writer from the restrictions of everyday language, the novel that pretends to render the stream of consciousness inevitably forces upon us a sense of the strangeness of words, and this awareness will lead quite naturally to a focusing on the words themselves rather than on the mental reality they purport to represent.

The shift from world to mind and finally out of mind to the words on the page is most strikingly displayed in the writings of James Joyce. While it forces from the reader the assent to illusion, the willing suspension of disbelief, *Ulysses* also points to itself, makes us equally conscious of the words that provoke our assent. Dublin, Bloom's mind, Joyce's words—these all exist between the covers of his book, a book that must be seen as the culmination of a tradition and the beginning of the reaction against that tradition.

v

The psychological novel sought to retain the objectives of realism while redefining what is most real to human consciousness, but language, once liberated, often left the world altogether. Words were often used to point to a reality beyond both thought and action. But because symbols are always symbols *of* something, the attempt to turn prose fiction into symbolic poetry is often grounded in an acceptance of the basic beliefs of realism. The language of this fiction—notwithstanding its strangeness, its poetry—is still used as a means rather than as an end in itself. Words become instruments for pursuing a reality that eludes both observation and introspective insight.

While the world of symbolic fiction may not obviously resemble any world of common experience, may even contain elements of the fantastic, it nevertheless points to something beyond itself, takes itself seriously as a representation of life. Readers need only convert the unknown into the known to see that they are at home in this world. The equations of symbolic fiction may be complex, may avoid simple allegory, may even be irreducible, resisting all paraphrase, but ultimately they seek "to capture reality and bring it back alive."

These fictions point to earlier modes of narrative, which sought to abstract from experience that which had ultimate meaning. Erich Auerbach compares this type of narrative, which he sees embodied in the Old Testament story of Abraham and Isaac, to the circumstantial realism of Homer, seeing both styles as basic types that recur in the history of narrative art.[19] Robert Scholes and Robert Kellogg, in *The Nature of Narrative*, seek to follow this basic distinction by dividing narratives into empirical and fictional modes, the former category subdivided into historical and mimetic writing and the latter into romantic and didactic tales: "While empirical narrative aims at one or another kind of truth, fictional narrative aims at either beauty or goodness."[20] Another way of phrasing this distinction would be to say that empirical narrative deals somehow with the actual while fictional narrative is primarily concerned with the ideal. Insofar as symbolic fiction points to the ideal rather than the objects of the senses, it may be seen to be in opposition to empirical forms such as history or realistic fiction. Yet insofar as it too wishes to make a statement, albeit oblique, about the nature of reality, symbolic fiction is compatible with the epistemological naiveté of literary realism.

Of course, the use of symbols can only be considered in terms of degree. Most great novels in the realist tradition make use of the symbolic properties of poetry, incorporating them into the narrative to serve their own ends. Ursula Brumm, however, has noted that the realistic novel does not use symbols in the same way as does the symbolic novel:

> The outstanding difference between such "realistic" symbols and the symbols of modern literature is that, unlike the latter, the former are not compact images that make a single strong sensual impression, but are often extensive and not easily delimitable.[21]

Brumm also points out that the symbolist, focusing on symbols that are not grounded in any concrete situation, real or imagined, "dematerializes the world, and in so doing deindividualizes it, deprives it of specific characteristics."[22] It is possible that this process of abstraction will come to affect not only the realist's material world but also the transcendent world of the symbolist, in which case the reader, rather than being forced out of a world of things and into a world of ideas, will be returned to the book and the words it contains.

vi

Another response to the failure of realism to meet the needs of modern writers and their audiences—perhaps the most extreme response of all— is the rejection of fiction altogether and the espousal of the aims of journalism, biography, autobiography, and history. This literature differs from most nonfiction writing of the past in that it consciously uses the techniques and conventions of the realistic novel to examine existing persons and situations. Often novelists by profession, such writers perhaps find the shifting reality behind contemporary events more fascinating than any imagined reality.[23] The "new journalism," the "nonfiction novel," the thinly disguised autobiography masking as fiction are all examples of the novelist's incursion into realms of fact usually explored by historians, journalists, and biographers. Obviously, the criteria by which we judge such performances must be even more rigorously truth-oriented than those we use for the most realistic of novels. Theories of plausibility or even probability are no longer acceptable. Such works, unless their aims are otherwise qualified, ask to be judged as accurate accounts of what happened, and they are subject to the same tests of verification as other reports of actual occurrences.

These works need not betray a rejection of the methods of literary realism. In discussing Norman Mailer's *The Armies of Night*, David Lodge notes that this example of the nonfiction novel "implies no disillusionment on the author's part with the novel as a literary form; on the contrary, it reaffirms the primacy of that form as a mode of exploring and interpreting experience."[24] What *is* challenged by this work, however, is the advisability of fabrication. While nonfiction novelists retain the liberty of technique of the fiction writer, at the same time they owe their final allegiance to the facts.

Obviously, the reader's attitude toward such works as Agee's *Let Us Now Praise Famous Men*, Capote's *In Cold Blood*, Frank Conroy's *Stop-Time*, or Mailer's *The Executioner's Song* is quite different from his attitude toward traditional realistic fiction.[25] The realistic novel always pretended to be nonfiction; the nonfiction novel, however, does not ask readers to suspend their disbelief but to test the work against other empirical evidence and to discover that the writer is working with facts and not fictions.

Finally, in spite of their dissatisfaction with fiction, nonfiction novelists, like realists, use language to point to a reality that lies beyond the printed page. One points to the events we can read about in our daily newspapers, while the other to events, though imagined, that are plausible and perhaps descriptive of the truths of the human heart.

The importance of the nonfiction novel when it is considered as a reaction against the realistic tradition is really determined by the questions it puts to that tradition. If realists are sincere about their desire to "capture life," why do they tolerate invention? "What invented story can compete with 'true facts'—of concentration camp stories, the Battle of Stalingrad or the richness and constructed subtlety of any well-constructed monograph?" asks Nathalie Sarraute.[26] When fiction *pretends* to be something else (i.e., history, autobiography) it seems to lose its own *raison d'être*: Why should a writer attempt to duplicate the achievements of other fields? Finally—and this question should be considered along with the other contradictions of the realistic aesthetic already noted—why does the realistic novel insist on both its mimetic inventions *and* its autonomy as a work of art? The nonfiction novel is instructive on this point because it recognizes the contradiction of a "caged reality." The frame in which journalists seek to place their work is constantly broken. Their art not only is used to represent, to imitate life, but also is caught up in the texture of life itself. The Mailer who writes of the march on the Pentagon is, after all, the same Mailer who goes to jail. Both his toads and his garden are real.

vii

Psychological fiction, symbolism, and the nonfiction novel may all be seen as reactions to the realistic tradition, as forms of antirealism if we accept the notions of "middle distance" and compromise—following Stern, Scholes, and Lodge—as the defining characteristic of the realistic novel. But we also noted that each of these forms shared with realism a tendency to point to some "object"—psychological, transcendental, or actual—outside of the work of literature itself. At the same time, these forms seem to suggest the possibility of a more radical kind of antirealism, a literature that turns back on itself, a literature that instead of simply relocating reality—placing it in the mind, in some ideal world, or in actual, everyday events—challenges the basic assumptions underlying *any* equation between literature and life. Scholes and Kellogg tell us that "meaning, in a work of narrative art, is a function of the relationship between two worlds: the fictional world created by the author and the 'real' world, the apprehendable universe. When we say we 'understand' a narrative, we mean that we have found a satisfactory relationship between these two worlds."[27] Fiction that looked at itself, that was reflexive, would not be creating yet another fictional world that needed to be related to the "real" world: it would take as its "object" the *relationship* between "real" and fictional worlds. It would be a species of criticism in fictional form. Call it metafiction. Or call it the reflexive novel, the novel about the novel—onanistically or perhaps incestuously using its own imaginative energy to sustain itself.

Instead of presenting a fictional situation requiring of the reader a "willing suspension of disbelief," the reflexive novel focuses on the fiction-making process itself: it openly examines the conventions of the realistic novel and asks the reader to do likewise. Although it often parodies traditional realism, its parody is an analytical tool for self-examination. Its relationship to the tradition it attacks, then, is much more complex than that of any of the narrative forms thus far examined. Unlike those other forms of anti-realism, the reflexive novel does not simply replace one notion of reality with another. It elucidates the conditions that must be met before we can speak of the relationship between art and life. In order to do this, the reflexive novelist must work closely with the assumptions of traditional realism. Gabriel Josipovici goes so far as to identify this concern with tradition as a central feature of modernism in general. In doing so, he is also suggesting the importance of the reflexive attitude in all modernist work: "There is no better way of defining the achievement of Picasso, Stravinsky or Eliot than to say that it is an exploration both of the medium in which they are working and of the traditional exploration of that medium."[28] Both types of exploration require a highly developed historical consciousness about the artistic possibilities of the medium in which one works.

Inevitably, the self-conscious writer makes the reader equally conscious of the mind behind the fiction. It is tempting to suggest that when the reality of the fiction-making process is substituted for the illusions of character and plot, when artifice is acknowledged as artifice, a new, nonillusory reality appears—the real fiction. Virginia Woolf's comment on *Tristram Shandy* perhaps does justice to that formidable parody of a novel: "The usual ceremonies and conventions which keep reader and writer at arm's length disappear. We are as close to life as we can be."[29]

MAKING STRANGE

i

Realists want to make "life" the object of their representations. They want their words to evoke the feelings of actual experience. But not quite, because they know that we tend to lose interest in mere life. If we didn't, there would seem to be little reason to read novels or to write them. Art, even an art dedicated to the representation of reality, wants to present us with an extraordinary experience, an experience that does not duplicate life but that arouses in us a higher level of attention than we are willing to give to most of the events of our daily existence.

Realists are faced with the difficult task of both representing these events and, at the same time, liberating them from the tedium of the unfamiliar. The conquest of reality creates new dangers for the realists:

Once they have acquired the ability to make their readers say, "Yes, this is life," they must guard against putting those readers to sleep. Wallace Stevens tells us that "one's grand flights, one's Sunday baths,/One's tootings at the wedding of the soul/Occur as they occur,"[30] but our moment-by-moment experience contains more Mondays than Sundays and is seldom anything to shout about. Geoffrey Hartman has written that now, following the conquest of reality, it is the familiar world that must be saved—saved from familiarity:[31] "A great novel does not breed familiarity; a bad novel is simply one that betrays the mystery, rapes the past, and lets us pass too quickly to another person or mind."[32] Every writer would echo André Gide's polite request to his reader: "Please do not understand me too quickly."

The Russian formalists have defined art in terms of its ability to separate itself from ordinary experience by "making strange": "The technique of art is to make 'unfamiliar' objects, to make forms difficult, to increase the difficulty and length of perception because the process of perception is an aesthetic end in itself and must be prolonged. *Art is a way of experiencing the artfulness of an object; the object itself is not important*.[33] Although theories that emphasize form rather than content tend to be critical of realism, it is interesting to note that the concept of "making strange" has been most prominently employed in discussing the work of Tolstoy. This suggests that defamiliarization is a property of all great art, realist as well as its alternatives.

Although he does not acknowledge the connection in his writings, Morse Peckham has attempted to support this axiomatic truth of the formalists with the discoveries of experimental psychology. Such discoveries indicate that "any perceptual experience is organized by a preexistent pattern in the mind . . . . As far as human beings are concerned, experience is not chaotic and cannot be, at least for long."[34] From this observation Peckham concludes that any theory of art that asserts that "experience comes to us in a chaotic blizzard of phenomena," and that from this chaos art makes order, is wrong.[35] Ordinary experience is already ordered—indeed, this is what makes it ordinary: Those preexistent perceptual patterns, call them habits of mind, make it possible for us to assimilate any new experience into the categories of thought we *bring* to the experience. What this means, of course, is that it is a natural tendency of the human mind to overlook the uniqueness of any experience, to force all new phenomena into previously acquired categories. The mind does this so that we may act without constantly reflecting on the uniqueness of every perception.

Given this understanding of the laws of ordinary experience, Peckham sees art as a means of assuaging "man's rage for chaos," his desire to break out of the confines of his conceptual *stasis*. The artist "presents the unpredicted; he offers the experience of disorientation."[36] Living every moment of our lives in this state of disorientation would render action impossible. But art recognizes the pathological dangers of a life totally committed to orderly experience: "It is the damaged personality, it is the neurotic, it is above all the psychotic whose behavior exhibits an uncontrollable and passionate rage for order, psychogenic death," the desire for death being "merely the desire for the most perfect order we can imagine, for total insulation from all perceptual disparities."[37]

Both formalists and behavioralists agree that art achieves its purpose only by making the familiar seem strange or by disorienting our experience in such a way that we are able to reawaken our sense of the uniqueness of individual acts of perception. For the realist, this means art must distort even as it attempts to represent. But what if the realist's customary methods of distortion become themselves habits of mind? If the techniques of making an object seem unfamiliar become themselves familiar—as they must, since reading itself is an experience subject to the assimilative and ordering actions of the mind—then new techniques of defamiliarization must be devised if art is to continue to free man from what Stevens calls the "malady of the quotidian."[38]

Imagine an art devoted exclusively to exploring its own strangeness, to exposing its discontinuity with ordinary experience, while at the same time asserting its own very real existence. Such an art has been elaborately imagined and to a certain extent realized by the theory and practice of Bertolt Brecht.

ii

Brecht's concept of "alienation" (*Verfremdung*) is a translation of the Russian formalist's notion of "making strange" (*ostrannenie*).[39] The similarity between the two concepts is strengthened by Brecht's own theoretical writings. Explaining the A-effect, he says: "What is obvious is in a certain sense made incomprehensible but this is only in order that it may then be made all the easier to comprehend. Before familiarity can turn into awareness the familiar must be stripped of its inconspicuousness; we must give up the assumption that the object in question needs no explanation."[40] Brecht's debt to the formalists is even more apparent when he attempts to show the practical application of the concept of alienation. In describing the actual performance, he says that it is the actor's object "to appear strange and even surprising to the audience. He achieves this by looking strangely at himself and his work. As a result everything put forward by him has a touch of the amazing.

Everyday things are thereby raised above the level of the obvious and the automatic."[41] It seems clear that for Brecht Russian formalism offered a theoretical justification for initiating a program of non-Aristotelian, nonillusionist drama—what Brecht called "epic theater."

One of the most interesting paradoxes of twentieth-century literature has been the opposing movements of drama toward narrative forms ("epic theater") and of narrative toward dramatic forms (*"show, don't tell"*). It is as if both drama and narrative were determined to be what they were least equipped, formally, to be. Because it employs real people moving in real space, drama cannot but show. Because it employs words and only words, narrative cannot but tell. As a representation of life, drama would always seem to have the advantage over narrative. It seems strange, then, that the strongest impulse toward anti-realism should appear in the theater.

What Brecht adds to the formalist idea is an intellectualization of the aesthetic experience. The praise of the unfamiliar for its own sake is not, after all, unlike the romantic predilection for the strange and exotic. Brecht discards the romantic overtones of Russian formalism by stressing the *critical* nature of an act of perception that is deprived of the safeguards of familiarity. The new audience must be a thinking audience, even if, in order to think, the spectator must give up the emotional satisfactions of empathy and illusion.

Of course, for Brecht this renewal of the critical activity is placed in the service of Marxism, and it would certainly be a distortion of his theories of discuss them apart from the social and political ends they were meant to serve. But as I noted before, nonillusionism in art tends to imply an epistemological skepticism, a skepticism that, in itself, cannot provide the artist with grounds for social and political commitment. Nor can Brecht's theater be said to create the kind of politically conscious audience that he had envisioned. Rather than examining Brecht's theories in relation to his political views, which would involve a comparison of two kinds of alienation—*Verfremdung* and *Entfremdung*—I prefer to consider these theories simply as one kind of alternative to illusionism. It seems clear that Brecht's influence should be finally measured in terms of his aesthetic innovations rather than by his attempt to establish an effective mode of political drama.[42]

All of Brecht's innovations may be seen as attempts to remove "the fourth wall": the spectator must never be allowed to think that what he is watching is anything more than a play. Actors are not to be confused with the characters they represent. Brecht learned a very stylized technique of acting from the Chinese theater, which he sought to incorporate into the productions of his own plays. In addition, the structure of the

well-made play is broken down into a series of episodes. The element of
spectacle is encouraged. The sources of light and music are made visible
to the members of the audience, who are encouraged to adopt a detached
attitude toward the performance they are witnessing.

Without diminishing our sense of Brecht's originality, Lionel Abel has
attempted to relate Brecht to a tradition in the theater that goes back to
the Renaissance. According to Abel, Shakespeare, Calderón, Marlowe,
and Molière all offer us a "metatheater" that stands in opposition to both
tragedy and illusionism.[43] Metaplays clearly indicate that their characters are of the playwright's invention. The truth of such plays derives not
from existing characters and situations but from the presentation of "the
reality of the imagination."[44] Abel's most convincing demonstration is
his reading of *Hamlet*, in which he sees the hero's philosophizing about
action as "a projection of the playwright's difficulty in making his hero
tragic."[45] The inability to write tragedy is seen to arise from two conditions present in the Renaissance—the artist's self-consciousness about
his art and his disbelief in any cosmic or natural order.[46] Whether one
agrees with Abel's notion of the Renaissance or not, these two conditions
clearly define Brecht's position in the twentieth century.

Abel defines metatheater in terms of its espousal of two ideas: "The
world is a stage, and life is a dream."[47] Most of the difficulty he has in
attributing these beliefs to Brecht could be resolved if he would qualify
his definition by recognizing that metatheater proceeds *as if* the world is
a stage and life is a dream. For Brecht the innate theatricality of life is
not a belief but a working hypothesis. The skeptic, it seems to me, is
always obligated to doubt the truth of his own skepticism. Brecht knew,
perhaps, that his communism was a refutation of the notion that the
world is a stage and life is a dream, but he did not allow this knowledge
to restrict either his political activity or the development of his dramatic
theory. In a sense, the life and opinions of Bertolt Brecht demonstrate
both the continuities and discontinuities of life and art.

iii

It should be possible to examine the ways in which the reflexive novel
employs techniques of alienation comparable to those of Brechtian
drama. The novel-within-the-novel will replace the play-within-a-play as
a means of indicating the artificial nature of a particular work. The
characters in a novel will seem "unreal," like those actors on the stage
who refuse to take their roles seriously. The novelist will return to the
liberties of narrative and reject drama. The readers of such fiction, like
Brecht's audience, will be encouraged to become critically detached

from the action. At the same time they will find it necessary to take on a more active role, to become involved at the level of artistic process rather than passively receiving the artistic product.

In addition to adapting Brechtian techniques to the novel, the reflexive novelist will invent new techniques to shatter the illusions of realism. The intrusive narrator will take on new roles. Footnotes and rough drafts will be incorporated into the fiction. The reflexive novelist will use nonnovelistic material, space-time dislocations, collage, alternative endings, and parody to remind the reader that a novel is something made. Language will be used in such a way that it calls attention to itself.

What will be made strange in this manner will be not only the conventions of the traditional novel but also the conventions of perception in general. The self-consciousness of the artist about inherited literary forms and about habitual modes of perception will, it is hoped, be transferred to the reader. The reflexive novel will then be seen as not only changing our attitudes toward the world but also changing the ways in which those attitudes are formed.

CHARACTERS AND PERSONS

> *Madame Bovary* is based on no actual occurrence. It is a totally *fictitious* story; it contains none of my feelings and no details from my life. The illusion of truth (if there is one) comes, on the contrary, from the book's impersonality. It is one of my principles that a writer should not be his own theme. An artist must be in his work like God in creation, invisible and all-powerful; he should be everywhere felt and nowhere seen.
>
> I am Madame Bovary.
>
> —Gustave Flaubert

i

Whether they concentrate on their characters' speech and actions or try to render the quality of their inner lives, the realists want us to believe that their characters have an extraliterary existence, a life of their own. They want us to forget "that literature is language, that stories and the places and people in them are merely made of words."[48] They want us to think of their characters as persons.

When reflexive novelists draw characters for us, it is usually their intention to force us to renounce the game of make-believe we play when

we read novels. Within their fictions, characters often become dehumanized counters, abstractions that are manipulated with the same
freedom as other nonhuman elements of the novel like plot, setting, or
symbol.

Within recent years, criticism of the novel has divided into two
camps—those critics who, following the methods of the "new criticism"
in dealing with poetry, focus on the language of fiction, and those who
find *character* the central feature of the novel. The latter group may
generally be seen as reacting both against critical techniques that fail to
do justice to their favorite realists and against modern novelists who no
longer seem concerned with adding to the number of fictional personages
in literature.[49]

Insofar as reflexive novelists write about the various *relationships*
between real and fictional worlds, they find both positions interesting
and representative of different ways of looking at literature and life. But
insofar as they reject the assumptions of realism, they tend to write
novels that are highly language-conscious yet skeptical of the power of
language to create a reality. Since they want to deal with the process of
creation itself and, by extension, with the acts of the imagination, they
tend either to create characters that are mere surrogates for the author or
to undermine the reality of all their characters and thereby draw attention to themselves. Both techniques serve to alienate readers insofar as
they force them to perceive all experience in terms of the act of writing.
To be is to write, and to be a character is to be an assortment of words on
a page.

ii

The aesthetic motives behind the modern novelist's approval of impersonal narration are many and varied, but it seems safe to assume that the
absence of the author was felt to enhance the presence of invented
characters. In other words, authorial intrusions were seen as disruptive
of the illusion of reality, which the realist wishes, at all costs, to maintain. To the extent that the removal of the teller from the tale is a defining
characteristic of modern novels, such novels constitute a continuation
rather than a rejection of the realist tradition. No one would deny that the
modern novel—by denying itself the privilege of omniscience and commentary, by "showing" instead of "telling"—has created some of the
most memorable characters in literature.

But even as they sought to present an unmediated vision of life,
modern novelists became more and more concerned with the problems of
their art. It is as if their voluntary movement toward silence made them

aware of all the questions they had forgotten to ask. Describing this predicament and one form its resolution takes, Sharon Spencer says that "it is as though the twentieth-century novelist, having been forced into concealment by the technical refinements introduced by Flaubert, James, Conrad, and Ford Madox Ford, is finding a way to assert himself back into the novel in disguised form as an artist-creator."[50] We immediately think of Stephen Dedalus and Herr Aschenbach, Marcel and Molloy; our century has no shortage of artist-heroes, and the *künstlerroman* is still a popular mode of fiction.

I should point out that the novel of the artist need not be reflexive, need not concern itself with the problem of the relation between reality and its representation. More often than not the novel of the artist emphasizes the artist's development within society and more or less takes the problems of art itself for granted. Stephen Dedalus is allowed to struggle with a poem, to present his aesthetic theory in *A Portrait of the Artist as a Young Man*, but these episodes are subordinated to the larger pattern of Stephen's development. One may, of course, expand Stephen's theory until it becomes a reflexive statement about Joyce's work as a whole, but to do so is to remove it from its original context.[51]

Although Maurice Beebe, in his study of the novel of the artist, concludes that "with Joyce . . . the archetype of the artist became firmly established, and later contributors to the genre have done little to alter that image,"[52] it would seem to be more accurate to say that the increasingly reflexive attitudes displayed by such novelists as Nabokov and Beckett have carried us much further toward a realization of the problems of art than Joyce ever intended to go. In Beckett, especially, we find a reduction of being to writing, an intensification of concern with the act of composition that is diametrically opposed to Joyce's easy faith in art and language. Beckett's parodies of Joyce's artist-god are more than entertainments. They alter our image of the artist.

In addition to the many artist-figures that are found in the modern novel, there are also those characters whose activities may said to represent symbolically the practice of writing. Conrad's Marlow, Quentin in *Absalom, Absalom!*, Mann's Felix Krull, and Nabokov's Luzhin in *The Defense* all illustrate ways in which artistic creation can be metaphorically discussed in terms of seamen's yarns, historical research, crime, and chess. In addition to establishing a continuity between art and other exercises of the imagination, such characters make possible new discoveries about the artistic process as these writers explore all the implications of their metaphors.

Yet another way in which authors may negotiate a return to their work is outlined by Nathalie Sarraute, when she notes that an anonymous "I," who is at once all and nothing, and who as often as not is but the reflection of the author himself, has usurped the role of the hero, occupying the place of honor. The other characters, being deprived of their own existence, are reduced to the status of visions, dreams, nightmares, illusions, reflections, quiddities or dependents of this all-powerful "I."[53]

Citing Proust, Genet, Rilke, Celine, and Sartre as practitioners of this narrative device, Sarraute rejects the notion that such a method indicates an adolescent egocentricity.[54] Rather than subscribing to solipsism, such a narrator simply makes use of the essential subjectivity of all experience to focus the reader's interest on a mind that, although it exists in the novel, is engaged in the process of structuring experience. Such "characters"—if we may call them that, since they have no identity apart from their function as a container for various impressions—deprive the other characters in the novel of all autonomous existence.[55]

Sarraute sees this device as a means by which the author attempts "to dispossess the reader and entice him, at all costs, into the author's territory."[56] Although the narrator should not be completely identified with the author, at least the illusions of realism have been replaced by a one-to-one relationship, a dialogue between narrator and reader. Such a dialogue was not possible when the only contact the reader had with the narrator was in the form of an authorial intrusion that separated itself from the story being told. With the use of the anonymous "I," story and dialogue become one.

iii

Geoffrey Hartmann tells his reader that there is only one fully developed character in the novels of Virginia Woolf, "and that is the completely expressive or androgynous mind."[57] Hugh Kenner says that "Flaubert, Joyce and Beckett are their own greatest inventions."[58] Both critics are describing that strong sense of authorial presence we find in modern novels, even in the works that seek to exclude the author by means of impersonal narration. Gods that are "everywhere felt, but nowhere seen" challenge the reader to find them out. It is often said that the practice of "showing" rather than "telling" creates a more active reader.[59] Rather than passively accepting the judgments of intrusive authors, readers must become imaginatively engaged in the process of understanding a given character. In a sense, the readers' task is to convert the showing into a telling, to reestablish the convention of omniscient narration by inferring what the authors' attitudes toward their creations actually are. But note that this whole process of inference is directed not toward understanding the characters of a story but toward understanding their makers. Impersonal narration turns authors into problems to be solved. Characters are not important for their own sakes but are clues, bits of evidence to be used in drawing an accurate portrait of the author's sensibility.

Wayne Booth has exposed the fallacy of impersonal narration and the objectivity it implies.[60] Writers never disappear from their work but only appear there in different disguises. They may appear as characters in the work or as an "anonymous I"; they may "appear" in the form of silence, especially when the reader has been conditioned to expect authorial intrusions. The absence of such intrusions only serves to heighten the reader's awareness of a silent maker.

Several modern novelists, either because they recognize the futility of the desire for impersonality or because such a condition no longer seems desirable, have returned to their novels with a vengeance. Prior to the twentieth century, only Lawrence Sterne had insisted upon occupying the space of his fiction with the aggressiveness of a Nabokov or a Beckett. These later writers—and add to the list Gide, Genet, most practitioners of the *nouveau roman*, Robert Musil, Mann in *Dr. Faustus* and *The Confessions of Felix Krull*, Jorge Luis Borges, Carlos Fuentes, Julio Cortázar, and the most interesting contemporary American novelists— can frankly find no character or story as interesting as themselves and the stories they tell of their own imaginative life.

Perhaps Sterne's self-aggrandizement, the joy he takes from the movement of his own mind, represents not a perversion of the novel but a realization of its true nature. E.M. Cioran observes that tragedy affects us as a reality independent of the writer: "the author has no influence over his heroes, he is only their servant, their instrument; they are the ones in control, and they prompt him to institute proceedings against themselves."[61] The novel, on the other hand, is seen as affecting us in an altogether different way: "The novelist is always uppermost in our minds; his presence haunts us; we watch him struggle with his characters; in the long run, he is the only one who holds our attention. 'What's he going to do with them? How will he get rid of them?' we wonder, our curiosity tinged with apprehension."[62] If Cioran's observation of the nature of the novel seems perverse, a rejection of the principles of realism on which the novel was founded, we must remember that Cioran, like ourselves, reads all novels from a modern perspective. A traditional novel is *changed* by our reading of reflexive novels. If readers will not accept this because it seems to distort the historical context in which the novel first appeared, let them consider how the eighteenth-century reader read Defoe, Richardson, or Fielding *after* the experience of *Tristram Shandy*. Seen in this way, the novel becomes the supreme instrument by which the mind meditates on itself. What it sacrifices in the way of an access to *things* and Cioran also catalogues these sacrifices with care and regret—it compensates for in terms of self-knowledge. Such knowledge, for Sterne and for the modern novelists mentioned, whether desirable or not, is *necessary*. Beside such knowledge, all the make-believe people and make-believe stories of the realistic novel seem to be childish attempts to avoid the self by inventing worlds we can no longer believe in.

Central to the reflexive novelist's attempt to confront the self has been a systematic devaluation of the fictional character. This has led many critics of modernism to speak of the "dehumanization," of the "loss of the self," in such writers.[63] This negative judgment is born of a confusion inherent in what I may call the mimetic fallacy: Characters are not persons. Must we be constantly reminded that the only contact a novel has with living beings is in its relationships with its author and its reader? It is one thing to speak of "characters" as if they were real persons, to talk of the "life" of a given novel, but it is another to forget the figurative nature of such language.

The notion of aesthetic distance may prove helpful here in showing why "dehumanization" is a misleading description of those modern novels which seek to be reflexive. Wayne Booth, in *The Rhetoric of Fiction*, has followed Edward Bullough's evaluation of distance: if a work is overdistanced, it will seem "improbable, artificial, empty, or absurd, and we will not respond to it. Yet if it is underdistanced, the work becomes too personal and cannot be enjoyed as art."[64] Yet Booth notes that "distance is never an end in itself; distance along one axis is sought for the sake of increasing the reader's involvement on some other axis."[65] By undermining our belief in their characters and thereby decreasing our involvement with them, reflexive novelists are not trying to cause us to lose interest in their work but to focus that interest along another axis. Such novelists, by overdistancing their readers' relationship with their characters, hope to reduce the distance between the reader and the writer.[66] If anything, rather than being "dehumanized," the reflexive novel runs the risk of being too personal.[67]

Brecht seems to be describing this shift of interest when he tries to gauge the effects produced by alienated acting:

The performer's self-observation, an artful and artistic act of self-alienation, stopped the spectator from losing himself in the character completely, i.e., to the point of giving up his own identity, and lent a splendid remoteness to the events. *Yet the spectator's empathy was not entirely rejected. The audience identifies itself with the actor as being an observer, and accordingly develops his attitude of observing or looking on.* [My italics][68]

Finally, Brecht rejects Aristotelian empathy less than he subverts it to serve new modes of communication. The self to which the spectators attach themselves is that of the performer *as* performer and *as* observer. Perhaps the way in which such performers avoid the personal is by observing the presence of their masks, but they cannot avoid the self as long as they recognizes that the mask is the face.[69]

The use of a dramatic analogy to describe reflexive fiction is singularly appropriate in that it stresses the element of *performance* in the act of composition. Richard Poirier has shown that many modern writers consciously distinguish between their finished work and the moment-by-moment victories of the process of creation, and wish to be judged in terms of the latter.[70] It is as if these writers' work had reality for them only in the moment of performance when they define themselves in terms of acts of language. It is for this reason that reflexive novelists often try to give their work the look of the moment in the study, the rough draft— that the reader might somehow experience the novel as an act, as something done with words by a particular person at a particular time and place.

If this talk of the personal and of performance suggests a relapse into the intentional fallacy, then it should be pointed out that we have not left the text itself. The self we speak of is not made of mere words: It exists beyond the page. But mere words provide the only access we have to that self and we cannot go beyond what they say. If they provide us with an "objectification of the subjective," it is a subject that is only as open to us as words will allow. All that such writers ask is that we stop treating the products of their labor as if they were some form of natural phenomena.[71]

Perhaps we are now in a position to explain the apparent contradiction implied by Flaubert's comments on *Madame Bovary*. His belief that writers should not make themselves their own theme and his assertion that, nevertheless, "Madame Bovary, c'est moi" can be made compatible if we note that the kind of identification implied by the second statement is that of a writer who recognizes that writing is ultimately an expression of the self. Hugh Kenner reminds us that *Madame Bovary* is, after all, "a novel about a woman who has read novels, kept as close as possible to the plot, the characterization, and the dialogue of the sort of novels she has read."[72] We should not miss the irony of the situation: The most famous creation of the father of realism turns out to be a parody of both the heroines of realistic novels and of the women who identify with such heroines. Flaubert, while working within the norms of realism, has managed to subvert that realism by making it look at itself instead of at the world.

THEMES OF THE REFLEXIVE

Verbs that have subjects and direct objects that are identical are reflexive. Compound personal pronouns are used as objects of transitive verbs or of prepositions when the objects denote the same person or thing as the subject; in this use they are called reflexive pronouns:

She dressed herself.

He hurt himself.

You corrected yourself.

I wrote myself a note. (indirect object)

This novel is about itself.

The reflexive is a "bending back," an action performed on the actor. Theoretically, any transitive verb can become reflexive, but some actions—suicide and masturbation, for example—seem necessarily reflexive. The suffix-*self* in the object is crucial, as if mere actors could avoid themselves as selves as long as they acted on others.

The reflexive is opposed to the intransitive, which cannot bend back, since it cannot move outward. The intransitive is pure activity without options: *He writes*.

What is the reflexive novel about? It is about itself. In order to avoid tautology, it must make its *action*—not its subject or object, which duplicate each other—its theme. The reflexive novel is *about* "bending back."

A list of the themes of the reflexive would be composed of a variety of gestures, each of which would be a form of "bending back." Since any verb can become reflexive, such a list cannot hope to exhaust the possible themes of the reflexive. But some gestures present themselves with greater frequency than others.

Consider Nietzche's image of "interiorization," the process by which man "turns *himself* into an adventure": "Lacking external enemies and resistances, and confined within an oppressive narrowness and regularity, man began rending, persecuting, terrifying himself, like a wild beast hurling itself against the bars of its cage."[73] Images of mere confinement are inadequate, intransitive; there must be a deflected movement outward, a bending back, a gesture of defiance or despair. The prison itself may have different names. The caged animal may merely find itself in the wrong place at the wrong time. Or it may believe that the cage is part of itself. It may be a prison house made of words instead of bricks. In any case, there must be a gesture against the bars.

With confinement comes poverty: "Lacking external enemies and resistances," the prisoner must make something out of nothing. The reflexive novel invariably involves a creation, and while what is created is most often a story, other objects may serve. The titular hero-maker of Robert Coover's *The Universal Baseball Association, J. Henry Waugh, Prop.* creates a game of numbers that eventually replaces the "reality" of the world outside Henry's apartment. What begins as a form of solitaire ends as a game larger than life: Henry becomes all those fictive ballplayers he has created.[74]

If the cell represents the human mind and what it can invent, then what is usually invented is another place and another time. Unable to go out into the world, the prisoner brings the world in, crowds the cell with play-figures and stories. Because of his poverty, the prisoner has no livable present. Unable to imagine a future that includes his release, he concentrates on the past, bends back in time. Real time, according to Sartre, is a synthesis of all three temporal dimensions, but an individual storyteller invariably distorts this real time by focusing on one dimension of time to the exclusion of others.[75] For the reflexive novelist the past is the essential value, what must be recovered. This past may take several forms. It may be the youth of the teller, as in Proust, or it may be that the teller is youth, seeking to discover an older system of values, as in Faulkner's Quentin. Or the past may simply be the literary past, the source of the prisoner's poverty being that he comes too late, after all of the stories have been told.

One of the paradoxes of the reflexive is stated in the juxtaposition of the theme of making with the theme of the past. In focusing on a past event, the storyteller initially surrenders his freedom. Only if he discovers that the past is irretrievable does he recover that lost freedom, that ability to make. In any case, he is likely to view his making as a remaking, a putting-back-together of a lost event, the parts of which have been scattered by time. His task is recovery, his material second-hand.

If the context of his story is the past, there is also an implied present, a storytelling situation. There is a bending back in time but also a

bending back of language. The process of denotation is commonly represented as a movement outward:

In the reflexive mode, the denotative process is arrested, turned back:

The proper point of critical departure for studying this form of reflexivity
would seem to be the structuralist or Saussurian position toward language: "At bottom, structuralism is a set of attitudes to and of language:
grammatology. . . . As science, structuralism is metalinguistic, language
studying language."[76] It is significant, too, that for the structuralist the
problem of *theme* is resolved formalistically: "The most characteristic
feature of structuralist criticism lies precisely in a kind of transformation
of form into content, in which the form of structuralist research . . . turns
into a proposition about content: literary works are about language, take
the process of speech itself as their essential subject matter."[77] The
structuralist brand of imprisonment would therefore posit the priority of
the signifier over the signified—the latter of which exists for us only
insofar as it is constituted by language. To know a story is to know the
words used to tell it. (To study a story is a semiological rather than a
semantic task, if semantics is understood as the study of meanings that
are somehow embodied by the text but exist apart from it.) Seen from one
point of view, the reflexive novel sets out to prove the limits of language,
the failure of semantics. But from a structuralist point of view, such a
novel neither succeeds nor fails but merely describes a fundamental
proposition about language.

In opposition to sign-centered structuralism is the phenomenological
approach, which seeks to go behind the words to a consciousness-
centered, transcendental subject. The "bending back" of the reflexive
mode points to a writer rather than to writing, a himself or a herself
rather than an itself. The difference between the two approaches lies
essentially in their conflicting descriptions of the meaning-giving activity: "Whereas existential phenomenology takes the high road on which
the fully conscious subject exercising his freedom brings meaning into
existence, structuralism takes the low road, on which a universal but

latent and unconscious human mind inscribes its deterministic architecture everywhere."[78] Insofar as phenomenology does not relapse into romantic biography, insofar as it does not reject language for thought but asserts the primacy of language even as it recognizes that the novel or the poem is a *made* thing, possessing a *maker*—however problematically that entity may be conceived—to that extent it offers us access to the reflexive mode. If structuralism can describe the prison, phenomenology explains the gesture against the bars, recognizes that the notion of imprisonment has meaning only if the writer can envision writing as a free act.

"The exceptional value of the work [Jean Genet's *Notre-Dame des Fleurs*] lies in its ambiguity. It appears at first to have only one subject, Fatality: the characters are puppets of destiny. But we quicky discover that this pitiless Providence is really the counterpart of a sovereign—and indeed divine—freedom, that of the author."[79] Sartre's description of *Our Lady of the Flowers* places that novel firmly in the tradition of the reflexive; furthermore; Genet's writing is literally enacted within the walls of a prison. Its images are consistently reflexive—masturbatory, narcissistic, suicidal. Imprisoned by walls and by words, Genet's narrator nevertheless attempts to assert his own freedom as he tells the love story of Darling and Divine: "Since it is impossible to make a ballet of it, I am forced to use words that are weighed down with precise ideas, but I shall try to lighten them with expressions that are trivial, empty, hollow, and invisible."[80] To rob language of its meaning, to destroy its referential character, is Genet's project. Readers are never allowed to immerse themselves in the story of Darling and Divine because the writer and his writing constantly intrude: "No other book," says Sartre, "not even *Ulysses*, brings us into such close physical contact with an author."[81] The characters in Genet's "dream" are transparent; the only reality of the book is the "I": "It is Darling whom I cherish most, for you realize that, in the final analysis, it is my own destiny, be it true or false, that I am draping (at times a rag, at times a court robe) on Divine's shoulders."[82]

The tension between imprisonment and freedom is reenacted through the themes of masochism and sadism that run throughout the novel. Genet is not merely the abject Divine but also her tormenter. And the violence is itself always verbal, as is the ambivalence of roles, expressed in the shifting of pronouns from the masculine to the feminine.

Perhaps the great theme of the reflexive novel is provided by the question "Who is writing?" As efforts at self-definition, such novels provide a commentary on *all* writing projects. If freedom is a matter of consciousness, then the themes of the reflexive add to rather than detract from such freedom, since their central aim is to provide a sustained self-examination of the writer and his writing. All writers, not only Sartre's Genet, operate under one essential rule: "The only rule underlying Genet's inventions and composition is Genet himself. For him, to compose is to recreate *himself*."[83] That this rule of self-creation can itself be challenged is the major topic of the later chapters of this book.

Notes

1. Albert Cook, *The Meaning of Fiction* (Detroit: Wayne State University Press, 1960).

2. Several critical studies in recent years have helped me to define my own position on what I am calling, following Cook, the reflexive novel. See especially those works listed in the bibliography by Sypher, Robbe-Grillet, Spencer, Poirier, Lodge, Caute, Scholes, Stern, Alter, and Kellman.

3. E. D. Hirsch, Jr., *Validity in Interpretation* (New Haven, Conn.: Yale University Press, 1967), p. 74.

4. See Maurice Beebe, *Ivory Towers and Sacred Founts* (New York: New York University Press, 1964), p. 304.

5. Dan Watt, *The Rise of the Novel* (Berkeley and Los Angeles: University of California Press, 1965), p. 291.

6. Linda Nochlin, *Realism* (Baltimore, Md.: Penguin, 1971).

7. J. P. Stern, *On Realism* (London and Boston: Routledge and Kegan Paul, 1973), p. 67.

8. Ibid., p. 73.

9. Nochlin, *Realism*, p. 14.

10. Ibid.

11. E. H. Gombrich, *Art and Illusion* (New York: Pantheon Books, 1961).

12. Stern, *On Realism*, pp. 122 ff.; also see David Lodge, *The Novelist at the Crossroads* (Ithaca, N.Y.: Cornell University Press, 1971).

13. See David Caute, *The Illusion* (New York: Harper and Row, 1971) and Roland Barthes, "Science versus Literature," in *Introduction to Structuralism*, ed. Michael Lane (New York: Basic Books, 1970), pp. 410–16.

14. Stern, *On Realism*, p. 31.

15. Ibid., p. 54.

16. In our century this term has been most completely appropriated by that school of postwar Italian filmmakers who favor a semi-documentary style, and for that reason seems inappropriate. Nevertheless, it is interesting that many of the most reflexive films of recent years have been made by directors whose debt of this neorealism may be easily traced—Fellini, Antonioni, Visconti, and Pasolini.

17. Attempts to speak of the influence of modern science on modern literature should be approached with caution: "Modern art has in no way been influenced by Einstein or Heisenberg or Wittgenstein. Most artists are too busy with their own problems to have the energy or the inclination to master an alien mode of thought, even if these things could be mastered without the proper training, which is highly dubious." Gabriel Josipovici, *The World and the Book* (Stanford, Calif.: Stanford University Press, 1971), p. xiv.

18. Josipovici, *World and One Book*, p. xiv.

19. Erich Auerbach, *Mimesis* (Princeton, N.J.: Princeton University Press, 1953), chap. 1.

20. Robert Scholes and Robert Kellogg, *The Nature of Narrative* (New York: Oxford University Press, 1966), p. 14.

21. Ursula Brumm, "Symbolism and the Novel," in *The Theory of the Novel*, ed. Philip Stevick (New York: The Free Press, 1967), p. 359.

22. Ibid., p. 360.

23. See Philip Roth, "Writing American Fiction," in *The American Novel Since World War II*, ed. Marcus Klein (New York: Fawcett Books, 1969), pp. 142–158.

24. Lodge, *Novelist at the Crossroads*, p. 12.

25. Ibid., p. 15.

26. Natholie Sarraute, *The Age of Suspicion*, trans. Maria Jolas (New York: George Braziller, 1963), p. 64.

27. Scholes and Kellogg, *Nature of Narrative*, p. 82.

28. Josipovici, *World and the Book*, p. xiv.

29. Virginia Woolf, *The Second Common Reader* (New York: Harcourt, Brace and World, 1960), p. 69.

30. Wallace Stevens, "The Sense of the Sleight-of-Hand Man," in *The Palm at the End of the Mind*, ed. Holly Stevens (New York: Vintage Books, 1972), p. 168.

31. Geoffrey Hartman, *Beyond Formalism* (New Haven, Conn.: Yale University Press, 1970), p. 70.

32. Ibid., p. 70.

33. Victor Shklovsky, "Art as Technique," *Russian Formalist Criticism*, trans. Leo T. Lemon and Marion J. Reis (Lincoln: University of Nebraska Press, 1965), p. 12.

34. Morse Peckham, *Rage for Chaos* (New York: Schocken Books, 1967), p. 33.

35. Ibid., p. 32.

36. Ibid., p. 79.

37. Ibid., p. 34.

38. Stevens is, with the possible exception of Flaubert, the most trenchant observer of the merely observable:

The houses are haunted
By white night-gowns.
None are green,
Or purple with green rings,
Or green with yellow rings,
Or yellow with blue rings. None of them are strange,
With socks of lace
And beaded ceintures.
People are not going
To dream of baboons and periwinkles.
Only, here and there, an old sailor,
Drunk and asleep in his boots,
Catches tigers
In red weather.

"Disillusionment of Ten O'clock," in *The Palm at the End of the Mind*.

39. For a discussion of Brecht's understanding of both terms, see Hans Egon Holthusen, "Brecht's Dramatic Theory," *Brecht: A Collection of Critical Essays*, ed. Peter Demetz (Englewood Cliffs, N.J.: Prentice-Hall, 1962), p. 108.

40. Bertolt Brecht, *Brecht on Theatre*, ed. and trans. John Willet (New York: Anchor Books, 1969), p. 361.

41. Ibid., p. 92.

42. See Martin Esslin, *The Theatre of the Absurd* (New York: Anchor Books, 1969), p. 361.

43. Lionel Abel, *Metatheatre* (New York: Hill and Wang, 1963).

44. Ibid., p. 59.

45. Ibid., p. 45.

46. Ibid., p. 77.

47. Ibid., p. 79.

48. William H. Gass, *Fiction and the Figures of Live* (New York: Vintage Books, 1972), p. 27.

49. See W. J. Harvey, *Character and the Novel* (Ithaca, N.Y.: Cornell University Press, 1965) for the most persuasive presentation of the role of character in the novel.

50. Sharon Spencer, *Space, Time, and Structure in the Modern Novel* (New York: New York University Press, 1971), pp. 93–94.

51. This is the approach taken in Robert S. Ryf's *A New Approach to Joyce: The Portrait of the Artist as Guidebook* (Berkeley and Los Angeles: University of California Press, 1962).

52. Maurice Beebe, *Ivory Towers and Sacred Founts* (New York: New York University Press, 1964), p. 299.

53. Sarraute, *Age of Suspicion*, p. 56.

54. Ibid.

55. Ibid., p. 71.

56. Ibid.

57. Hartman, *Beyond Formalism*, p. 75.

58. Hugh Kenner, *Flaubert, Joyce, and Beckett: The Stoic Comedians* (Boston: Beacon Press, 1962), p. xix.

59. The term *showing* is always misleading insofar as it attributes a visual quality to a medium that is exclusively verbal. Analogies with drama or the visual arts cease to be useful in the criticism of fiction when they obscure "obvious" truths about what a story is made of.

60. Wayne Booth, *The Rhetoric of Fiction* (Chicago: University of Chicago Press, 1961).

61. E. M. Cioran, *The Temptation to Exist*, trans. Richard Howard (Chicago: Quadrangle Books, 1968), p. 137.

62. Ibid., pp. 137–138.

63. See W. J. Harvey, *Character and the Novel*, and Wylie Sypher, *The Loss of Self*.

64. Booth, *Rhetoric of Fiction*, p. 122.

65. Ibid., p. 123.

66. The shifting of the relative distances between author, audience, and character is described in Walker Gibson's *Persona* (New York: Random House, 1969), pp. 51–53.

67. The dangers inherent in the approach are discussed in Oscar Büdel's "Contemporary Theatre and Aesthetic Distance," in *Brecht: A Collection of Critical Essays*, pp. 59–85.

68. Brecht, *Brecht on Theatre*, p. 93.

69. Perhaps the most extensive study of masks and role-playing is the work of sociologist, psychologist, and philosopher Erving Goffman, especially his *The Presentation of Self in Everyday Life* (Garden City, N.Y.: Doubleday, 1959) and *Frame Analysis* (New York: Harper and Row, 1974).

70. Richard Poirier, *The Performing Self: Compositions and Decompositions in the Languages of Contemporary Life* (New York: Oxford University Press, 1971), p. 87.

71. Such a request, perhaps, arises less from a desire for personal recognition than from the sense that "artificiality" is itself a value.

72. Kenner, *Flaubert, Joyce, and Beckett*, p. 22.

73. Friedrich Nietzsche, *The Birth of Tragedy* and *The Genealogy of Morals*, trans. Francis Golffing (Garden City, N.Y.: Doubleday Anchor Books, 1956), p. 218.

74. Robert Coover, *The Universal Baseball Association, Inc., J. Henry Waugh, Prop.* (New York: New American Library, 1971).

75. See Frederic Jameson, "Three Methods in Sartre's Literary Criticism," in *Modern French Criticism*, ed. John K. Simon (Chicago: University of Chicago Press, 1972), p. 195.

76. Edward Said, "Abecedarium Culturae," in *Modern French Criticism*, p. 363.

77. Fredric Jameson, *The Prison-house of Language* (Princeton, N.J.: Princeton University Press, 1972) pp. 198–99.

78. Vernon W. Gras, "Introduction," in *European Literary Theory and Practice*, ed. Vernon W. Gras (New York: Delta Books, 1973), p. 15.

79. Jean-Paul Sartre, *Saint Genet*, trans. Bernard Frechtman (New York: George Braziller, 1963), p. 447.

80. Jean Genet, *Our Lady of the Flowers*, trans. Bernard Frechtman (New York: Bantam Books, 1964), p. 70.

81. Sartre, *Saint Genet*, p. 449.

82. Genet, *Our Lady of Flowers*, p. 99.

83. Sartre, *Saint Genet*, p. 543.

2

Chance and Joseph Conrad's Theory of Fiction

Chance is an example of objectivity, most precious of aims, not only menaced but definitely compromised; whereby we are in presence of something really of the strangest, a general and diffused lapse of authenticity which an inordinate number of common readers. . . have not only condoned but have emphatically commended. They can have done this but through the bribe of some authenticity other in kind, no doubt, and seeming to them equally great if not greater, which gives back by the left hand what the right has, with however dissimulated a grace, taken away. What Mr. Conrad's left hand gives back then is simply Mr. Conrad himself.

—Henry James, *Notes on Novelists*

I invent the character of a novelist, whom I make my central figure; and the subject of the book, if you must have one, is just that very struggle between what reality offers him and what he himself desires to make of it.

—André Gide, *The Counterfeiters*

The Prismatic Bezel can be thoroughly enjoyed once it is understood that the heroes of the book are what can be loosely called "methods of composition." It is as if a painter said: Look, here I'm going to show you not the painting of a landscape, but the painting of different ways of painting a certain landscape, and I trust their harmonious fusion will disclose the landscape as I intend you to see it.

—Vladimir Nabokov, *The Real Life of Sebastian Knight*

It's true that most sciences are farcical except those which teach us how to put things together.

—Joseph Conrad, *Chance*

Recent discussions of reflexive novels often treat such works as expressions of a postmodern avant-garde development in fiction. Concentrating on the work of such older writers as Nabokov, Beckett, and Borges, and on the experimental fiction of younger American writers like Barth, Barthelme, Coover, Pynchon, and Gass, these discussions usually ignore the continuities between modern and postmodern fiction, preferring instead to stress the radically innovative nature of the major fiction written after the Second World War. If we look at the other arts, however—especially painting, sculpture, and music—we see that the movement toward what has been called "an interrogation of the medium" has been, from the beginning, an integral part of modernism itself. We are then forced either to admit that literature has lagged behind the other arts in seeking new forms of expression or to reevaluate the role of reflexivity in the work of the major modern novelists in the first part of the century.

Such a reevaluation might show that behind the work of the contemporary avant-garde there lies a tradition of fiction about fiction, a tradition that goes back to *Don Quixote* and *Tristram Shandy*, that is largely submerged during the nineteenth century's infatuation with naive realism but that appears in some of the works of the modern masters.

A consideration of Joseph Conrad's *Chance* in this tradition will perhaps serve to modify some current critical dissatisfaction with this novel, a dissatisfaction that derives in part from a failure to recognize the terms of its success. A different perspective can provide a different judgment, however, only if the reader is willing to accept the new perspective as a valid one. Of course, merely to be reflexive is no guarantee of success. The final test will be to discover how reflexivity is an integral part of this particular novel and not merely a trick without rewards.

It is interesting to note that many recurrent objections to *Chance* can be discarded or even transformed into virtues once it is acknowledged that Conrad's task here is to dramatize the difficulties of his art. (Not that he writes a poor novel and justifies it by announcing the difficulties of his profession; such a procedure could be used to save any novelist from censure and would hardly be acceptable. Rather, he is saying that a fictionalized account of the process of creation is as interesting, complex, and worthwhile a subject as anything else.) Douglas Hewitt's complaint, restated by so many critics that it becomes the chief "flaw" of the novel, that the technique of indirection seems to be there for its own sake, is directly to the point.[1] If Conrad's task is merely to tell the love story of Flora de Barral and Captain Anthony, then the technique of multiple narration supplemented by bold conjecture seems just so much excess baggage. Neither are the ends of verisimilitude furthered if this technique merely calls attention to itself, as it does in the critical description *tour de force*, so often pejoratively attached to the novel. But if technique is seen as the matter, not merely the manner, of the novel, then such complaints lose much of their force.

Other examples of misoriented criticism are important for what they reveal about the essential reflexivity of the novel. Albert Guerard complains about the weaknesses of the various narrators, their inability to give a satisfactory account of the story they tell,[2] but such a criticism is an acknowledgment of Conrad's success in dramatizing the disparity between the complexity of life and the finite capabilities of the interpreting mind. In noting Marlow's relative indifference to the story he narrates,[3] Guerard also inadvertently points to the tendency of the novel to see itself merely as a novel, a fiction, something that calls for and receives a certain degree of detachment.

F. R. Leavis is one of the novel's few defenders, yet he finds the title of the novel misleading. For him, "chance plays no notably different part from that it must play in any story offering a novelist a study of human nature."[4] Precisely! At one level *Chance* is working out theoretical concerns that are peculiar to the novel as a form, and at this level it should appear as a paradigm.

Other critics have also seen *Chance* as containing thematic or stylistic elements common to other work of the period. One sees in it a "normalizing of attitude and method" that aligns it with the popular magazine romance of the day.[5] For another the novel is an unsuccessful self-parody of the Conradian method.[6] One attempt to praise the novel uses a different approach, to see *Chance* as a "comedy of manners which deliberately parodies one kind of Victorian novel."[7] The dangers inherent in this type of interpretation are manifold: one is tempted to justify as parody what is in fact simply another inconsequential addition to that body of literature supposedly being parodied. Read either as a Victorian fiction or as a parody of that fiction, *Chance* is expendable. Nevertheless, observations along this line are not entirely unjustified. If certain themes and techniques seem familiar, even hackneyed; if they seem exaggerated to the point of intentionally satirizing Dickens or Conrad himself, this is as it should be in a novel that seeks to examine the generic problems of narrative fiction. In using familiar attitudes, Conrad has also effectively redirected the reader's attention toward problems of composition and away from the conventional fictional situations.

These different critical approaches, both positive and negative in their evaluation, suggest the need for a different view of the novel, one that would establish it as essentially reflexive in its attitudes.

Since the degree of self-consciousness required of such a novel seems at first antithetical to the proclaimed intentions of objectivity and impersonality of most modern fiction, certainly those of Ford Madox Ford and Joseph Conrad, it is important to show how, in the context of Conrad's work in general, such an apparent anomaly as *Chance* is possible. If we examine Conrad's fiction in search of a distinctive manner, something that clearly acts as a signature for his most typical work, we are most likely to concentrate on what Edward Said labels the "retrospective mode," that narrative structure which employs a narrator who is trying to come to terms with some event in the past.[8] The character of the narrator, the degree of his involvement with the events he narrates, the significance of the event itself—all these things may vary. What remains constant in Conrad's fiction is the double focus of past and present, the divided interest of teller and tale. It is true that in most of Conrad's fiction this division of interest is unequal. Marlow in *Lord Jim* or the teacher of languages in *Under Western Eyes*, while important as integrated commentators, do not usurp Jim or Razumov in the directed emphasis of the narratives. Nevertheless, these central narrators, and their more transparent counterparts in *The Nigger of the "Narcissus"* and *Nostromo*, are present in the novels under more disguises than reporter and commentator. As artist-surrogates intent on rescuing meaning from the flux of experience, they assume the roles of reporter and commentator while reflecting back upon the implied author's task.[9]

In *Chance* the distance between the event and the retelling of the event is so great that the possibility of attaining a "true" version of the original event is constantly in question. Not only is the event buried in the past, not only are Marlow's various sources of information either biased or unobservant, but Marlow himself—who has the advantage of being able to sort and evaluate all the different accounts—is out of his element. A sailor, unmarried, is supposed to interpret a story that evolves on land and that seems to call for the experience of a marriage counselor. This is not to say, however, that Marlow should be considered an "unreliable narrator." In order to make this accusation, the reader would have to have access to a "truth" behind the appearance that Marlow presents as his story. Such knowledge is not forthcoming to the reader; therefore, we accept what Marlow says, but we accept it for what it is—a *created* story, loosely based on a reality that eludes the grasp of art.

The obscurity of the original event is further emphasized by enhancing the immediacy of what E. K. Brown describes as the "objective theater"—in this novel, the scenes that involve Marlow and the "I"-narrator.[10] I use the term *scene* advisedly, for in the terminology of novel criticism what most establishes scenic properties is the sense of the immediacy of the action. The "action" here being primarily verbal, one might wonder at the propriety of calling these dialogues—dialogues they are, because the "I" can even make his silences heard—scenic. In Ring Lardner's "Haircut" we have a barber who tells a story, and nothing of what he tells is dramatically *shown*. Nevertheless, the story is dramatic, because the story of a small-town practical joker is framed by the immediacy of the barber shop, the barber, and his new customer. In much the same way Conrad turns summary into scene by giving life to the storytelling situations.

He uses several devices to accomplish this, and what is interesting is that these devices work on two levels: they serve as commentary on the Flora-Anthony story while focusing on Marlow as artist. The most obvious device is the presentation of Marlow as philosopher, usually expounding the nature of womanhood. Quite apart from the truth or falsity of his aphorisms or their relevance to the story of Flora de Barral, they do serve to stop the machinery of narration and to conjure up the appearance of Marlow in meditation. On another level Marlow will stop the narrative in order to insert an incident from personal experience, as when he recounts his meeting with de Barral. Again, aside from the question of its relevance to the story—and certainly the reader is struck by what little, *really*, can be made of that chance meeting—the episode again has the effect of a renewed concentration upon the narrator. Also, Marlow's use of conjecture should be considered at this point as another device for creating a sense of immediacy in the "objective theater." What all of these devices have in common is that they are each interruptions in the story of Flora de Barral. Considered in terms of both their frequency and their duration, these interruptions become no longer digressive, but supplant the original experience—whatever that was—as the focus of the novel.

Further evidence in the support of *Chance's* essential self-consciousness is found in the patterned reference to literary or theatrical terms. This is usually offered by Marlow, who alone sees the experience as "story." The very titles of the parts of the book—"The Damsel" and "The Knight"—carry literary associations for the reader. It should also be noted that, for the only time in his career, Conrad uses chapter titles, an obvious literary convention. Very early in his relationship to Flora and the Fynes, Marlow is quick to attach a fictive title to the experience—"the affair of the purloined brother,"[11] he calls it. Later, as Powell recalls his first voyage aboard the *Ferndale*, Marlow refers to the episode as "the sea-chapter," seeing it as a "member of a series, following the chapter outside the Eastern Hotel in which I myself had played my part." (p. 309). Also, Marlow's repeated attempts to classify the experience as tragedy or farce (p. 55), and his final description of it as a tragicomedy played upon a floating stage (p. 272), serve to place the events in a fictive context. Note that the appropriateness of the label *tragicomic* is not in question here. What is important is that Marlow thinks of the events in those terms.

He even gets support for this point of view from the unimaginative Fyne, who confesses that on the day of the governess's departure he followed the action from his window across from the de Barral house, as if he were "watching some action on the stage" (p. 114). Even Powell turns out to be, "like many seamen, an industrious reader," as is illustrated by his characterization of Flora as a "forsaken elf" and of Anthony as Othello (p. 424). That these comments are not obtrusive is a measure of the success with which Conrad has handled both a reflexive attitude and the account of a "real" experience. Anthony is Othello in terms of the psychological requirements of the situation, but he is also Othello, imaginary character.

The most subtle of the many literary references is found toward the conclusion, as dawn is approaching, and both Marlow and his audience are weary of their mutual and sustained struggle with life and art. Within two chapters Marlow is positioned four times within "the shadow of the bookcase" (pp. 325, 327, 350, 359). Against the objection that the narrator should be allowed to sit where he likes without encountering accusations of self-consciousness, I would reply that within the context of this discussion, as within the context of this novel, such repetitions warrant attention. As to the narrator's freedom to choose his own seating arrangement—that claim works both ways. Why should the reader suppose that the choice was haphazard? "Hang it all, for all my belief in Chance I am not exactly a pagan . . .–" (p. 447).

If this concentration on the reflexive elements in *Chance* seems to some a perverse distortion of what most readers see as essentially a love story, I would seek support for my position from one of the earliest and most perceptive critical discussions of the novel. In his essay "The New Novel" in *Notes on Novelists*, Henry James has fastened upon the essential texture of *Chance* and perhaps Conrad's fiction in general—by seeing narrative technique acting as the

> prolonged hovering flight of the subjective over the outstretched ground of the case exposed. We make out this ground but through the shadow cast by the flight, clarify it though the real author visibly reminds himself again and again that he must —all the more that, as if by some tremendous forecast of future applied science, the upper

airplane causes another, as we have said, to depend from it and that one still another; these dropping shadow after shadow, to the no small menace of intrinsic color and form and whatever, upon the passive expanse.[12]

In this context, the "passive expanse," the original experience of Flora and Captain Anthony, is, again in James's terms, "not only menaced but definitely compromised."[13] What James notices is simply that Conrad is after something other than an objectively rendered experience, that his book is primarily concerned with the process of creation rather than with the social or financial worlds of the late nineteenth century.

Fascinated by what he sees as the invoked difficulties of narration, James expresses the uniqueness of the novel by describing Conrad's practice of

> so multiplying his creators or, we are now fond of saying, producers, as to make them almost more numerous and quite emphatically more material than the creatures and the production itself in whom and which we by the general law of fiction expect such agents to lose themselves.[14]

By recognizing the relative materiality of the various narrators in Conrad's story, James is acknowledging the author's divergence from one of the central tenets of modern fiction, the injunction that the author should disappear. But James is also aware that the use of the narrator here differs sharply from the intrusions of earlier fiction: the illusion of objective authenticity is still there, but it is "authenticity other in kind" from that of the conventional Jamesian novel. James has perfectly captured the quality of this authenticity by examining the use of multiple narration through an analogy with a bucket brigade in which the original quantity of water or story is lost or distorted, and that which remains in the last bucket, the story as finally filtered through the "I"-narrator,

> has accordingly the form not of such and such a number of images discharged and ordered, but that rather of a wandering, circling, yearning imaginative faculty, encountered in its habit as it lives and diffusing itself as a presence or a tide, a noble sociability of vision.[15]

Expressed in the form of an imaginative faculty, taking that form itself as its subject, *Chance* becomes, in a sense, the most personal of Conrad's works—personal, not in the sense that biographical information is supplied or even in the sense that Marlow's process of telling is perfectly analogous to Conrad's own creative process, but personal as a reduction of those problems which most concern the man as novelist. In James's estimation, these problems are capable of taking on a life of their own, and it is important to recognize that this quality of felt life, even though it occurs in something more indefinable than character or incident, is not to be despised. Conrad is asserting here nothing less than the reality of the imaginative life.

If one is willing to grant that *Chance* takes the creative process as its theme, then it follows that certain problems of the artist will find expression there. In attempting to define these problems, I shall try to follow the method of the novel itself, that is, I shall leave the problems within the dramatic context in which they are found. I take it that it is only through the vivid and complex rendering of ideas by fictional illustration that the novel of ideas is able to justify its existence. What belongs to the essay, to the philosophical tract, should remain with those forms. I shall, however, refer to Conrad's letters, his critical essays and prefaces, when such outside sources seem to clarify or enlarge the significance of passages from the novel.

Certainly one of the most crucial problems that Conrad faced as a novelist is dramatized in *Chance* in his complex treatment of point of view. As has been noted before, the use of a limited point of view in the modern novel should not be considered as merely an aesthetic device, since the abjuration of omniscience is clearly related to our present world view, which emphasizes the fallibility of human knowledge and the subjective nature of experience.[16] Conrad consistently indicates that novelists are not exempt from such restrictions; that they, like other persons, see only what their vision permits them to see, and even *that* "truth" is distorted in its contact with the perceiving mind. From this evolves the solipsistic position that ". . . a novelist lives in his work. He stands there, the only reality in an invented world, among imaginary things, happenings, and people. Writing about them, he is only writing about himself."[17] Conrad goes on in this passage to insist, however, that this solitary reality in the novel is not to be confused with the author's own personality, which remains "a figure behind the veil."[18] The author may, as Conrad insists in the Author's Note to *Chance*, "give himself (and his morality) away in about every third sentence,"[19] but this surrender is accomplished obliquely in most cases. What is significant in Conrad's fiction is not so much that Conrad tells us about himself as that he finds it necessary to posit a "self" before the narrative can take shape.

In his interesting study *Joseph Conrad and the Fiction of Autobiography*, Edward Said finds a recurrent theme in Conrad's letters and short fiction that may be expressed in terms of an either/or proposition: Either experience carries no meaning, or meaning is created through the assertion of a created self.[20] The typical Conradian hero attempts to structure the universe, to give it meaning, only to become the victim of his own illusions. Another critic finds that in Conrad's fiction "each man is his own artist! Each one is following an artistic vision of the facts, an imaginative re-creation of reality."[21] What the artist does, then, in ordering experience is analogous to the process by which any person gives meaning to his or her world. The validity of these similar illusions may vary, but the final criterion is not to be found in their value as imitations; indeed, in this view, imitations are impossible.

By examining the role of self in the creation of art and seeing its relation to the illusions of Conrad's heroes, we begin to see exactly what writing a novel about the creative process entails. *Chance* is more than a rather personal *tour de force* and becomes instead a concentrated expression of what may be Conrad's central concern as a novelist—to show a person creating both a self and a world and living with that self in that world:

> After all, the creation of a world is not a small undertaking except perhaps to the divinely gifted. In truth every novelist must begin by creating for himself a world, great or little, in which he can honestly believe. This world cannot be made otherwise than in his own image.[22]

Difficult as this task appears, Conrad neglects to mention yet another difficulty. Before the world can be created in the self's own image, the self itself must be created, and the particular self that creates *Chance* is Charlie Marlow—ex-sailor, raconteur, and amateur philosopher. In looking at Marlow, I think it is important neither to minimize nor to exaggerate the importance of establishing his exact relation to his creator. To say that Marlow "does not present psychological problems and . . . does not belong to the inner substance of these stories"[23] is to vitiate the significance of that relation; to insist on discovering Conrad's real attitude toward women by trying to find the author somewhere within or behind or beyond or above his creation is to ask far more than the novel is prepared to offer. In some very obvious ways Marlow is not Joseph Conrad; in some equally obvious respects we can see why Conrad considers him "a most discreet, understanding man."[24] If we see Marlow in the proper perspective, that is, as an artist, limited by the intractability of experience, then accusations of unreliability are beside the point. Marlow is simply doing the best he can with the material. Conrad chooses here a self that is neither greater nor smaller than his own—only different.

Marlow's function in *Chance* will be missed if we expect him to conform to the role he established for himself in *Lord Jim*, "Youth," or *Heart of Darkness*. This role has been clearly defined by Scholes and Kellogg, who see variations of the approach in Faulkner, Fitzgerald, and Warren:

> The story of the protagonist becomes the outward sign or symbol of the inward story of the narrator, who learns from his imaginative participation in the other's experience. Since the imagination plays the central role, the factual or empirical aspect of the protagonist's life becomes subordinated to the narrator's understanding of it. Not what really happened but the meaning of what the narrator believes to have happened becomes the central preoccupation of this kind of narrative.[25]

In *Chance*, however, the factual or empirical aspect of the protagonist's life is not merely subordinated to the imagination of the narrator; it is submerged, forgotten. As William York Tindall puts it, the emphasis, "falling no longer on what he [Marlow] makes of a problem, falls now on what he makes."[26] The Marlow of *Chance*, if seen in the company of the Quentin Compson of *Absalom, Absalom!*, of Nick Carraway, or of Jack Burden, seems strangely detached from the story he narrates. And compared to Thomas Sutpen, Jay Gatsby, or Willie Stark, Roderick Anthony seems too shadowy to deserve the title of protagonist. Seen, then, in terms of this particular narrative mode—which Conrad himself helped to create in the earlier Marlow stories—*Chance* is a distinct failure. It is only by accepting Marlow's withdrawal from the story he tells, only by recognizing the essential reflexivity of the novel, that *Chance* becomes for the reader a unique statement and illustration of the problems of the artist.

The role of the "old" Marlow is that of *histor*, who seeks to reconcile various accounts and interpretations of a past experience in order that he himself might impose a finality of form to that experience. But even in those earlier fictions, we are left with a sense of the inadequacy, the incompleteness of Marlow's accounts, comparable to the effect Conrad recognized and admired in the work of Henry James:

> One is never set at rest by Mr. Henry James's novels. His Books end as an episode in life ends. You remain with the sense of the life still

going on; and even the subtle presence of the dead is felt in that silence that comes upon the artist-creation when the last word has been read. It is eminently satisfying, but it is not final. Mr. Henry James, great artist and faithful historian, never attempts the impossible.[27]

The failure implicit in the earlier fiction—Marlow's failure to render *absolute* justice to the visible universe—is made explicit in *Chance* as the conditions surrounding the *histor* become more and more unfavorable to the discovery of truth. Simply in terms of the facts available, Marlow is presented with only meager outlines, and his appeal to hearsay—which is his prime source of information in *Lord Jim*—is reduced to necessary conjecture.

The final interview with Flora, which seems to give Marlow all that he needs for a precise historical account, is in fact a device for conceding the slender basis of Marlow's suppositions. Marlow's promise of an additional source of information appears at the beginning of chapter 4, and when it comes, toward the end of the novel, we have long ceased to expect it. "By the time she had brought in a lighted lamp I had heard all the details which really matter in this story" (p. 443). But many of the details of *Marlow's* story cannot be acquired from Flora or from anyone else. Flora, like Powell, remains ignorant of many aspects of the story, and surely Marlow tells all of what he knows to the "I"-narrator alone. (Indeed, Marlow's concealment of the circumstances surrounding de Barral's death in that final interview has many of the characteristics of the "true lie" as found in the final scene of *Heart of Darkness*.)

Marlow's most extended use of conjecture, although he is granted a sophisticated omniscience throughout the novel, comes in the account of the relationship between the governess and her "nephew," an account based only on the slenderest of observations and judgments on the part of the Fynes. Although the "I"-narrator is "struck by the absolute verisimilitude" (p. 102) of Marlow's conjectures, his comment to Marlow reveals that he is completely aware of the fictive nature of the story he is listening to: "You have a ghastly imagination" (p. 102).

Marlow's imagination is the true source of the story, as indeed it must be in the Conradian epistemology. This imagination is characterized by the habit, or weakness, or gift of visualizing a segment of a story for itself (p. 177), and this habit or weakness or gift is freely exercised whenever direct knowledge is unavailable. When Fyne asks Marlow if he sees now (understands), Marlow's reaction is literal:

I saw, all sorts of things! Immediately before me I saw the excitement

of little Fyne—mere food for wonder. Further off, in a sort of gloom
and beyond the light of day and the movement of the street, I saw the
figure of a man, stiff like a ramrod, moving with small steps, a slight
girlish figure by his side. (P. 245)

Lest we become too absorbed in the sense of reality of Marlow's picture,
however, we should remember that Conrad works equally hard to undermine this sense of reality. The man and the girl are "figures from Dickens—pregnant with pathos" (p. 162).

Marlow's role as *histor* is suitably parodied in the scene with Flora on
the pavement. Faced with his own curiosity and the unliklihood of
stumbling on more facts, Marlow attempts to justify his interview with
Flora:

> The trouble was that I could not imagine anything about Flora de
> Barral and the brother of Mrs. Fyne. Or if you like, I could imagine
> *anything* which comes to the same thing. Darkness and chaos are first
> cousins. I should have liked to ask the girl for a word which would
> give my imagination its line. But how was one to venture so far? I can
> be rough sometimes but I am not naturally impertinent. (Pp. 210–11)

One wonders what excess Marlow has in mind as "impertinence" if he
himself is absolved from that censure in the question-and-answer ex-
change that follows. All attempts to justify psychologically Marlow's
good fortune in obtaining facts here must fail, and even at that Marlow
admits that "if you were to disentangle the words we actually exchanged
from my comments you would see that they were not so very many,
including everything she had so unexpectedly told me of her story. No,
not so very many" (p. 231). Even more impressive is Conrad's treatment
of the scene of the interview. Life literally streams by Marlow and Flora
on that busy street corner, interrupting the narrative and making the
artist's task all but impossible. "The ugly street-noises swelling up for a
moment covered the next few words she said. It was vexing" (p. 216). If
the scene, with its many interruptions, is read as a dramatization of the
problems the novelist faces as he attempts to select and order a fragment
of experience, the "reality" of the scene is not impaired. The reflexive
attitude simply makes the scene available on another level.

The chance of the self's distortion of reality is of course multiplied in
the narrative by the use of several narrators, all limited in their capacity
for observation and by personal biases. No less than ten characters
contribute to Marlow's "knowledge" of the story, and only half of this
number are questioned by Marlow himself. A diagram of the chain of
communication perhaps better indicates both the variety of sources and
Marlow's distance from the experience he seeks to recreate.

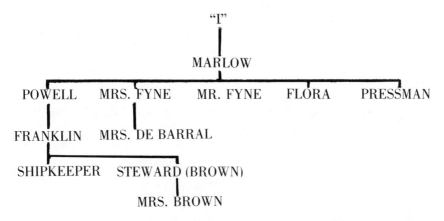

As can easily be seen, Powell's youth at the time of his shipping aboard the *Ferndale*, his contempt of general ideas (p. 23), his ignorance of the background for the "sea chapter"—all contribute to make him something less than the perfect observer. The Fynes' lack of imaginative sympathy (p. 143), Mrs. Fyne's preoccupation with her book, her relationship with her brother, and Mr. Fyne's relationship with his wife are factors that make these people, Marlow's second most important source of information, blind to the significance of much of what they witness.

Perhaps Marlow's most limited informant is his friend the pressman, who might have provided him with information concerning de Barral had he not found him "a dull dog" (p. 86). Although he is able to describe to Marlow the financier's last-minute gesture of defiance at the trial, "the pressman disapproved of that manifestation. It was not his business to understand it. Is it ever the business of any pressman to understand anything? I guess not. It would lead him too far away from the actualities which are the daily bread of the public mind" (p. 87). But Marlow's interest does not lie in these actualities, nor is his the public mind. In a moment of detached contemplation in a bar with the pressman, Marlow projects himself "into the feelings of a man [de Barral] whose imagination wakes up at the very moment he is about to enter the tomb" (p. 87). The contrast between the pressman's facts and Marlow's projection of self into those facts is an important distinction for the artist, the distinction between "information" and "knowledge":

Information is something one goes out to seek and puts away when found as you might do a piece of lead: ponderous, useful, unvibrating, dull. Whereas knowledge comes to one, this sort of knowledge, a chance acquisition preserving in its repose a fine resonant quality. (P. 88)

Marlow also says that this knowledge is not something "had," but rather that it is something that *exists within* one (p. 88). Perhaps these two antithetical forms of knowing are what Conrad has in mind in the passage of *A Personal Record* that speaks of a novel as "a conviction of our fellow-men's existence strong enough to take upon itself a form of imagined life clearer than reality and whose accumulated verisimilitude of selected episodes puts to shame the pride of documentary history."[28] Whatever the distortions the subjective consciousness imposes upon reality, it is, nevertheless, precisely this engagement of the self that heightens the mere information given and creates of it a work of art.

E. M. Forster has noted that all novels contain clocks, that the manipulation of time cannot be avoided by the storyteller.[29] This manipulation can take two forms: Writers can expand or compress the duration of chronological time, or they can disrupt the experiential sequence of a given action. Both distortions are integral parts of Conrad's art, and *Chance* employs these distortions and comments reflexively upon their use.

The problem of time expansion and compression is handled in part by the novelist's use of summary and scene, and, as I have previously noted, *Chance* is, in one sense, made up of two scenes that correspond to the two parts of the book, the first scene involving Powell, "I," and Marlow, and later Marlow's telling "I" of his adventures with the Fynes. This, at least, is the appearance of Part I. In fact, however, the "I"-narrator has played the artist and given the reader in one expanded scene what he received from Marlow "in several stages, at intervals which are not indicated here" (p. 41). The second part of the novel actually is delivered to the "I"-narrator in his rooms when Marlow comes by for an evening visit. The tale is not finished before dawn. Conrad's defense of Marlow's long-windedness in the preface to *Lord Jim* may also be invoked here,[30] if the reader seeks realism; nevertheless, the justification of Marlow as an agent of verisimilitude still seems unconvincing. In this role, Marlow surely creates more problems than he solves.

If we move beyond the "objective theater" to the story within the story, we are struck by the lack of immediacy in much of what Marlow presents. But what we have is not so much condensation as *extended summary*, if such an expression can be used. Conrad, in a by-no-means rare show of wit, defends the length of the novel in his Author's Note:

A critic has remarked that if I had selected another method of composition and taken a little more trouble the tale could have been told in
about two hundred pages. I confess I do not perceive exactly the
bearings of such criticism or even the use of such a remark. No doubt
that by selecting a certain method and taking great pains the whole
story might have been written out on a cigarette paper. For that
matter, the whole history of mankind could be written thus if only
approached with sufficient detachment. The history of men on this
earth since the beginning of ages may be resumed in one phrase of
infinite poignancy: They were born, they suffered, they died. . . . Yet
it is a great tale! But in the infinitely minute stories about men and
women it is my lot on earth to narrate I am not capable of such
detachment. (P. x)

On the one hand, storytellers must be selective if they are to rescue
meaning from the experience they examine; on the other, they wish to
present life in all its fullness. To accomplish this, Conrad seeks not only
to achieve a balance between summary and scene but also to add immediately to mere summary by projecting it from a vividly rendered
storytelling situation.

Most of the narrators of the story, in spite of their other limitations,
seem to respect the integrity of the moment. Either this is true, or
Marlow has again stepped in and invoked the author's privilege of filling
out what comes to him in fragments and summary form. Both actually
seem to be the case, since Powell's narrative, which opens the story,
comes directly from Powell and is fully rendered, whereas we surely get
a fuller picture of Captain Anthony at the Fynes than Flora is able to
provide on the street.

The immediacy of a scene from Flora's life should be indirectly pro-
portional to the immediacy of the objective theater, that is, there being
only so much "life" to go around, scenes from Flora's life should become
more vivid as Marlow's presence becomes more transparent, his interruptions less frequent. Such is not always the case. An objective description of de Barral's attempt to poison Anthony is what Powell is able
to provide toward the end of the novel, and it is one of the most vividly
rendered scenes in the book. But Marlow's presence in the scene, his
continual interjection of psychological comment, enhances rather than
disrupts the visual immediacy of the scene. Powell is able to see only the
surface, and the interest of the scene, the dramatic interest, lies elsewhere. "The inwardness of what was passing before his eyes," says
Marlow "was hidden from him, who had looked on, more impenetrably
than from me who at a distance of years was listening to his words"

(p. 426). Conrad and Marlow together create a kind of "authorial intrusion" that is neither distracting nor nondramatic, but is rather an expansion of the dramatic present that allows past and future to enter and contribute another dimension of immediacy to the scene.

Conrad is certainly correct in seeing almost all of his art defined through his use of "unconventional grouping and perspective."[31] By insisting upon the use of a narrator who reflects upon the past, he poses for himself the problem both of maintaining a distance from the past, a distance that is necessary if he is to comment on the action, and of rendering the past alive. Perhaps his most successful device for achieving this dual effect is the time-shift, which takes care of both problems—first by making the reader aware of the artistic control of the narrator by breaking the actual sequence of events, and second by enhancing the immediacy of the past through a juxtaposition of present and past, which tends to obscure the relative positions in time of separate events.

Marlow expresses the necessity of escaping the moment through reference to Powell's "surprise" at encountering his own past:

> The surprise, it is easy to understand, would arise from the inability to interpret aright the signs which experience (a thing mysterious in itself) makes to our understanding and emotions. For it is never more than that. Our experience never gets into our blood and bones. It always remains outside of us. That's why we look with wonder at the past. (P. 282)

When we are unable to make the moment intelligible, all that is left is the retrospective glance at someone who is "other," or at our younger self, that is also "other" now.

If curiosity is the first tool of the storytellers, memory is the second. In his essay on James, Conrad sees that "the only possible form of permanence in this world of relative values" is the "permanence of memory."[32] Not that the original event remains intact in the memory of the event—our experience tells us that this is impossible—but as memory always forces upon the person who remembers some of the artifices of the creative act, the memory itself becomes a work of art, which is commonly said to achieve a kind of permanence.

As Tindall has noted, "a narrator who scrambles times, finds matter less important than its arranger. No longer itself, matter becomes things for arrangement, for abstraction."[33] Marlow's broken time sequence, his arrangement of events, may more clearly reveal the truth of the story of Flora de Barral, but what truth adheres to the story is imaginative truth, and the use of the time shift is not justified by reference to the original sequence but by reference to Marlow's attempt to create a world "in which he can honestly believe."[34]

Whatever relative significance we assign to the language of fiction when comparing it to the language of poetry, it remains obvious that words exist in the novel differently from such aspects of fiction as story, plot, character, or setting. In all novels language is the medium through which these other elements are presented, regardless of the fact that the burden that words carry differs from novel to novel. Any discussion of *Chance* in terms of its presentation of Conrad's critical assumptions must deal with the uses of language.

Since Conrad is dealing, for the most part negatively, with the problem of making art out of life, this discussion must center mainly on the limits of language. In a letter to William Ernest Henley, quoted by Baines in his biography, Conrad writes of the difficulties of finding an adequate expression: "Words blow away like mist, and like mist they serve only to obscure, to make vague the real shape of one's feelings."[35] And again, at the close of the letter:

> Satis. Enough words. The postman will carry away this letter, the mist shall blow away and in the morning I shall discern clearly what tonight I am trying to interpret into writing—which remains. Let it remain, to show with what thundering kick the gods of life shut the door between our feeling and its expression. It is an old tale, the eternal grievance. If it were not for the illusion of the open door— sometimes—we would all be dumb, and it wouldn't matter, for no one would care to listen.[35]

The temptation of silence carries its greatest force when the writer finds the door between feeling and expression locked and all keys inadequate. In another letter to Hugh Clifford, after cautioning the writer to exercise the utmost care in selecting his words, since "things 'as they are' exist in words," and "the whole of the truth lies in the presentation," Conrad goes on to give a careful analysis of a passage of Clifford's writing. He objects strongly to the use of *frightened* in the passage, saying that it is "inadequate to express the true state of that man's mind. No word is adequate. The imagination of the reader should be left free to arouse his feeling."[37]

In recognizing the limits of language, Conrad also does homage to the truth of silence in certain situations. No word at all is truer than a lie. If the novelist's primary task is not to make us hear but to make us see, then Conrad is confronted with the conflict between the aims of his art and the means for achieving those aims. One resource at his disposal is the use of a nonverbal language, but even this must be presented verbally in the novel.

> She [Flora] tried to read something in his [Anthony's] face. . . . But she was not yet capable of understanding its expression. . . . She had not learned to read—not that sort of language. (P. 331)

> Everything he [Anthony] had said seemed somehow to have a special meaning under its obvious conversational sense. (P. 222)

> All her [Mrs. Fyne's] mental energy was concentrated on the nature of that memorable glance. The general tradition of mankind teaches us that glances occupy a considerable place in the self-expression of women. Mrs. Fyne was trying honestly to give me some idea, as much to satisfy her own uneasiness as my curiosity. . . . "It was horribly merry," she said. (Pp. 170–71)

Although Mrs. Fyne may consider her struggle with language successful, there is nevertheless something lost as experience seeks to find its expression in language. This "something lost" is precisely the quantity that stands between Flora's life and Marlow's work of the imagination.

Conrad says that with the right word and the right accent he will move the world:

> Yes! Let me only find the right word! Surely it must be lying somewhere among the wreckage of all the plaints and all the exultations poured out aloud since the first day when hope, the undying, came down on earth. It may be there, close by, disregarded, invisible, quite at hand. But it's no good. I believe there are men who can lay hold of a needle in a pottle of hay at the first try. For myself, I have never had such luck.[38]

Such submission before the limits of language seems to go beyond the relationship of Conrad to his chosen language. We may wonder at his choice, yet not doubt that for him it was the best of all possible choices. Language, like life, does not yield to the mind seeking truth: "Dark and, so to speak, inscrutable spaces being met with in life, there must be such places in any statement dealing with life" (p. 101).

In *Chance* Conrad successfully dramatizes the deceptive nature of language in his chronicle of de Barral's financial exploits, which were made possible on the strength of a mere word—*thrift*. While denigrating the capacity of words to convey truth, Conrad also works to show the *power* of language. Although words are, as J. Hillis Miller puts it, "a fabrication of man's intellect . . . a part of the human lie,"[39] and as such function as the material for the construction of illusions, it is these very illusions, here and elsewhere in Conrad, that alone are capable of capturing our devotion.

The question of the truth of language can be expanded to involve the question of the truth of illusions in Conrad generally. This truth must be considered limited, but again we must remember that in Conrad it is only the self-imposed order of an illusion that rescues experience from chaos. Faced with both the limitation and the necessity of language, the teller of the tale must choose the course of least distortion. "In his [Powell's] own words to me, he felt very 'enthusiastic' about Mrs. Anthony. 'Enthusiastic' is good; especially as he couldn't exactly explain to me what he meant by it" (p. 407).

Certainly the most significant problem of language in *Chance* is the ubiquitous sound of Marlow. In transmitting not only his own impressions but also his conversations with others, Marlow inevitably sets the tone and chooses most, if not all, of the words. Albert Guerard has very perceptively noted the relation between narrative method and language in the novel:

> The method, we shall see, marks a slight extension over that of *Lord Jim* in the degree to which scenes are vivified through Marlow's speculations on them; conjecture replaces hearsay. Thus the slighter *Chance*, rather than *Lord Jim* or *Nostromo*, anticipates the full Faulknerian extension of the impressionistic method. The amount of meditative comment screening the naked scene, the degree and the amount of interposition, gives Marlow at times the very accent and rhythm of the Faulknerian overriding voice.[40]

In spite of his dissatisfaction at times with the sound of Marlow, Guerard clearly sees the effect aimed at. From the perspective of the self-conscious novel, we can see that effect both establishing again the essential reflexivity of the novel and dramatizing the problem of transforming experience into language. One may examine any scene from Flora's history that is concretely rendered to discover the implications of Marlow's voice. Since it comes to the "I"-narrator and the reader in the form of a polished fragment from a novel (which it is, of course), the scene either will give proof of the artistry of the original narrator-observer—something that knowing the various narrator-observers, the reader cannot accept—or of the liberties that Marlow has taken with his material. The difficulties of establishing the source of information in some sections of the novel—many of the scenes on board the *Ferndale*, for example, could have come from either Flora or Powell—point to the uniformity of tone and style in Marlow's story. This uniformity is given a natural cause in the case of Powell, who, as a man of the sea, possesses, like Marlow, "a turn of mind composed of innocence and skepticism" and "an unexpected insight into motives, as of disinterested lookers-on at a game" (p. 33). But it should also be remembered that these are the attributes of an older, more experienced sailor and not those of the young Powell. And, unlike the Marlow of "Youth," Powell does not possess the full meaning of his past. It is Marlow's task to bring each segment of the story up to his own level of understanding.

But this can be accomplished only through a marriage of matter and manner. In a letter to Edward Garnett, Conrad is quick to recognize the incongruities of H. G. Wells's criticism of *An Outcast of the Islands*. Wells admired the matter but deplored the manner. But what transmits to Wells an appreciation of the novel? "What? It can be nothing but the expression—the arrangement of words, the style—Ergo: the style is not dishonorable."[41] The question of whether or not anything remains of a novel once we have given an exhaustive study of its style is an interesting question in itself, but for my purposes Conrad's answer to the question is sufficient. Nothing remains. As in Conrad's novel there is no dimension beyond the novel as given, so in Marlow's story there is no *other* story. If the autonomy of a work of fiction, its independence from actuality, seems obvious, it does not follow that these remarks on *Chance* could be applied, in the same way, to any novel, because traditionally an important part of the novel's appeal comes from its abjuration of autonomy, its insistence that it *is* an imitation of reality. So inured are we to the necessity of proffering the suspension of our disbelief, that a novel like *Chance*, which challenges us to concentrate on the mechanisms of its art, strikes the reader as a new kind of realism. What could be more realistic than the artifact that begins by calling attention to itself as artifact?

If we admit that in *Chance* Conrad is primarily concerned with dramatizing the problems of the novelist, we can still hope to show that the story of Flora de Barral and Captain Anthony—the son of the poet, you know—is not an accident, that the theme of *that* story is inextricably connected to the fortunes of the artist as old sailor. Whatever the role of chance in life, there is very little room for it in Conrad's art.

Bruce Harkness has argued persuasively that the narrators of Flora's story must be considered as performing a dual function.[42] They not only provide Marlow with facts and impressions, but they are all to some degree responsible for the *conditions* of Flora's life. Not merely passive observers, they act to shape the history they are recounting. Mrs. Fyne invites her brother for a visit, only to set the stage for a clandestine romance by ignoring him while he is there. The pedestrian Fyne visits Anthony at the Eastern Hotel, a visit that casts a shadow over the Anthonys' married life. Powell saves Anthony's life and brings the story to a climax. Marlow would perhaps like to think that he saves Flora's life at the quarry, but in fact it is the Fyne's dog that acts upon the story in that situation. In what may appear to be a gratuitous appendage of a happy ending, Marlow does act in the story by playing matchmaker. I would suggest that this final act should be considered a sort of deus ex machina, an outrageous, last-minute attempt on the part of the artist to tamper with life. What these examples show is that the causal agents of the life as well as of the tale are the same. Considered in their dual role as actors and writers of "history," the narrators serve to unite the themes of life and art.

To speak of the art in the life of Flora and Captain Anthony is to see how the problems of Marlow as storyteller and the problems of existence coalesce. Both Carleton Anthony and his son are acquainted with "all the supremely refined delicacy of tenderness," but upon reading the older Anthony's poetry, Powell is able to discern a certain difference, which Marlow interprets: "The father, fastidious, cerebral, morbidly shrinking from all contacts, could only sing in harmonious numbers of what the son felt with a dumb and reckless sincerity" (p. 332). While Roderick Anthony's own vision of Flora as a "wisp of mist" is comparable to the vision of a poet whose "poems read like sentimental novels told in verse of a really superior quality," he discovers that life will not yield to his illusion, and it is this discovery of his folly that seems to make life possible for him.

To speak of the life in Marlow's art is to see the fine balance, or tension, with which the claims of life and art are met. Never mere essay, "*Chance* is that rare thing, a work of fine spiritual significance and a technical *tour de force*."[43] In spite of its many indiscreet, narcissistic disclosures, *Chance* somehow manages to pay homage to life after all. We may even understand Marlow's comment on hearing of Captain Anthony's death: " 'You don't say so!' I cried quite affected as if I had known Captain Anthony personally" (p. 438).

At one point in the story, Marlow is interrupted by the "I"-narrator and accused of merely seeking amusement through gossip. Marlow's reply to this charge may be read as an eloquent apology for art, a justification that derives its force from its attempt to show that the practice of art can enhance our response to life:

> surely life must be amused somehow. It [gossiping] would be still a very respectable provision if it were only for that end. But from that same provision of understanding, there springs in us compassion, charity, indignation, the sense of solidarity; and in minds of any largeness an inclination to that indulgence which is next to affection. (P. 117–18)[44]

NOTES

1. Douglas Hewitt, *Conrad: A Reassessment* (Cambridge: Bowes and Bowes, 1952), p. 98.
2. Albert Guerard, *Conrad the Novelist* (Cambridge, Mass.: Harvard University Press, 1958), pp. 258–59.
3. Ibid., p. 269.
4. F. R. Leevis, *The Great Tradition* (London: Chatto and Windus, 1948), p. 223.
5. Guerard, *Conrad the Novelist*, p. 255.
6. Fredrick Karl, *A Reader's Guide to Joseph Conrad* (New York: Noonday Press, 1960), p. 244.
7. J. W. Johnson, "Marlow and *Chance*: A Reappraisal," *Texas Studies in Language and Literature* 10 (Spring 1968): 91.
8. Edward Said, *Joseph Conrad and the Fiction of Autobiography* (Cambridge, Mass.: Harvard University Press, 1966).
9. Wayne Booth, *The Rhetoric of Fiction* (Chicago: University of Chicago Press, 1961), pp. 71–76. Perhaps Booth's most important contribution to the vocabulary of novel criticism is the term *implied author*. While absolving the critic of the task of making biographical conjectures, the term nevertheless acknowledges the presence of the author in his work. This author is of interest to the literary critic rather than the biographer, since he is *always* a *created* figure and since all the essential features of his personality are within the covers of the book under examination.
10. E. K. Brown, "James and Conrad," *Yale Review* 55 (Winter 1946): p. 269.
11. Joseph Conrad, *Chance* (New York: Norton Library, 1968), p. 148. Subsequent references to this edition will appear in the text.
12. Henry James, *The Future of the Novel*, ed. Leon Edel (New York: Vintage Books, 1956), pp. 281–282.
13. Ibid., p. 282.
14. Ibid., pp. 280–81.
15. Ibid., p. 284.
16. Robert Scholes and Robert Kellogg, *The Nature of Narrative* (New York: Oxford University Press, 1966), pp. 274 ff.
17. Joseph Conrad, *Joseph Conrad on Fiction*, ed. Walter F. Wright (Lincoln: University of Nebraska Press, 1964), p. 119.
18. Ibid.
19. Ibid., p. 207.
20. Said, *Conrad and the Fiction of Autobiography*, pp. 12–13.
21. Karl, *Reader's Guide*, p. 61.
22. Wright, ed., *Conrad on Fiction*, p. 79.
23. Richard Curle, *Joseph Conrad and His Characters* (London: Bowes and Bowes, 1957), p. 65.
24. Wright, ed., *Conrad on Fiction*, p. 167.
25. Scholes and Kellogg, *Nature of Narrative*, p. 267.
26. William York Tindall, "Apology for Marlow," in *From Jane Austen to Joseph Conrad*, ed.

Robert C. Rathburn and Martin Steinmann, Jr. (Minneapolis,: University of Minnesota Press, 1958), p. 285.

27. Wright, ed., *Conrad on Fiction*, p. 88.

28. Ibid., p. 130.

29. E. M. Forster, *Aspects of the Novel* (New York: Harcourt, Brace and World, 1927), p. 29.

30. Joseph Conrad, *Lord Jim*, ed. Thomas Moser (New York: W. W. Norton, 1968), p. 1.

31. Wright, ed., *Conrad on Fiction*, p. 44.

32. Ibid., p. 84.

33. Tindal, "Apology for Marlow," p. 284.

34. Wright, ed., *Conrad on Fiction*, p. 79.

35. Jocelyn Baines, *Joseph Conrad: A Critical Biography* (London: Weiden and Nicholson, 1959), p. 218.

36. Ibid.

37. Wright, ed., *Conrad on Fiction*, pp. 20–21.

38. Ibid., p. 118.

39. J. Hillis Miller, *Poets of Reality* (Cambridge, Mass.: Harvard University Press, 1966), p. 36. Miller's book also contains an excellent discussion of *The Secret Agent*.

40. Guerard, *Conrad the Novelist*, pp. 266–67.

41. Baines, *Critical Biography*, p. 166.

42. Bruce Harkness, "The Epigraph of Conrad's *Chance*," *Nineteenth-Century Fiction Studies* 9 (December 1954), 217–18.

43. Edward Crankshaw, *Joseph Conrad: Some Aspects of the Art of the Novel* (London: John Lane, 1936), p. 132.

44. See the preface to *Almayer's Folly* for a similar defense.

3

William Faulkner's *Absalom, Absalom!*: Fiction as History

Fiction is history that might have happened. History is fiction that did happen.

—André Gide

Men, like poets, rush "into the middest," *in medias res*, when they are born; they also die *in mediis rebus*, and to make sense out of their span they need fictive concords with origins and ends, such as give meaning to lives and to poems.

—Frank Kermode, *The Sense of an Ending*

History may be, in a philosophical sense, a fiction, but it does not feel like that when we miss a train or somebody starts a war.

—David Lodge, *The Novelist at the Crossroads*

We make history, both by performing those acts which constitute the subject matter for accounts of the actions of the past and by writing those accounts. *History* can refer to either the deed done or the account of the deed. It is a peculiarity of the term, however, that the account of the event takes a special priority over the event itself, and not merely in the sense that for most of us historical knowledge is so much a matter of knowing accounts rather than events that we even fail to acknowledge the distinction. The more decisive priority of history as a recording of events over history as events recorded is established once we grant the obvious fact that it is the historian's decision to record an event that makes that event *history* in both senses of the term. And this fact perhaps justifies us in our failure to distinguish between the past and the past recaptured. We cannot calculate Homer's debt to Achilles, but the hero's debt to the poet-historian is fixed—and absolute.

On the other hand it should be noted that historians begin to surrender their priority—call it their freedom—as soon as they first exercise it. Once chosen, the event begins to dictate the substance of the historical account. Their moment of freedom gone, or at least powerfully circumscribed, historians then seek to become subservient to the past, to become as free as possible of the task of making choices.

Of course, there will still be choices to make, but historians like to think—and, in a sense, they are correct—that these choices are directed by the past itself. Still, they do well to retain some freedom, for there will come a moment when the past is silent, and since they know that there are no real silences in history, that the silence is only *there*, in their histories, they will try to fill the void with a guess that they will call a hypothesis.

A hypothesis is a fiction. It may remain a fiction, or it may subsequently be proved or disproved when more facts are known. It may be proved unacceptable without the acquisition of new facts if it is examined and found incompatible with such facts as are already available. The hypothesis is one kind of union of fact and fiction, because finally, although it is a fiction, it is not a totally free fiction: some hypotheses are acceptable and some are not.

Literary fictions are free. Literary fictions that are free but like to pretend they are not are called novels. A novelist's business is to impersonate the historian, and yet these impersonations are games, contracts entered into by writers and readers whereby we pretend that the novel is what it is not and what, strangely, we do not really wish it to be. Novels, after all, are neither written nor read as substitutes for some desired but as yet unattainable histories. What we want is the sense of life, certainly, but life as it is imagined, not as it is lived.

I may question this disjunction and say that the sense of life that I desire is obtainable only as something lived *and* as something that engages the imagination. The reader of novels, then, seeks neither an escape from reality nor its duplication, but rather an experience that is itself a part of life by virtue of its independence from representation. The life that the novel describes is the life that it creates, and that life is no less *there* than the events that compose our histories. In fact, it is *all* there, in a way that even the most complete historical study is not. It is curious, then, that we continue to pretend that histories are somehow more important to us than novels.

While no readers of the novel *Absalom, Absalom!* think they are reading history, some have thought that Quentin Compson and Shreve

McCannon, the last of a long line of redactors, are engaged in a historical investigation of the legend of the Sutpen family, and that this investigation itself is central to the novel. Some, like Cleanth Brooks, see the novel as dramatizing the process of historical reconstructions, as dealing directly with the nature of historical truth and with "the problem of how we can know the past."[1] But perhaps the novelist, as inventor of stories, might be more interested in the process of creation than in the process of historical reconstruction. While it might be true that Faulkner wants to tell us that "history is really a kind of imaginative construction," that all histories are really fictions—and it is understandable that the novelist, whose profession is lying, should take the lies of others as a matter of course—we should not miss an even more central idea, that all fictions are fictions before they are anything else.[3]

The real problem with Brooks's account of the novel—and this failure is shared by most other critical accounts as well—is that finally it is unable to explain the specific form of the novel and how that form is expressive of content. Hyatt Waggoner says that the chief effect of the form is to cause us to feel that we are participating in a search for the truth: "*Absalom* draws us in, makes us share its creative discovery as few novels do."[4] While it would be easy to agree with this emphasis on reader-participation, Waggoner's perspective of the novel as a discovery—albeit creative—of something behind the fiction reveals the fact that he still feels that he is dealing with a traditional mimesis. Olga Vickery recognizes the story as legend rather than history, but at the same time cautions us not to mistake the dream for the reality. According to her, the lesson of the novel is that if man "tries to impress an ideal pattern on experience, it is at the expense of humanity, his own and that of others."[5] Such an interpretation fails to acknowledge the bond between Thomas Sutpen's "designs," Miss Rosa Coldfield's "demonizing," Quentin's own obsessions, and the novel that the reader holds in his hands; art itself is seen, in this novel, as an imposition of an ideal pattern on experience, made at the expense of humanity. One of the most perceptive readings of this novel is Ilse Dusoir Lind's "Design and Meaning in *Absalom, Absalom!*," but unfortunately the essay breaks into two parts, one on meaning and one on design. Lind has discovered that *the Sutpen tragedy as communicated* (as opposed to what?) has no objective existence, that it is the collective product of the workings of the minds of three major narrators and one collaborator,[6] but she fails to draw from this the necessary conclusions concerning the meaning of the novel. The Sutpen tragedy exists only as it is communicated, and that existence is objective: the words on the page are real words. But to say that the novel is an exploration of the meaning of history is to lose this insight and to make the form or design of this novel extraneous.[7] And finally, in saying that the novel is the collective product of its various narrators is to refine the author quite out of existence when, in fact, his presence is felt on every page.

In *The Limits of Metaphor*, James Guetti speaks of *Absalom, Absalom!* in a way quite different from that of the critics I have been considering. Guetti sees the novel as primarily illustrative of the modern artist's preoccupation with the "problematic quality of the artistic structure or structures."[8] More specifically, he sees the narrative structure of the hunt becoming in Faulkner a metaphor for "a search for the right words, a matter of telling and retelling, and the narrative difficulty is that of using language in such a way as to prevent one's recognition of the arbitrariness and exclusiveness of composed linguistic systems."[9] While I might object to Guetti's formulation of the problems facing Faulkner—I believe that the novelist is trying to *lead* his reader to the discovery of the "arbitrariness" and "exclusiveness" of his novel, for example—nevertheless, this critic's *way* of discussing the work explains many aspects of our own experience of the novel. I would say that his approach leads us to consider that the novel is not really about what it seems to be about, except this formulation of his approach would not really distinguish it from those offered by other interpreters of this novel: the novel doesn't *seem* to be about the meaning of history, either. It seems more appropriate to say that Guetti has recognized that the novel is *about* what it *is*—a search for the right words. The language Guetti uses to describe the novel will sound strange to us only to the extent that we have forgotten what novels are and how they are made. (For some, this will even include their lost awareness *that* novels are made.)

Absalom, Absalom!, as I see it, is primarily a description of the conflict between life and art, between words and things; it is an examination of some of the central assumptions of fictional realism. Faulkner follows the tradition of fictional realism in that he pretends to be doing the job of the historian. But, more important, he parodies that tradition by presenting us with a self-acknowledged fiction, a novel that uses the history-making process as a metaphor for the fiction-making process. Brooks is at least partially correct: Faulkner's subject is history, art, society, and all that the mind of man creates. But both the language and the structure of the novel suggest the centrality of the aesthetic rather than the historical experience.

My reading of this novel is in many ways similar to the one given by Richard P. Adams: "*Absalom, Absalom!* is usually approached as if it were essentially history, or at any rate as if Faulkner's method in it were essentially historiographical. . . . The answer . . . is that Faulkner is not using a story to teach us history. He is using history and historiography as tools in telling a story."[10] It becomes important that we do not confuse vehicle and tenor in Faulkner's metaphorical structure. Adams avoids this by recognizing that the telling of the story is at least as important as the story told and that, therefore, all critical accounts of *Absalom, Absalom!* must establish the centrality of Quentin Compson: "Miss Rosa's frenzy, Mr. Compson's puzzlement, and the anguish of Charles Bon and Judith and Henry Sutpen are more or less objective correlatives of Quentin's frustration and despair."[11] This formulation has the advantage of offering an explanation of the design of the novel, but it suffers from its failure to recognize that once we have recognized that *Absalom* is a complex allegory devoted to an examination of the problems of literary creation, there is no reason to focus on the psychology of Quentin, to claim that "the 'history' of the book is perhaps more concerned with the fictional biography of Quentin than with that of Sutpen."[12] Quentin, like Sutpen and all of the other characters in the book, is above all a *created* character, and serves, like the others, as an "objective correlative" of the author's own frustration and despair. Once this is recognized, it becomes possible to view *Absalom, Absalom!* as Faulkner's most personal and revealing novel as well as his greatest.

Recorded history, like fiction, is composed of words. Since persons and events are not words, the historian cannot be said to deliver the past unmediated. But surely this similarity between the historian and the novelist is not a sufficient reason to confuse history with fiction. Nor is the style or structure of historical writing an adequate means of differentiating it from fiction. Many novelists write like historians, and a historian, if he chose to do so, could write Faulknerian prose and still be writing history.

Margaret MacDonald, in an attempt to isolate the unique characteristics of fiction, finds that unlike the nonfiction writer, the "storyteller both creates a story, a verbal construction, and the contents of that construction," and that for the novelist, these two activities are inseparable.[13] J. M. Cameron, in defining the poetic as the fictitious, makes a similar observation: "The poetic description has the form of a description; but it exists only as *this* description, these words in this order. What is said and how it is said are thus not distinguishable in the way they are in other forms of discourse."[14] Perhaps what we really mean when we say that the content of a poetic utterance is identical to its form—and I would hold that this is as true of prose fictions as it is of lyric poetry—is that there is no separable content, behind the words, that might have been expressed differently. We can choose between two descriptions of an existing thing on the basis of the correspondence of the utterance to the reality, but when there is no reality apart from the words, the words are the only reality.

What we mean by *creative writing* is not the imaginative selection of words and phrases and arrangements, but the creation of fictive worlds, which lie neither beside nor beyond the language that depicts them but solely *in* the language itself. Now this is equally true of all fictions, and what distinguishes reflexive storytellers from others is their sustained effort to make us aware of the nonexistence of their fictive world outside of language.

One way that Faulkner does this in *Absalom, Absalom!* is to emphasize the immateriality of the figures in the Sutpen legend, who are variously presented as ghosts, phantoms, shades, and shadows. Another way is to make the reader aware of the unreality of the storytelling situation itself. Combining these two methods of exposure, Faulkner's novel moves dialectically toward a comprehensive view of the kind of reality that *is* available to the novelist.

The reader is introduced to the laws governing the shifts from story to storyteller early in the novel as Miss Rosa Coldfield begins to conjure up the ghost of Thomas Sutpen. "As though in inverse ratio to the vanishing voice, the invoked ghost of the man whom she could neither forgive nor revenge herself upon began to assume a quality almost of solidity, permanence."[15] If Sutpen can have no existence without the presence of those who imagine him, it is equally true that all of those who imagine him depend upon him for their existence. Each storyteller is, like Quentin, either an "empty hall" or a "barracks filled with backward-looking ghosts"(p. 12). Insofar as the narrator is successful in realizing the presence of the Sutpen family, he begins to lose whatever tenuous life he possesses. The "inverse ratio" suggests a kind of law of the conservation of reality that operates throughout the novel. But the circularity of cause and effect lends an air of unreality to all figures in this novel, both the imagined and the imagining.

It is the task of novel readers to discover the unity of method and matter in the novel they are reading. In this novel this task itself is dramatized as the search for the relationship between the created and the creator, between the story of the Sutpens and the story of the making of the story of the Sutpens. This relationship is primarily expressed by the interdependence of creator and created, which is shown by presenting all characters as belonging to both classes.

It is Judith, by mixing the metaphors of puppet and weaver, who first seems to recognize her dual identity as both created and creator:

> You get born and you try this and you dont know why only you keep on trying it and you are born at the same time with a lot of other people, all mixed up with them, like trying to, having to, move your arms and legs with strings only some strings are hitched to all the other arms and legs and the others all trying and they don't know why either except that the strings are all in one another's way like five or six people all trying to make a rug on the same loom only each one wants to weave his own pattern. (P. 127)

Judith is offering General Compson's wife the last letter she received from Charles Bon, not that it may be understood or even read but that something might *occur*, if it is nothing but the passing of a letter from one hand to another, an event that might affirm the reality of beings who, because they recognize the limitations on their freedom—not succumbing to fate but acting as if they were free while knowing that the pattern or design they intend can never be realized—are able to question the reality of the self, which depends for its existence on beings equally frustrated in their attempts at self-realization.

Judith is here trying to break out of the circle, to send out from the confines of this fictive world something real, something that escapes the dehumanizing process represented later in the passage by the words carved on the tombstone, which "cant be *is* because it never can become *was* because it cant ever die or perish." The only way *to be* (and Faulkner constructs a fairly coherent ontology around conjugations of this verb) is to be able to die and not-be, but Judith cannot exist because she cannot cease to exist. Ironically, this letter, which was to enable her and the others to resist the process of summing up, which is represented by the scratches on a never-dying block of stone, becomes a part of a novel, which, like the block of stone, "cant be *is* because it never can become *was* because it cant ever die or perish." The imperishable quality of art insures its lack of continuity with life. We murder to immortalize.

The other characters in the Sutpen Legend are only partially aware of their dual status as free creators and as fated characters in the fiction they create. But it is this partial awareness that provides the key to the unity of the novel. In a sense, the problems of artistic creation are with us throughout the story, not merely in the last chapters, where Quentin and Shreve make up their version of the story. All of the characters, even

Wash Jones, try to compose the worlds in which they live. The truest link between the story told and the telling of the story—between Quentin and the characters from the Sutpen legend—is not Quentin's emotional commitment to Southern values or even his identification with Henry through their common obsession with the idea of incest, but in the sharing of the acts of the imagination. As Faulkner tells us, in a crucial shift to third-person narration and the omniscient point of view, both Quentin and Shreve are "dedicated to that best of ratiocination which after all was a good deal like Sutpen's morality and Miss Rosa Coldfield's demonizing" (p. 280). The creation of the story in Cambridge is analogous to Sutpen's "design" and Miss Rosa's satanic epic, even to the extent that Quentin at least, like Sutpen and Miss Rosa, seems destined to live and act within his fiction. Whatever differences may exist in the degree to which the separate artist-figures fail to actualize their visions, these visions—and, as I hope to show, Faulkner's own--have a great deal more in common with each other than with the ineluctable reality that always and necessarily exists beyond the reach of fiction.

In one sense Quentin and Shreve are the creators of the Sutpen legend, since they give us the story in the form present to the reader of the novel. But in another sense, they are the final link in a causal chain initiated by Thomas Sutpen. Quentin alone seems to recognize this: "Yes, we are both Father. Or maybe Father and I are both Shreve, maybe it took Father and me both to make Shreve or Shreve and me both to make Father or maybe Thomas Sutpen to make all of us." In this climactic passage Quentin recognizes that interdependence between the created and the creator, that law by which the imagining mind is at last possessed and then usurped by that which it imagines. Thomas Sutpen then becomes not tragic hero nor arch-fiend but arch-creator, father of all the living and the dead.

It is Quentin—whose images are no doubt colored at this point by Rosa's account—who first sees Sutpen as creating *ex nihilo* the world that he will inhabit:

> Then in the long unamaze Quentin seemed to watch them overrun suddenly the hundred square miles of tranquil and astonished earth and drag house and formal gardens violently out of the soundless Nothing and clap them down like cards upon a table beneath the up-palm and pontific, creating the Sutpen's Hundred, the *Be Sutpen's Hundred* like the oldentime *Be Light*. (Pp. 8–9)

What is here stressed simultaneously with the arrogance and independence of Sutpen's act is the artificiality of his creation. Sutpen "abrupts" upon this scene, which is as "peaceful and decorous as a schoolprize water color" (p. 8), with nothing more than a pack of cards, counters in a game of solitaire. Like Adam, he names the objects of his world, "his own get and all the get of his wild niggers after the country began to assimilate them" (p. 61), but he forgets that the word is not the thing, that some things have no name, that some names name no things.

Sutpen's "design" is nothing more nor less than an attempt to show that "some things have to be whether they are or not," a vain attempt to weave his pattern on the loom, even after he realizes the futility of his effort to make the world outside correspond to the pictures in his head. Sutpen first expresses this realization when he talks to General Compson during his visit home during the war, a visit itself which, since it involves the absurd task of transporting the huge tombstones to Sutpen's Hundred, is a continuation of the design even after that design has been exposed as an illusion. "You see, I had a design in my mind. Whether it was a good or a bad design is beside the point; the question is, where did I make the mistake in it, what did I do or misdo in it, whom or what injure by it to the extent which this would indicate" (p. 263). According to General Compson, Sutpen's tragedy occurs not because his design fails but because he could not anticipate the failure. In his "innocence" he had "believed that the ingredients of morality were like the ingredients of a pie or cake and once you had measured them and mixed them and put them into the oven it was all finished and nothing but pie or cake could come out" (p. 263). Cleanth Brooks is perhaps correct in seeing this as an innocence that flourishes in a secularized society.[16] Sutpen is certainly viewing the design from a secular point of view by refusing to consider it in terms of good and evil, and by refusing to see its defeat as a form of retribution. His belief in the power of the mind or imagination to master the world is also a rejection of the irrational forces of life. All designs and recipes are abstractions of human invention; Sutpen's design fails not because it was "wrong," but because, like any other mental construct, it must fail. Finally, Sutpen is not the fully secularized man, because while he would reject the old myths, he would still retain the belief in the power of myths to control and pattern our lives. There is finally some truth in Miss Rosa's demonizing, for like Satan, Sutpen would possess God's creative power but forgets that only the dreams of the gods are real.

Although of all the characters Sutpen has the greatest illusions about his own powers as creator, he also has an awareness of himself as one of the created. This double identity as both creator and created is expressed in his telling of his own story to General Compson:

he was not talking about himself. He was telling a story. He was not
bragging about something he had done; he was just telling a story
about something a man named Thomas Sutpen had experienced,
which would have been the same story if the man had had no name at
all, if it had been told about any man or no man over whiskey at night.
(P. 247)

Sutpen is here creating with words what he had created through the
actions of his life—himself. But he is aware that this verbal account is
not to be identified with the real man, for he is not talking about himself
but telling a story.

If we doubt that it would have been the same story if it had been told
about no man, then we should be reminded that this "if" is ironical, that
the story *is* about no man, that it is fiction and not history. It is as if
Sutpen's perspective suddenly shifts and he is able to see himself for
what he really is—a character in a fiction. If Sutpen, who creates and
peoples the world of the story, is himself—as Miss Rosa calls him—"a
walking shadow," then the process of dehumanization, which here becomes Faulkner's method of characterization, should be complete.
Cleanth Brooks notes that the long perspective of history is "anti-
historical: make it long enough and any 'sense of history' evaporates.
Lengthen it still further and the human dimension itself evaporates."[17]
But not quite. To the extent that an audience can no longer believe in the
reality of a storyteller's story, to that extent they must confront the reality
of the storyteller himself: Alone, and with no place to hide, the storyteller can only be present, imagining.

The process by which Faulkner dramatizes the reflexive nature of the
act of creation is extended to the other characters in the Sutpen Legend.
Sutpen's second wife, Ellen, creates the "vicarious bridal" (p. 77) for
her daughter and Charles Bon even before the engagement, and the
quality of her creation reflects the quality of her mind: It is seen as a
fairy tale enacted by a fashionable ladies' club (p. 76). When she is
finally frustrated in her design and takes to her bed, it is "not at the
upset of the marriage but at the shock of reality entering her life: this the
merciful blow of the ax before the beast's throat is cut" (p. 79). She dies
when her world dies, and later her actual death leaves no body to be
buried (p. 126).

Judith accepts the part her mother writes for her because she exists at
that time in the selfless state between childhood and womanhood, which
Mr. Compson describes as

that state where, though still visible, young girls appear as though

seen through glass and where the voice cannot reach them; where they
exist . . . in a pearly lambence without shadows and themselves
partaking of it; in nebulous suspension held, strange and unpredict-
able, even their very shapes fluid and delicate and without substance.
(P. 67)

Even allowing for the distortions of his peculiar brand of romantic mis-
ogyny, we can probably say that Mr. Compson is wrong only to the extent
that he fails to include the male characters in this dreamlike state.
Judith is insubstantial not by reason of her female adolescence but
because she is a character in the novel.

The lover, Charles Bon, is likewise seen as a character in the Sutpen
legend, "a myth, a phantom: something which they created themselves;
some effluvium of Sutpen blood and character, as though as a man he did
not exist at all" (p. 104). He is a hero out of *Arabian Nights* (p. 96) or
Lothario (p. 102); Polynices, the unacknowledged son and brother to
Judith's Antigone. We are not allowed to see Bon and Judith as lovers in
the flesh but only as "two shades pacing, serene and untroubled by
flesh" ((p. 97).

But if Bon is a created figure, he also creates. With Henry he creates
Judith—"just the blank shape, the empty vessel in which each of them
strove to preserve not the illusion of himself nor his illusion of the other
but what each conceived the other to believe him to be" (pp. 119–20).
Bon alone attempts to create Henry by treating him as a docile plate, a
sort of *tabula rasa*, on which he, Bon, not nature, can draw whatever he
wishes (p. 111).

Henry is also created by Quentin as "that gaunt tragic dramatic self-
hypnotized youthful face like the tragedian in a college play, an
academic Hamlet waked from some trancement of the curtain's falling
and blundering across the dusty stage from which the rest of the cast had
departed last commencement" (p. 174). Henry is seen as a tragedian,
the creator of the drama, and Hamlet, an actor in it.

The sole living links between the past and the present, between the
Sutpen story and the telling of that story are Henry and Miss Rosa
Coldfield. Quentin's encounter with Henry—the climax of the story if it
is viewed as history—is not even given. It is as if Henry, out of the
context of legend and into the realm of Quentin's experience, cannot—
like Bon's letter to Judith—sustain examination in a full light (p. 89). He
remains, in spite of Quentin's encounter with him, a part of the legend
rather than a figure in life. To Quentin, the experience of meeting him is
like an encounter with a character from a dream.

Rosa Coldfield is the only character who has existed in both fictional worlds and who has both narrated the story of the Sutpens and played a role in that story. She therefore provides the most important link between the two worlds.

Insofar as Miss Rosa lives in the past, Sutpen and his progeny live in the present. Yet she is constantly aware of the intangible quality of the remembered past. As a child she was only conscious of watching the "miragy antics of men and women" (p. 162), of a "Casandra-like listening beyond closed doors" (p. 27), where the reality of events was always beyond the understanding of the child-voyeur, who, chameleonlike, tried to blend herself in her surroundings and lose her identity in order that she might freely observe and yet not take part in the reality around her (p. 27).

She is finally drawn into this reality by the murder of Charles Bon, but even this event is a "shot heard only by its echo" (p. 153). Although she will try to verify the event or at least confirm the existence of Bon by trying to feel his weight in the coffin as they carry him to his grave, she will be unable to do so. "I do not even know of my own knowledge that Ellen ever saw it, that Judith ever loved it, that Henry ever slew it: so who will dispute me when I say, Why did I not invent, create it?" (p. 147). Rosa gains nothing in knowledge by her participation in the actions she describes. Her own involvement is as legendary to her as it is to Quentin, to whom she recounts her story.

In his *Philosophical Fragments*, Kierkegaard contrasts the contemporary disciple of Christ with the disciple at second hand, and finds that the problems of belief are essentially the same. Due to the paradoxical assertion that Jesus is both God and man, the contemporary disciple of Christ possesses no essential advantages. The kind of truth offered is not subject to the verification of an eyewitness.

In much the same way, Miss Rosa is not any closer to the reality behind her experience for having been there. The reason for this is twofold: (1) The kind of reality she seeks cannot be obtained from the events themselves, since it has no objective existence, and (2) she was not *there*, anymore than she is *here* with Quentin, telling her story. She, like the other narrators in the story, is a disembodied voice; she is composed solely of the words that she utters.

The disembodied voice of each of the narrators corresponds to the ephemeral nature of the various "telling scenes" or "objective theaters" of the novel. The fictive present has three locations: the office in Miss Rosa's home, the veranda of the Compson home, and the dormitory room

in Cambridge, Massachusetts. These scenes represent the "real" world
of the novel, the places where the words are spoken. The reader is made
constantly aware of the scenes, either by the indirect form of the report-
age of the past, by the speaker's openly hypothetical comments on the
story, or by reference to the physical nature of the storytelling scene
itself and the appearance of the characters in that setting. An examination of some of the physical properties of these scenes will demonstrate
that they do not, in fact, give solidity and reality to the storytelling
situation.

Images of deadness and sterility dominate the scene of Miss Rosa's
telling. Miss Rosa herself has been "dead" for the forty-three years since
Sutpen's insult, and "the dim hot airless room" on a "long hot weary
dead September afternoon" has been closed and fastened against the
light for an equal length of time. The teller is dressed in black; her "legs
hung straight and rigid as if she had on iron shinbones and ankles"
(p. 7). Although no one knows for whom she mourns—for sister, father,
or "nohusband"—it is clear that she might easily be in mourning for
herself. Locked in the "dim coffin-smelling gloom" (p. 8), Quentin listens to a disembodied voice that possesses qualities of its own apart from
the speaker. It is "like a stream, a trickle running from patch to patch of
dried sound, and the ghost mused with shadowy docility as if it were the
voice which he haunted where a more fortunate one would have had a
house" (p. 8). Himself a ghost, Sutpen must have no contact with a
physical world but only with the ghostlike voice of Miss Rosa.

As Quentin listens to the old woman's story, he muses on the relationship of the act of storytelling to dreams and finally to art. The passage
seems to be one of the most directly reflexive statements in the novel:

> It should have been later than it was; it should have been late, yet the
> yellow slashes of mote-palpitant sunlight were latticed no higher up on
> the impalpable wall of gloom which separated them; the sun seemed
> hardly to have moved. It (the talking, the telling) seemed (to him, to
> Quentin) to partake of that logic- and reason-flouting quality of a
> dream which the sleeper knows must have occurred, stillborn and
> complete, in a second, yet the very quality upon which it must depend
> to move the dreamer (verisimilitude) to credulity—horror or pleasure
> or amazement—depends as completely upon a formal recognition of
> and acceptance of elapsed and yet-elapsing time as music or a printed
> tale. (P. 22)

In listening to the story unfold, Quentin has entered the rhythm of the
fiction, which here moves faster than the rhythm of the day in the
darkened room. Like dreams, fictions require that we *knowingly* surren-

der our own time for that of the illusion. The emphasis on "formal recognition and acceptance" tells us that this is the willful surrender that makes possible the illusion of the sense of life, the sense of "elapsed and yet-elapsing time." "It should have been later than it was" is an expression of the impossible desire for one time, a time in which the telling and the tale exist in harmony within the same world.

And yet, curiously, it is the telling that here exists as a work of art exists—out of time—while the tale itself seems to move in accordance with the rhythm of life. The tale has stolen life from life and left the dreamer wondering if he wakes or sleeps. The answer can only be that the dreamer himself is dreaming within that larger dream which is the novel. He cannot escape, any more than Sutpen can escape, his own fictional nature. But he can, like Sutpen, live as he imagines or is imagined. He can act *as if* he lives in a single, harmonious time where fact and fiction are one.

I have read this remarkable passage as an attempt by Faulkner to provoke his readers to examine not only the relationship of the narrator and listener to the story but also their (the readers') own relationship to the novel and, by implication, to any novel. What do we mean when we say that fiction is a representation of reality or that we, as readers, suspend our disbelief? These are questions that any theorist of the novel might ask but that Faulkner asks in the context of this novel. One answer that seems to be given here is that the realists' problem derives from their failure to recognize that the reality they are said to represent must first be created. Another answer seems to be that all readers' surrender to the illusion must be a calculated act, whereby at least part of their minds begrudgingly recognize the disparity between their worlds and the world presented to them by the artist. Having recognized this disparity, they may then, however, commit themselves to make-believe, recognizing, as they do so, that they have merely traded one dream for another.

Faulkner continues to undercut the reality of the storytelling scenes when he moves to the Compson veranda for chapters 2 through 4. Less distinctly rendered than Miss Rosa's office, the veranda hardly exists at all: it is usurped by the voice of the third-person narrator, by Mr. Compson's version of the story, and finally, at the beginning of chapter 4, by Quentin, who imagines Miss Rosa alone in her house, waiting to take the trip to Sutpen's Hundred. The most clearly rendered object on the veranda is the porch light, which Mr. Compson turns on in order that Quentin may read Charles Bon's letter to Judith—"the single globe stained and bug-fouled from the long summer and which even when clean gave off but little light" (p. 89). By this light Quentin reads "the faint spidery script not like something impressed upon the paper by the once-living hand but like a shadow cast upon it which had resolved upon the paper the instant before he looked at it and which might fade, vanish, at any instant while he still read" (p. 129). Certainly the lack of adequate light contributes to the shadowy quality of the letter itself. The role of the subject in the act of perception—a role that is at least partially conditioned by the circumstances under which this act is performed—is all-determining. For the letter, to be is to be perceived; inhuman, the words of the letter are shadows that only are when they appear. Later, I wish to examine more closely Faulkner's orientation toward philosophical idealism. For the moment, it should be sufficient to note that the past is given existence by the perceiver in the storytelling situation, and yet this situation is as poorly lighted as Miss Rosa's office. It exists in the same world of shadows as the letter itself.

It might be helpful to seek to understand the mode of existence of this letter as well as that of the other "documents" in the novel. It appears as a kind of intrusion of the reality of the past, like Hawthorne's scarlet letter. It wants to be an object, a thing, something more solid than the voices of the various narrators. It is the thingness of the letter that Judith emphasizes when she gives it to General Compson's wife. Yet it loses its pretensions as a thing in the phenomenal world and becomes a "dead tongue," yet "gentle sardonic whimsical and incurably pessimistic" (p. 129). Paradoxically, perhaps, it becomes human as it speaks, but loses its presence, its being-in-the-world, as it gains in humanity. Is this not another way of dramatizing the disparity between dead "realities" and live fictions?

The most intensely realized storytelling scene is located in Cambridge, the fictional present of the last four chapters of the novel. Because these chapters constitute the primary theater of creation in the novel, it will be necessary to deal with them in some detail. But first it is important to examine the physical characteristics of the scene.

Immediately, we notice certain parallels with the other scenes I have been describing. In spite of the fact that Faulkner returns us again and again to the scene, interrupts the flow of the narrative within the narrative in order to make us completely aware that this inner narrative is not reality but a story told, the scene of the telling itself is familiarly insubstantial. The sitting room, the scene of chapters 6 through 8, is "tomblike: a quality stale and static and moribund beyond any mere vivid and living cold" (p. 345). Early in the evening Quentin and Shreve are removed from the reality of "this strange iron New England snow," cloistered in the "warm and rosy orifice above the iron quad" (p. 217). As the evening progresses, however, "this snug monastic coign, this dreaming and heatless alcove of what we call the best of thought"

(p. 258) is penetrated by the cold outside. But this contact with the outside, instead of enlivening the room, only serves to increase its resemblance to a tomb, whose coldness is "beyond any mere vivid and living cold."

Quentin and Shreve participate in the sterility of the scene: Quentin speaks in a "flat, curiously dead voice, the downcast face, the relaxed body not stirring except to breathe" (p. 258). Shreve is wrapped like a mummy against the cold in both bathrobe and overcoat (p. 346).

As in the other storytelling scenes, the sitting-room is dimly lit. The light will be extinguished shortly when the boys go to bed, and "the iron and impregnable dark" becomes one with "the iron and icelike bed-clothing lying upon the flesh slacked and thin-clad for sleeping" (p. 360). It is in this cold and this darkness that Quentin at last finishes "reading" his father's letter, which, like Bon's letter, is an intrusion of reality upon the deathlike scene. Ironically, of course, the letter is composed of Mr. Compson's comments on death.

In the last chapter, after Shreve's recreation of the final episode of the Sutpen story—the burning of the Sutpen mansion—"Quentin did not answer, staring at the window; then he could not tell if it was the actual window or the window's pale rectangle upon his eyelids" (pp. 376–77). Finally, the problematic nature of reality, which has been the concern of all of the narrators of the story, envelops the storytelling scene itself. The deadness of the narrators comes to match that of the characters in the story they tell.

In spite of this physical deadness, or perhaps because of it, the room in Cambridge is filled with creative activity. Quentin and Shreve, who are "as free now of flesh" as Sutpen himself (p. 295), persist in their attempt to give shape and meaning to the fictive past,

> the two of them creating between them, out of the rag-tag and bob-ends of old tales and talking people who had perhaps never existed at all, anywhere, who, shadows, were not shadows of flesh and blood which had lived and died but shadows in turn of what were (to one of them at least, to Shreve) shades too, quiet as the visible murmur of their vaporizing breath. (P. 303)

The allusion here to Plato's notion of art as an imitation of an imitation seems to point to an acceptance of the philosopher's rejection of art on the grounds that it is untruthful. But freed of the demand of veracity—as the artist here is freed of flesh—art can perhaps *create* a kind of truth. Even Shreve, who does most of the talking in these last chapters and who insists on a kind of detached and game-playing attitude (p. 280), is enlivened by the effort to give life, panting, "as if he had to supply his shade not only with a cue but with breath to obey it in" (p. 344).

Their efforts to give life to the shadows go beyond any attempted reconstruction of the past, any search for historical truth; in fact, they finally must seem antithetical to any such search. All of the narrators in the story seem to recognize the futility of such a search, in spite of the facts in their possession:

> They are there, yet something is missing; they are like a chemical formula exhumed along with the letters from that forgotten chest, carefully, the paper old and faded and falling to pieces, the writing faded, almost indecipherable, yet meaningful, familiar in shape and sense, the name and presence of volatile and sentient forces; you bring them together in the proportions called for, but nothing happens; you reread, tedious and intent, poring, making sure that you have forgotten nothing, made no miscalculations; you bring them together again and again nothing happens; just the words, the symbols, the shapes themselves, shadowy inscrutable and serene, against that turgid background of a horrible and bloody mischancing of human affairs. (P. 101)

In this long passage, Mr. Compson acknowledges the disparity between the life of the past as it was lived and the words, symbols, and shapes that compose the ingredients of a historical account, the "chemical formula" that might be compared to Sutpen's "moral recipe" in that both fail to do justice to the texture of life. By the same token, fictions, because they are only made of words and symbols and shapes, cannot *discover* the real.

As Quentin and Shreve continue the search for the meaning of the story, they become increasingly aware that what they want from the past is not historical truth, which always differentiates between the knower and the known. Also, they do not wish that they had been there—that they had stood beside Judith and Clytie when their father bid them goodbye. As he imagines, Quentin thinks "he could see it; he might have been there. Then he thought *No. If I had been there I could not have seen it this plain*" (p. 190). As an object of historical knowledge, Sutpen is always beyond the knower's grasp. But the problem is the same, essentially, when Sutpen becomes the object of sense experience: he is still the other, always mysterious, always eluding the understanding. He is no more comprehensible to those who were there—General Compson and Miss Rosa, for example—than he is to Quentin and Shreve. But it is important to recognize that Quentin does not achieve a greater clarity of vision by persisting in a historical search. What he sees, and sees plainly, is what he has made.

Which is more real—what we discover or what we make? Shreve seems to recognize a hierarchy of modes of being when he paraphrases Miss Rosa: " . . . there are some things that just have to be whether they are or not, have to be a damn sight more than some other things that maybe are and it don't matter a damn whether they are or not" (p. 322). This first group of things are the necessary creations of the imagination; they derive their necessity and their significance from the maker, while the members of the second group remain contingent because value is not conferred upon them. This second group exists—the idealist's position is not taken—but it exists at a lower level of being.

What seems to be in the offing here is yet another attempt to establish the cognitive value of art, yet another theory of poetic truth. Hyatt Waggoner sees Faulkner, in *Absalom, Absalom!*, defending a higher form of knowledge, a higher mode of being than that presented by history or naturalistic fiction. For Waggoner's Faulkner, "fiction is neither lie nor document but a kind of knowledge which has no substitute and to which there is no imaginative shortcut."[18] But what is the nature of this knowledge?

Perceived as what David Grossvogel calls an "extra-fictional dialogue between author and reader,"[19] *Absalom, Absalom!* reveals the truth that behind every fiction there lies an existing creator and an existing reader. There will be those who will be dissatisfied by this meager knowledge, those who will want to know what really happened at Sutpen's Hundred or who, like Shreve, will want to know the truth about the South. Or about the human heart. Such readers fail to recognize that the truths of this novel are not essentially of this order: they are rarer and in a sense more fundamental. They come only when novelists surrender their pretensions to these other kinds of truth. What is gained through that surrender, that open acknowledgment that any formulation of experience is a falsification of that experience, is the knowledge that at least this book exists, as something written and something read, and that the writer and reader are aware of that book as book. This knowledge leads to other discoveries.

I have been dealing with ways in which the writer of *Absalom, Absalom!* is recognized as existing. Such a recognition goes beyond any authorial intrusions into the narrative, although these are present too. The persistent demonstration that their characters have no independent existence is the most effective method writers can use in affirming their own presence in a novel. It can now be shown that Faulkner also acknowledges the presence of his reader—by placing reader surrogates within the novel.

Even if an author forgoes, in the interest of a compromise with Jamesian illusionism, any attempt to address his reader directly, he may

nevertheless compensate for this loss in direct communication by
dramatizing his relationship with his reader. In *Absalom, Absalom!* this
is accomplished by analogy: the reader is to *Absalom, Absalom!* as the
various narrators of the story are to the Sutpen legend. Like Faulkner's
reader, these narrators are each attempting to "decipher" the meaning of
a "text." It might even be argued that all plausible readings of the novel
are embodied in the novel itself through the interpretations of various
narrators. Certainly all critical interpretations seem to rely more heavily
on one narrator's account than another's. If we read the novel as a moral
fable, we are preceded in this interpretation by Rosa Coldfield. If we
view the work as an attempt at modern tragedy, Mr. Compson is our
guide. Psychological interpretations, leaning heavily on the themes of
incest and miscegenation, follow Quentin's lead.

Shreve's reading—perhaps because it seems to best represent the
disinterestedness of the critic—is probably the favorite with most
readers of the novel. Even as she refuses to accept Shreve's vision of the
legend as complete, Ilse Dusoir Lind compares that vision to the Dilsey
section of *The Sound and the Fury*, calling both the "normal" view of
reality.[20] Hyatt Waggoner flatly rejects Shreve's view as final, "because
there is no final one explicitly stated anywhere in the book. There are
only other points of view and the implications of the form as a whole."[21]
This is not so much a rejection of the notion that the reader is represented by different characters in the story as an assertion that all the
readers we find there are inadequate: they tell us how *not* to read the
story. Other critics have also taken this view. For example, Brooks finds
that "Shreve sounds like certain literary critics who have written on
Faulkner. It was a stroke of genius on Faulkner's part to put such a
mentality squarely inside the novel, for this is a way of facing criticism
from that quarter and putting it into its proper perspective."[22] Behind
the views of both Waggoner and Brooks lies the assumption that there *is*
a correct perspective, a truth about the Sutpens that is to be arrived at by
accepting parts of each narrator's view and rejecting the rest, or by
observing the "implications of the form as a whole."

A more radically skeptical approach to the novel is presented by
Duncan Aswell in "The Puzzling Design of *Absalom, Absalom!*" According to Aswell, the novel is so structured that although "our disbelief is
almost wholly suspended as we read it for the first time, a close study of
the text will lead the reader to total skepticism."[23] It can be argued that
the difficulties in following the text's complex design prevent any suspension of disbelief on the first reading, but I also feel that Aswell's
observations on the effects of subsequent readings are correct. He also
goes as far as to suggest that the errors in Faulkner's "Genealogy" are
intentional, are attempts to "evoke the capriciousness of human experi-

ence and the arbitrariness of structuring it in ordered works of art."[24] Faulkner's chronology is seen as the work of a drunken and crazy Kinbote.[25] Personally, I would guess that Faulkner's errors are more a result of indifference to matters of "fact" than a conscious attempt to provoke skepticism, but certainly the desire to emphasize the problematic nature of the relationship between art and life seems central to the writer's intentions.

Aswell's reference to the most famous reader in modern fiction is also instructive. Charles Kinbote's reading of John Shade's poem "Pale Fire" introduces questions concerning the possibilities of an extrafictional dialogue between author and reader that are anticipated by Faulkner's treatment of the problem in *Absalom, Absalom!* If the act of reading can itself be dramatized, can take on a kind of solidity and life, what is to prevent this act from becoming the major object of the author's concern? The result, as Kinbote suspects, may be "the monstrous semblance of a novel,"[26] but it might also be something more than a novel and more than another work of criticism.

When the act of reading is dramatized (or fictionalized) the result will be an increased awareness on the part of the reader of the continuity of creation and critique, of real and fictional worlds. In *Absalom, Absalom!* this continuity is nowhere more strongly asserted than in the scene describing the Christmas departure of Charles Bon and Henry Sutpen from Sutpen's Hundred. Both Quentin and Shreve, who together have created the scene, merge with their fiction: "So that now it was not two but four of them riding the two horses through the dark over the frozen December ruts of that Christmas Eve: four of them and then just two—Charles-Shreve and Quentin-Henry" (p. 334). In his introduction to the Modern Library edition of the novel, Harvey Breit comments that there are really five riders, representing the "sum of all the readers throughout the world" (p. xii). We can feel that Faulkner expects his reader to provide the fifth rider. But in order to do so, the reader must make an imaginative leap: he must project himself into the story and, at the same time, acknowledge the artificiality of such projections. This is made possible by recognizing the analogy that contends that the reader is to the novel as the various narrators are to the Sutpen legend. Five riders are reduced to two—Faulkner and his reader—and the horses they ride they have made together.

Both Walter Slatoff and Claude-Edmonde Magny have seen this peculiar intimacy between author and reader as effected by Faulkner's style. For Slatoff, who has certainly provided the closest examination of that style, Faulkner's prose creates a series of tensions in the reader that engender "not a detached contemplative or evaluative act, but rather an empathetic experience, a comprehension from within. He is not so much to observe and judge characters, as to feel what they feel, as nearly as possible, to be them."[27] I have suggested, however, that the reader is in a much more complex relationship with the characters in *Absalom!* On the one hand, identification with the characters is rendered impossible by Faulkner's continual questioning of their reality. On the other hand, Slatoff is certainly correct in noting that Faulkner's style invokes a peculiar *complicity* on the part of his readers. Many critics have noted, impressionistically, that this style induces something akin to a hypnotic trance. I would suggest, however, that in *Absalom!*, in the absence of any "real" characters, Faulkner uses this technique to bring the reader closer to an awareness of the author.

A comparison with some of Faulkner's other works will be instructive. Unlike such experiments in mixed, imitative style as *The Sound and the Fury* and *As I Lay Dying*, *Absalom!* is characterized by a more or less uniform prose style. Faulkner draws his reader's attention to this fact: Quentin thinks that Shreve sounds just like Mr. Compson, and Shreve later makes the same observation with regard to Quentin's discourse. Such a style—and the remarks made about it in the novel—works against the reader's acceptance of the work as traditional mimesis. It functions as a device of alienation comparable to those mentioned earlier in my discussion.

Claude-Edmonde Magny describes Faulkner's style as a kind of "glue" meant to entrammel the reader.[28] Speaking of the special effort that Faulkner requires of his reader, she observes that an involvement with the texture of his prose

> forces us to pass through the other side of the carpet—to the side where he, the author, is busy knotting the threads of his plot; it obliges us to adopt his point of view—that of immediate and unambiguous knowledge, that of the creative vision. If he is sometimes deliberately obscure, it is never because of disdain for the reader; on the contrary, his enigmas are so many means of assuring our complicity. *In a word*, thanks to them he forces us to put ourselves in his place, to become the author of what we are reading.[29]

Although Magny's comments here are directed toward the Faulkner *oeuvre*, they seem most applicable to *Absalom!* It is the novel that most involves the reader in a recreation of the acts of the imagination, which are in turn identified with the mysteries of the aesthetic experience. For both author and reader, creation is critique.

It should also be noted that the cumulative effect of so many adumbrative hypotheses attached to the central narrative of *Absalom, Absalom!* is to give a kind of roughness to the entire work. Walter Slatoff, again writing of Faulkner's style, says that "the finished work becomes, in a sense, the record of a process, the record of the artist's struggle with his materials, rather than the record of his victory over his materials."[30] A work that is "the record of a process" rather than a complete and static product would seem to elicit a more active response from its readers. Again, it would seem to require of readers that they "pass through the other side of the carpet" and recognize that the center of the action is not located in the minds or actions of the fictive characters but in the consciousness of the writer himself. It is this consciousness—which, for the reader, can only have objective existence as words on the page—that constitutes both the meaning and design of *Absalom, Absalom!*

Take any scene prefaced with a cue such as "Quentin could almost see her . . ." or "it seemed to Quentin he could actually see them"— Quentin imagining Miss Rosa alone in her house, waiting to be taken to Sutpen's Hundred; or Henry and Charles facing each other for the last time; or the ragged and starving Confederate Army in retreat. Examine this scene closely, both in terms of its language and in terms of the effects it has on the reader. These scenes become "real" for the reader in precisely the same way that any scene in fiction captures and fills the imagination. Language always *seems* to point to something beyond itself, even when we know that this something is totally imagined. What distinguishes *Absalom, Absalom!* from traditional realism in fiction, even from Faulkner's other novels, is its persistent exposure of illusion as illusion.

At the beginning of chapter 8, Quentin and Shreve construct the scene in which Thomas Sutpen tells Henry that Charles Bon is his brother. The reader is made to see—through a remembrance attributed to Henry— Judith and Charles walking in the garden amid jasmine, spiraea, honeysuckle, Cherokee roses. Then, suddenly, Faulkner reminds us that this scene is not staged in time and space but solely in the mind:

> It would not matter here in Cambridge that the time had been winter in that garden too, and hence no bloom nor leaf even if there had been someone to walk there and be seen there since, judged by subsequent events, it had been night in the garden also. But that did not matter because it had been so long ago. It did not matter to them (Quentin and Shreve) anyway, who could without moving . . . and with no tedious transition from hearth to garden to saddle, who could already be clattering over the frozen ruts of that December night and that Christmas dawn . . . not the two of them there and then either but four of them riding the two horses through the iron darkness, and that not

mattering either: what faces and what names they called themselves
and were called by so long as the blood coursed—the blood, the
immortal brief recent intransient blood which could hold honor above
slothy unregret and love above fat and easy shame. (P. 295)

Facts do not matter when one (Quentin, Shreve, author, or reader) is
free of flesh. How strange it is that we should wish to be bound by facts,
by history, by "tedious transitions," by all the accumulated weight of
"reality" while we read fiction. Isn't it better to give up all that life that
we may move as the mind moves, that we may be free to contemplate
what the mind makes?

The above passage ends with a series of abstractions that are promi-
nent throughout the novel—honor, love, shame. According to Robert H.
Zoellner, the high frequency of occurrence of abstractions "becomes a
direct and aesthetically efficacious reflection of the ontology of *Absalom,
Absalom!*"[31] More to the point, I think, is Jean-Jacques Mayoux's explanation of Faulkner's style in terms of his idealistic conception of the
nature of reality: "If finally ideas and representations are what make up
the human world . . . there are no separations between the most concrete, the most physical sensations and abstractions of all degrees."[32] To
live in the mind is to reduce all experience to the level of abstraction. Of
course, if Faulkner does adopt an idealistic conception of reality, then
he finally is committed to a depiction of what is. By describing "the
presence of the imagination to itself"[33] rather than the world outside, he
is merely directing his language toward consciousness as the sole source
of reality. His art is then still essentially representational and, instead of
providing a created world of words, provides an accurate description of
the place where we all live.

It is tempting to accept this formulation of the aims of *Absalom,
Absalom!*, partially because it seems to be an appropriate description of
Faulkner's other work, and partially because it places this novel in a
recognizable context of reaction against realism and naturalism. We can
use terms like *impressionism* or *expressionism* or *subjectivism* to locate
this novel within artistic movements of the twentieth century. More
important, perhaps, such a formulation satisfies our desire for an art that
offers *explanations*.

But Faulkner eschews explanations in favor of an insistence on the
problematic nature of reality. Just as deftly as he disappoints his reader's
expectations concerning the depiction of a world outside, he also refuses
to deny the possibility of such a world. To express this refusal differently, and in terms of the novelist's craft—just as he exposes his novel as

mere artifice, he also suggests a mode of being that lies beyond the reach of mind and fiction.

Rosa Coldfield is reliving the moment in which she arrives at Sutpen's Hundred just after the murder of Charles Bon. She would mount the stairs to Judith's room, she would see what Henry has done, but Clytie stops her. "Dont you go up there, Rose." And then Clytie touches her. Time stops, fiction stops—at least as much as language, which moves in time and is not real, can stop:

> Because there is something in the touch of flesh with flesh which abrogates, cuts sharp and straight across the devious channels of decorous ordering, which enemies as well as lovers know because it makes them both—touch and touch of that which is the citadel of the central I-Am's private own; not spirit, soul;the liquorish and un-girdled mind is anyone's to take in any darkened hallway of this earthly tenement. But let flesh touch with flesh, and watch the fall of all the eggshell shibboleth of caste and color too. (P. 139)

It is as if Rosa is awakened from a dream. For the reader, it is *as if* (we are still dealing with mere words) not only "the eggshell shibboleth of caste and color" falls but also all the designs and abstractions that separate him from his own life. This touch of flesh with flesh, which Rosa experiences, is all that Charles Bon wants from his father—"the physical touch even though in secret, hidden—the living touch of that flesh warmed before he was born by the same blood which it had bequeathed to him to warm his own flesh with, to be bequeathed by him in turn to run hot and loud in veins and limbs after that first flesh and then his own were dead" (p. 319). The touch of flesh with flesh resists the mind's ordering, what Rosa calls the "trashy myth of reality's escape" (p. 143). It is *as if,* by describing "the presence of the imagination to itself," Faulkner is able to suggest a presence that is not imagined, that "abro-gates, cuts sharp and straight across the devious channels of decorous ordering" that inform both our histories and our fictions.

NOTES

1. Cleanth Brooks, *The Yoknapatawpha Country* (New Haven, Conn.: Yale University Press, 1963), p. 309.

2. Ibid., p. 311.

3. Brooks's chapter, which is one of the best discussions of the novel, contains several nice

instances of critical insight that are finally damaged by his failure to recognize the *kind* of novel he is dealing with:

(1) "More than most characters in literature, Thomas Sutpen is an imaginative construct" (p. 309). If all that is meant here is that more than most novelists Faulkner here openly acknowledges that he is dealing with a character, i.e., an imaginative construct and not a person, then I fully agree. But as all characters in fiction are totally imaginary, the use of "more" or "less" suggests a confusion about the differences between characters and persons. It is, of course, a confusion that mimetic fictions encourage, but that is precisely what *Absalom, Absalom!* is not.

(2) "It [*Absalom*] may also be considered to yield a nice instance of how the novelist works, for Shreve and Quentin both show a good deal of the insights of the novelist and his imaginative capacity for constructing plausible motivations around a few given facts" (p. 311). Again, Brooks seems to confuse history and fiction. What are the novelist's facts? Is writing fiction a matter of making a big lie out of a little fact? While the novelist may not create *ex nihilo*, his *given* need not take on all the messy particularity of an anecdote at the dinner table or a letter in a trunk.

(3) "To note that the account of the Sutpens which Shreve and Quentin concoct is largely [!] an imaginative construct is not to maintain that it is necessarily untrue" (p. 312). Brooks is certainly correct in emphasizing the conjectural nature of the Quentin-Shreve story. But the novel is sufficiently complex in its treatment of the nature of truth to justify at least a passing attempt on the part of the critic to explain how *any* imaginative construct could possibly be true.

4. Hyatt Waggoner, *William Faulkner: From Jefferson to the World* (Lexington: University of Kentucky Press, 1959), p. 168.

5. Olga Vickery, *The Novels of William Faulkner* (Baton Rouge: Louisiana University Press, 1959), pp. 224–25.

6. Ilse Dusoir Lind, "Design and Meaning in *Absalom, Absalom!*" in *William Faulkner: Three Decades of Criticism*, ed. Frederick J. Hoffman and Olga W. Vickery (New York: Harcourt, Brace and World, 1963), pp. 281–82.

7. Ibid., p. 279.

8. James Guetti, *The Limits of Metaphor* (Ithaca, N.Y.: Cornell University Press, 1967), pp. 120–21.

9. Ibid., p. 4.

10. Richard P. Adams, *Faulkner: Myth and Motion* (Princeton, N.J.: Princeton University Press, 1968), p. 173.

11. Ibid., pp. 181–82.

12. Ibid., p. 175.

13. Margaret MacDonald, "The Language of Fiction," in *Contemporary Studies in Aesthetics*, ed. Francis J. Coleman (New York: McGraw-Hill, 1968), p. 272.

14. J. M. Cameron, *The Night Battle* (Baltimore, Md.: Helicon Press, 1963), pp. 136–37.

15. William Faulkner, *Absalom, Absalom!* (New York: Modern Library, 1951), p. 13. [Subsequent references to this edition will appear in the text.]

16. Brooks, *Yoknapatawpha Country*, p. 297.

17. Ibid., p. 317.

18. Waggoner, *From Jefferson to the World*, p. 169.

19. See my introductory chapter.

20. Lind, *Design and Meaning*, p. 286.

21. Waggoner, *From Jefferson to the World*, p. 158.

22. Brooks, *Yoknapatawpha Country*, p. 313.

23. Duncan Aswell, "The Puzzling Design of *Absalom, Absalom!*" *Kenyon Review* 30 (Winter 1963): 67.

24. Ibid., p. 82.

25. Ibid., p. 80.

26. Charles Kinbote, *Pale Fire* (New York: Lancer Books, 1963), p. 168.

27. Walter Slatoff, *Quest for Failure: A Study of William Faulkner* (Ithaca, N.Y.: Cornell University Press, 1960), p. 246.

28. Claude-Edmonde Magny, *The Age of the American Novel: The Film Aesthetic of Fiction Between the Two Wars*, trans. Eleanor Hochman (New York: Frederick J. Ungar, 1972), p. 197.

29. Ibid., p. 207.

30. Slatoff, *Quest for Failure*, p. 256.

31. Robert H. Zoelner, "Faulkner's Prose Style in *Absalom, Absalom!*" *American Literature* 30 (January 1959): 500.

32. Jean-Jacques Mayoux, "The Creation of the Real in William Faulkner," trans. Frederick J. Hoffman, in *Three Decades*, p. 171.

33. Ibid.

4

Virginia Woolf's *The Waves:*
A Voice in Search of Six Speakers

I have of course always been struggling with this thing, to say what you nor I nor nobody knows, but what is really what you and I and everybody knows, and as I say everybody hears stories but the thing that makes each one what he is is not that. Everybody hears stories and knows stories. How can they not because that is what anybody does and what everybody tells. But in my portraits I had tried to tell what each one is without telling stories. . . .

The landscape has its formation and as after all a play has to have formation and be in relation one thing to the other thing and as the story is not the thing as any one is always telling something then the landscape not moving but being always in relation, the trees to the hills the hills to the fields the trees to each other any piece of it to any sky and than any detail to any other detail, the story is only of importance if you like to tell or like to hear a story but the relation is there anyway.

—Gertrude Stein, *Lectures*
in America

What is the point of hinting that she [Virginia Woolf] might better have a little more of Arnold Bennett than she does? And what is the point of paraphrasing *The Waves*, of trying for your own circles of ebb and flow to compete with hers? I was immensely moved by this novel when I read it recently and yet I cannot think of anything to say about it except that it is wonderful. The people are not characters, there is no plot in the usual sense. What can you bring to bear: verisimilitude—to what? You can merely say over and over that it is very good, very beautiful, that when you were reading it you were happy.

—Elizabeth Hardwick, *Seduction*
and Betrayal

It is as if she [Emily Brontë] could tear up all that we know human beings by, and fill these unrecognizable transparencies with such a gust of life that they transcend reality. Hers, then, is the rarest of all powers. She could free life from its dependence on facts; with a few touches indicate the spirit of a face so that it needs no body; by speaking of the moor make the wind blow and the thunder roar.

—Virginia Woolf, "*Jane Eyre* and *Wuthering Heights,*" in *The Common Reader*

We know human beings in part by the way in which they are represented in fiction. When we say that Catherine and Heathcliff could never be found in the world, we might really be thinking that they could not be found in Trollope. The pages of nineteenth-century fiction are an essential part of what gets torn up during a sympathetic reading of *Wuthering Heights*. The "gust of life" the common reader senses in Brontë's figures is derived from the energy of the writing—writing that forgoes the momentum automatically supplied by convention, which must therefore create its own energies. In freeing life from its dependence on facts, the writer has also freed it from the conventions of nineteenth-century realism, which are "facts" only insofar as they are undisputedly present in the novels of Emily Brontë's contemporaries.

In describing the nature of her precursor's accomplishment, Virginia Woolf uses the language of magic. Brontë is provided with rare powers that enable her to transcend reality, present bodiless spirits, make the wind blow and the thunder roar with words. The language is familiar, but for that very reason it should not be allowed to lose its metaphorical status. Novelists are not really magicians; they do not create worlds. They do create sentences, sequences of sound, which, if not wind or thunder, are at least as palpable as those.

By focusing on this particular quality of *Wuthering Heights*—its "magical" rejection of nineteenth-century realism—Woolf comes close to describing her own relation to the tradition of the English novel, and it seems safe to say that no other novelist in the twentieth century devoted as much time and energy to the study of that tradition. Her most radical break with realism, *The Waves*, is an antinovel by virtue of the fact that, instead of experimenting with totally new material or of being a "play-poem," it depends most heavily on the conventions of novel writing, and it is best understood in its reaction to those conventions. Woolf's experiments in form always have to be understood in relation to her knowledge of the Victorian/Edwardian novel and her thorough understanding of its nature. In no other novelist of her stature are the creative and scholarly faculties so closely intertwined.

For Virginia Woolf writing seems to be an adjunct to reading, a way of setting up a dialogue with a deaf text. The writing comes *after*, as answer, as response. We write in order to understand what we have read: "Perhaps the quickest way to understand the elements of what a novelist is doing is not to read but to write; to make your own experiment with the dangers and difficulties of words."[1] Learning by doing, such readers return to the foreign text, attuned to the complexities of language and ready to exercise the same sort of skills they have employed in writing: "To read a novel is a difficult and complex art. You must be capable not only of great fineness of perception, but of great boldness of imagination if you are going to make use of all that the novelist—the great artist— gives you."[2] Reading creatively and writing critically, the reader-writer establishes a relationship between two texts *and* two activities. As beneficiaries of both the nineteenth-century novels Virginia Woolf read and the twentieth-century novels she wrote, the present reader is obligated to maintain a double focus on her work, to see it primarily as a response to her reading.

She read mainly about the world that earlier writers saw or thought they saw or pretended to see. She recognized that all writers must be read in terms of their vision and that the most important act of adjustment that the imaginative reader is called upon to perform is ocular. And yet merely to see as writers see or think they see or pretend to see is not enough: "The thirty-two chapters of a novel . . . are an attempt to make something as formed and controlled as a building; but words are more impalpable than bricks; reading is a longer and more complicated process than seeing."[3] The novelist creates sentences, words are not bricks, and reading is not seeing. If the realistic novel is, for reasons of its own, devoted to obscuring such obvious truths, the novels of Virginia Woolf, especially *The Waves*, seek to reawaken our abilities to experience reading and writing for what they really are.

To the extent that we become involved with Lily Briscoe's attempt to capture a moment in time with paint, become so involved, perhaps, that the act of painting tends to displace the temporal—there represented by the narrative of *To the Lighthouse*—to that extent we are prepared for the "inward turn of narrative" that *The Waves* provides. For in that novel Virginia Woolf sacrifices most of the conventions of the novel, even those newer conventions which she herself helped to establish in her earlier work. Here readers must "read," for there are none of those comforting, familiar transparencies which allow them to pretend they are merely seeing.

Perhaps the most striking technique of alienation Woolf employs is the descriptive interludes that preface each sequence of the novel. While these passages bear certain superficial similarities to both the "Time Passes" segment in *To the Lighthouse* and the brief descriptions that begin each section of *The Years*, more is lost than is gained by placing too much emphasis on these similarities. In each of these novels Virginia Woolf has posed an entirely different set of problems to be solved. These descriptive passages only appear similar when they are extracted from the contexts of the novels in which they appear. In *To the Lighthouse*, the "Time Passes" segment functions primarily as a concretization of the passing of time. The descriptive passages in *The Years* serve to enlarge both the spatial and temporal scene of the story of the Pargiters. Although the interludes in *The Waves* deal with the passage of time and attempt to stretch the world of the novel beyond the circle of the soliloquies, they are primarily examples of a strategy of alienation and as such function as a part of the reflexive context.

The interludes are usually either praised as realistic descriptions or condemned as prose-poems that have no place in a work that purports to be a novel. As in the case of the controversy over point of view in *The Waves*, both those who defend and those who attack the passages usually base their arguments on the premise that the novel must concern itself with the representation of reality. For Josephine O'Brien Schaefer, the interludes "bear witness to Virginia Woolf's awareness that any description of reality must include the non-human as well as the human."[4] The thesis of Schaefer's book—that Virginia Woolf's novels do *not*, as is often implied, slight the claims of the exterior world—provides an explanation for the use of the interludes: they serve to remind us that there is a world outside the human world of the soliloquies. A more sophisticated argument along the same lines is Frank D. McConnell's effort to see the interludes as "highly effective attempts to present a phenomenal world without the intervention of human consciousness, a world of blind things which stands as a perpetual challenge to the attempts of the six monologists to seize, translate and 'realize' their world."[5] McConnell then goes as far as to compare Woolf's phenomenological method with that of such writers as Robbe-Grillet and Sarraute.[6]

Both of these interpretations, insofar as they assert that the interludes are an attempt to represent the nonhuman world of things, fail to recognize that only the human can describe, that there is no knowable or expressible world of things apart from human consciousness. Rather than providing a contrast to the soliloquies, the interludes present another way of showing the limits of language.

One striking difference between Virginia Woolf's method of description and that found in the novels of Robbe-Grillet is the frequent use of figurative language in the interludes, especially simile, which perhaps draws attention to itself more than any other figure of speech. The rise and fall of the waves is like the sighing of a sleeper.[7] The rising of the sun is like a woman lifting a lamp (p. 179). The birds in the garden move like skaters rollicking arm-in-arm (p. 194). The waves are like turbaned warriors advancing menacingly on flocks of sheep (p. 227). Sometimes the simile takes on epic proportions, advancing far beyond any descriptive efficacy and providing the kernel of a story that is not told. The waves leave "a black rim of twigs and cork on the shore and straws and sticks of wood as if some light shallop had floundered and burst its sides and the sailor had swum to land and bounded up the cliff and left his frail cargo to be washed ashore" (p. 125). Obviously the sailor does not stand for anything *in* the scene. In fact, he draws attention away from any attempt at visualization.

It should also be noted that each of the similarities I have collected take humanity as its vehicle. If the referents for the passages are portions of the nonhuman world, it should be noted that both the form and the content of the descriptions are such that we never lose sight of the human, since the simile form draws attention to its own artificiality and the content of the comparisons suggests that the nonhuman is perhaps understood only in terms of the human.

Rhoda's complaint—which would seem to be directed as much toward language as toward perception—is nowhere more applicable than in the interludes: "'Like' and 'like' and 'like'—but what is the thing that lies beneath the semblance of the thing?" (p. 288). Human perception and language are limited by the appearance of things and by words that are only words and not the things themselves. Rhoda's failure to leave the human world except at death would seem to mirror the failure of writers to get outside their own perceptions, outside their own language. The interludes—because they *try* to get outside human consciousness, try and fail—serve to reinforce the impression presented by the soliloquies themselves of humanity locked within its own perceptions and its own language.

If the interludes and the soliloquies do not stand in direct opposition to each other—the nonhuman versus the human—the question of their precise relation remains unanswered. Joan Bennett is certainly correct when she notes that the interludes disturb the willing suspension of disbelief, that they remind readers of the art of the storyteller and thereby contribute to the breaking of the illusion.[8] The critic would be wrong, however, to assume that this illusion is sacrosanct. Insofar as the interludes serve the rhetorical function of breaking up the reader's immersion in "the story," they provide their own justification in a reflexive text. But do they perform other services as well?

Woolf seems to have first considered the interludes as a symbolic commentary on the action of the soliloquies. To cite the most obvious example—the course of the sun across the sky parallels the passage of time in the lives of the characters. But as she became more involved with the revision of the novel, she discovered that the images in the interludes resisted symbolic formulation: ". . . this is the right way of using them [the images]—not in set pieces, as I had tried at first coherently, *but simply as images* [my italics] never making them work out; only suggest. Thus I hope to have kept the sound of the sea and the birds, dawn and garden subconsciously present, doing their work underground."[9] To use the images *as* images is to decrease their referential or symbolic character. To insist too strongly on the correspondence between the position of the sun and the stages of her characters' lives is to forget what the soliloquies never let us forget—that these characters have no lives apart from the telling of them. It is the telling, then, that is measured by the sun's progress, and not merely in a figurative sense but also literally. The day that passes in the interludes is the day of our reading of *The Waves*.

It could, of course, be argued that the time it takes to read the novel is not something objectively given in the novel, that "reading" is obviously an activity of the reader, not of the writer, nor an activity controlled by the book itself. But surely to stretch out our reading of a short story over several weeks or to read *Ulysses* in a day is to do more than merely exercise our prerogatives as readers. It involves a distortion, if not of the work itself, at least of our experience of the work. In the performing arts, of course, the experience of the work is totally in the hands of the creator and the performers. The audience is entirely at their mercy. But perhaps the dramatic or pseudo-dramatic character of *The Waves* is primarily a device for encouraging us to view this novel as a sort of performance. It would be typical of reflexive works in general to seek to establish control over the reader's experience and to provide an immediacy of experience that we normally associate with the performing arts.

The kind of correspondence that we find between the interludes and the soliloquies is a correspondence between images *as* images and texts *as* texts. In her diary entry Woolf makes it clear that she is after an effect of simultaneity. The sounds of the sea, the birds, the dawn, and the garden should seem to continue as background music to the soliloquies, not as something separate and foreign but something that should appear as a part of the soliloquies themselves. And it is the *sound* of the interludes that should echo through the soliloquies, that is, images taken not as visual or auditory images, as something described through words, but images understood as words in a text. If we think of images as representations—visual, as in "The surface of the sea slowly became transparent and lay rippling and sparkling until the dark stripes were almost rubbed out," or auditory, as in "The birds sang their blank melody outside,"—then it becomes obvious that the imagery of the interludes is predominantly visual—the breaking of the waves, the chirping of the birds, and the blowing of the wind being virtually the only sounds represented. If these are the sounds that are to echo through the soliloquies, then by far the greater part of the interludes, which deals with the play of light and shadow, is to be left out. Woolf's intention, however, seems to be that the interludes be taken whole, without any distinction being made as to the visual or auditory nature of the image understood as representation. In order for this to be possible, images must be understood as words, and the sounds we are to hear are sounds of words, texts taken as texts rather than representations or descriptions.

If the interludes are neither representations nor descriptions nor symbolic correspondences, the question then arises as to whether or not they are in need of exegesis. A text that is only a text would seem to be only what it appears to be. Looking and understanding then appear to be one act. But if the text is self-referential rather than nonreferential, interpretation is still necessary. In *The Waves* it is not that there are no correspondences between elements but that the system of correspondences occurs only within the text taken as text. Symbols, in other words, will appear, but they will only function to clarify the nature of the text itself.

Taken as a self-referential symbol, the sun in the interludes is more than a source of light. At dawn it is denaturalized by the epiclike simile of a woman lifting a lamp. Later, the woman herself will become the source of light: "The girl who had shaken her head and made all the jewels, the topaz, the aquamarine, the water-coloured jewels with sparks of fire in them dance, now bared her brows and with wide-opened eyes drove a straight pathway over the waves" (p. 255). Thus humanized, sunlight is no longer a natural phenomenon but an active process, a making of what we see. Objects *are* what light makes them appear to be. In early morning light, "everything became softly amorphous, as if the china of the plate flowed and the steel of the knife were liquid" (p. 194). Later, "the sun fell in sharp wedges inside the room. Whatever the light touched became dowered with a fanatical existence. A plate was like a white lake. A knife looked like a dagger of ice. Suddenly tumblers revealed themselves upheld by streaks of light. . . . And as the light increased, flocks of shadow were driven before it and conglomerated and hung in many-pleated folds in the background" (p. 251). As in a painting, light is the presence that makes all other presences possible. Indeed, the objects in the house are seen as objects in a painting are seen, are made to exist in precisely that way. With the sinking of the sun and the coming of night, "all the colours in the room had overflown their banks. The precise brush stroke was swollen and lopsided; cupboards and chairs melted their brown masses into one huge obscurity" (p. 340). It is as if what is described is not a scene but a painting of a scene, a device that takes us two removes from "reality" by making the brush strokes visible. The sun is presented both as artist and as hidden subject of the painting. One thinks of Monet's assertion that light is his real subject.

On another level the interludes are used to comment on the form and substance of the soliloquies. Aside from direct references to such images in the soliloquies as the beast stamping and the bird on the stake, references that presuppose the existence of an omniscient narrator, the interludes also provide self-referential symbols for the form of the soliloquies themselves. The birds' songs in each of the interludes provide a sort of introduction to the soliloquies that follow. Just before the farewell party for Percival, each bird "sang stridently, with passion, with vehemence, as if to let the song burst out of it, no matter if it shattered the song of another bird with harsh discord" (p. 250). But later "their songs ran together in swift scales like the interlacings of a mountain stream whose waters, meeting, foam and then mix, and hasten quicker and quicker down the same channel brushing the same broad leaves. But there is a rock; they sever" (p. 251). The soliloquies that follow this passage reenact the pattern described. The section begins with each voice separate and alone, but gradually the voices actually seem to engage in conversation. The section closes as the voices again break apart.

Of the objects that reappear in several of the interludes, the most enigmatic is the mirror. Its conventional use as metaphor for mimesis is expanded to express something beyond a mere copying process: "The looking-glass whitened its pool upon the wall. The real flower on the window-sill was attended by a phantom flower. Yet the phantom was part of the flower for when a bud broke free, the paler flower in the glass opened a bud too" (p. 226). If we think of the novel as a mirror, then we discover the same distancing effect that a "painting of a painting" provides. When a mirror is turned upon a mirror, what is reflected is the process of mirroring itself.

In addition to providing a break in the narrative and thereby shattering the illusion, the interludes also give the novelist a perspective outside of the soliloquies in which to take an overtly omniscient view. As has been shown, the soliloquies themselves imply an omniscience, but by actually taking the stage, Woolf makes her presence even more strongly felt. Jean Guiguet has perhaps caught the peculiar effect of the interludes when he suggests that they resemble stage directions.[10] In realistic drama, of course, such directions and the directing hand would remain behind the scene, in the script. Here, the script *is* the scene.

Many readers who accept the interludes, just as they accept the "Time Passes" section in *To the Lighthouse*, as justified experiments in poetic prose, are nevertheless disconcerted when they approach the major portion of *The Waves*, which is composed of a series of "speeches" by each of the six characters. Readers who are familiar with the rapid shift of perspective in much modern fiction, who have read Woolf's earlier work or Faulkner's *As I Lay Dying*, might feel that they have been cheated: although the text tells them that they are moving from one voice to another, the uniformity of the prose style might lead them to think that the progress of the English novel toward greater and greater realism has been temporarily arrested. And not only does Woolf refuse to use style as a means of individualizing character; she also does not attempt to imitate the speech patterns appropriate to a character at a particular age. The reader of modern fiction can appreciate the opening of *A Portrait of the Artist as a Young Man* as a successful attempt at imitative style that exposes previous presentations of childhood consciousness as highly artificial:

> Once upon a time and a very good time it was there was a moocow coming down along the road and this moocow that was coming down along the road met a nicens little boy named baby tuckoo. . . .
> His father told him that story: his father looked at him through a glass: he had a hairy face. . . .
> When you wet the bed first it is warm then it gets cold. His mother put on the oil-sheet. That had the queer smell.[11]

But after such an "advance" in realism, what are readers to make of the voice of Bernard, age six or seven, describing his bath?

> Water pours down the runnel of my spine. Bright arrows of sensation shoot on either side. I am covered with warm flesh. My dry crannies are wetted; my cold body is warmed; it is sluiced and gleaming. Water descends and sheets me like an eel. Now hot towels envelop me, and their roughness, as I rub my back, makes my blood purr. Rich and heavy sensations form on the roof of my mind; down showers the day—the woods; and Elvedon's Susan and the pigeon. Pouring down the walls of my mind, running together, the day falls copious, resplendent. (P. 192)

While the *contents* of this consciousness, its preoccupation with sensation, its prelogical associations, might suggest the mind of a child, the form in which it is presented is certainly too sophisticated to be mistaken for a child's language. Unless readers simply wish to conclude that Woolf tries to make her children sound like children but fails to do so, they must somehow explain the purpose of this particular convention in the novel. It may be, as Jean Guiguet has suggested, that to define the nature of this unchanging voice is "to solve the whole problem of *The Waves*."[12]

In "Mr. Bennett and Mrs. Brown," Woolf declares that "a convention in writing is not much different from convention in manners. Both in life and in literature it is necessary to have some means of bridging the gulf between the hostess and her unknown guest on the one hand, the writer and his unknown reader on the other."[13] Woolf then goes on to complain that the difficulty of writing modern fiction derives in part from the absence of any immediately recognizable code from which writers can begin their discourse. The conventions of the naturalistic novel will not suffice, since they prevent writers from getting beyond talk about the weather. On the other hand, the reading public knows no other code by which to come to terms with its authors. But by 1930, many of the battles for what we have come to call the stream-of-consciousness novel had been fought and won. Writers like Joyce, Richardson, Faulkner, and Woolf had persisted in their efforts to establish a new code of communication with their readers until, in fact, those readers came to know what to expect, which means that the novel again found itself in the position with respect to its audience that Woolf had described in her essay, namely, that in which "a convention ceases to be a means of communication between writer and reader, and becomes instead an obstacle and an impediment."[14] It is doubtful that so many censures and misunderstandings concerning point of view in *The Waves* would have arisen had not Virginia Woolf herself helped to establish the conventions of stream-of-consciousness fiction in her earlier novels—conventions that she saw fit to discard and replace with new ones. When *The Waves* is judged and condemned, it is not because it fails to meet the standards imposed by Edwardian fiction—the novels of Bennett, Wells, and Galsworthy—but because it fails to follow the conventions and duplicate the achievements of *Mrs. Dalloway* and *To the Lighthouse*.

In 1942 David Daiches expressed an opinion that is perhaps still held by the majority of Woolf's readers: *The Waves* is seen as a "curiously artificial piece of work."[15] "Instead of the multicoloured and rapidly shifting streams of consciousness which we are shown in the earlier novels, we get here the set monologue in which each character formalizes his impressions and attitudes into what for Virginia Woolf is

quite a rigid piece of prose."[16] *Artificiality, formality, rigidity* are the
key terms for expressing the critic's disfavor, since for Daiches Virginia
Woolf is above all a realist, no different in her intentions—to reveal life
as it is—from the Edwardian writers she condemns. For Daiches, life as
it is is best expressed as in *To the Lighthouse*. But by being able to ask
such questions as—again in "Mr. Bennett and Mrs. Brown"—" . . .
what is reality? And who are the judges of reality?"[17] Woolf sets herself
against those who pretend to know life as it is. Mrs. Brown is neither her
boots nor her thoughts as represented in interior monologue. Mrs.
Brown, life—and this is really what Woolf's essay is all about—is that
which never gets into the pages of a novel.

Daiches's realistic bias is nowhere more clearly represented than in
his comments on point of view in *The Waves*. For him, "though the
reader comes to accept this type of artificial monologue as one of the
conventions of this kind of writing, it is difficult for him to accept the
necessity of the convention."[18] One is entitled to ask, I believe, to what
kind of writing *The Waves* belongs. I suspect, since Daiches gives no
definitions or examples, that he simply means the bad kind, the artificial
kind. It is difficult to accept the notion of the *necessity* of a convention
unless you ascribe some a priori purpose to art. In Daiches's case, of
course, such a purpose is forthcoming—the representation of life as it is.

An even more curious phenomenon in more recent criticism has been
the attempt to defend *The Waves* on realistic grounds, either by denying
that Woolf employs a uniform prose style or by explaining that uniformity
in realistic terms. The first of these strategies must be immediately
rejected. Even if a quantitative analysis of the style of Bernard's
speeches and Rhoda's were to reveal slight differences between those
characters' use, say, of *-ing* verb forms, such an analysis would have
nothing to do with our experience of the novel, with which every atten-
tive reader would concur in describing as composed of the experience of
one style, in which language is used to differentiate characters only in
terms of content, only in terms of particular images that are associated
with particular characters.[19]

Those critics who recognize the uniformity of style as a problem often
take extreme measures to justify it in terms of a realistic aesthetic. For
Susan Gorsky, the undifferentiated nature of the monologues indicates
the possibility of what she calls a "cosmic communication—the internalization of another's unexpressed thoughts and experiences."[20]
Troubled by what could only seem a lapse from a realistic perspective,
James Naremore gives what is perhaps the most fanciful account of
Woolf's intentions: "It is as if Virginia Woolf were asking her reader to
suppose that the six types she has arranged in the novel can at any

moment be represented by six detached spokesmen who are continually going through the process of self-revelation. These voices seem to inhabit a kind of spirit realm from which, in a sad, rather world-weary tone, they comment on their time-bound selves below."[21] All this sounds suspiciously like a novel of the occult or science fiction, realistic science fiction, to be sure, in which readers are asked to suspend their disbelief for all sorts of extraordinary occurrences. William Golding has written a novel employing "cosmic communication" called *The Inheritors,* and we have enough ghost stories to keep us permanently in touch with the spirit realm.

Instead of multiplying Woolf's characters by two, Naremore would have done better to have divided by six, which is precisely the operation performed by James Hafley, who concludes that the speeches "are not to be considered as stream-of-consciousness monologues. Rather, these soliloquies are transcriptions of the feelings, perceptions, and thoughts of six persons by a central intelligence—that of the author," and that "the point of view is omniscient—one person is arranging and telling everything."[22] If Hafley is correct—and I think he is, in the main—then Woolf's so-called dramatic method in the novel is a sham. Instead of removing herself entirely from the text, as the series of speeches would suggest, the author has—by the omnipresence of a fixed, poetic style—made herself felt in every line, obliterating the individual contours of character by imposing her own voice on the vacuum created by the departure of individualizing styles.

Jean Guiguet has reached similar conclusions concerning this method of narration, which for him employs neither a transcription nor a translation of inner life but its "poetic correlative"—

a way of writing, a style, which is essentially that of the writer, freed from any preoccupation with realism, calling on all his resources, knowledge and skill with words to obtain an equivalent to the sort of reality he is trying to express. What Bernard, Rhoda, Louis, etc. "say" is just what they do not say, it is not even what they think or what they feel, whether clearly or confusedly, but what will affect the reader's sensitivity and intelligence so as to make him conceive and feel, as though by direct experience, the conscious or subconscious reality which might form the stuff of their true interior monologue, in the usual sense of the term.[23]

Both Hafley and Guiguet see that it is impossible to read *The Waves* as a "realistic" presentation of the consciousnesses of six different characters. For Hafley, the technique Woolf employs can be compared to the use of the omniscient narrator in eighteenth and nineteenth centuries, a technique that has largely been condemned by James, Sartre, and other modern writers. For Guiguet, the narrative stance is essentially lyrical and symbolic. The speeches evoke a sense of the reality Woolf is presenting without recourse to what the character is actually thinking or feeling.[24]

As far as these two critics may appear to be from those readings which attempt to view *The Waves* as an example of the stream-of-consciousness novel, they are nevertheless still tied to the notion that the novel seeks to express the inner lives of six imaginary people. There is, in other words, for both critics, a life "out there" that the novelist is trying to capture, be it through a godlike omniscience or through symbolic representation. But what Guiguet calls "the stuff of their true interior monologue," which the reader is supposed to experience directly, is nonexistent. Of course, it is literally nonexistent, since Bernard and the others are fictional characters; but it is also nonexistent for purposes of reading the novel. The reader is not being asked to jump from the language of the novel to an extra-fictional reality beyond. There are no characters in the novel in either Mr. Bennett's sense or in Mrs. Woolf's sense. What is reality? It is that which doesn't get into a novel, except insofar as a novel represents an act of writing. In the sense in which the novel is evidence of this act, there is one "character" left in *The Waves*. This is perhaps the way to understand Geoffrey Hartman's assertion that "there is only one fully developed character in Mrs. Woolf's novels, and that is the completely expressive or androgynous mind."[25] What this mind seeks to express is itself.

When Virginia Woolf, in *A Writer's Diary*, says that *The Waves* might be called an autobiography,[26] she is to be taken seriously—and literally. A novel may be said to be autobiographical if it attributes to its characters certain elements taken from the life of its creator. Expressed in such general terms, we can easily accept the notion that all novels are to some degree autobiographical. And we can also easily accept the notion that since the late eighteenth century, authors' lives have taken on a new degree of importance in their creative work. What may be less easily accepted is the notion that in *The Waves* Virginia Woolf is attempting to present her life as a writer in a more immediate way than through the creation of a story or characters who in some way stand for herself. Rather than drawing the portrait of the artist, she is turning the mirror of her art on herself as she pretends to draw such a portrait. The central problem in *The Waves* involves defining what we find in that mirror.

In the initial stages of composition, when Virginia Woolf was considering the angle of vision from which to present her narrative, she had first thought of using an anonymous woman as narrator: "Autobiography it might be called. . . . In its leaves she might see things happen. But who is she? I am very anxious that she should have no name. I don't want a Lavinia or a Penelope: I want 'she'. . . . Also I shall do away with exact time and place."²⁷ Some months later she asked herself, "Who thinks it? And am I outside the thinker? One wants some device which is not a trick."²⁸ The selection of a narrator in any fiction is a trick, an act of impersonation. The implied narrator is no less fictive than any other character who speaks and acts within the context of a novel, since writers must always limit themselves when they choose this phrase rather than that. Against the created narrator and what he or she says, there is always the creator and what she or he doesn't say, always that person outside the work who is never simply the one voice we hear. If we grant that Virginia Woolf is attempting some sort of autobiography, then we may see more clearly why at first she wants a nameless narrator and why later she wants to discard the narrator altogether and write drama. By refusing to define herself as this particular voice, by being all these voices, she is able to attack the notion that the self is a single entity that can be precisely defined and limited. In a sense her point of view enables her to use only the elements of lyric and drama that suit her purpose. As in a lyric, she presents a self; but by employing a dramatic form she also refuses to limit that self to a single voice. She is able to realize that compromise between poetry and the novel toward which her efforts are directed: "this appalling narrative business of the realist, getting on from lunch to dinner; it is false, unreal, merely conventional. Why admit anything to literature that is not poetry—by which I mean saturated. The poets succeeded by simplifying: practically everything is left out. I want to put practically everything in: yet to saturate."²⁹ This broad statement of her intentions in *The Waves* covers many other qual-ities of that novel as well as the choice of point of view, but mainly it justifies her dramatic-lyric method. The opposition between the novel and the poem—an opposition of a shallow inclusiveness and a "saturated" treatment of a limited subject—is partially resolved through point of view. If the subject of *The Waves* is autobiographical, that is, the writer writing, saturation is achieved by conceiving of the separate characters as a single unit, a solitary self; inclusiveness is then ap-proached (it can only be approached, since art *is* selection) by fragment-ing the self, by giving it six voices that are different and yet the same.

These technical and philosophical considerations find their counter-part in some of the speculations of the "characters" in *The Waves*. Again, it is important to recognize that by depriving her readers of any sense of the characters' independent existence, Woolf is not representing her own ideas and feelings through her characters, but, rather, is using the novel form as a means of presenting without mediation the act of self-creation through language.

Bernard defines the self in terms of the language it employs. As is always the case, Bernard's voice holds a special status among the voices that we hear—not that *he* represents the self of the novelist, for to take this view is to again impose a single, defined narrator, which is precisely the kind of limiting of the self that Woolf seeks to avoid. His voice, however, is the most self-conscious, the most actively engaged in the process of composition. What he tries and fails to compose is simply the novel we are reading, and yet he is extremely important in that his failure helps us to define the measure of Woolf's success.

For Bernard, a failure in life and failure in art are one, since he has no life apart from his phrase-making, no ability to write except through his contact with a concrete world: "I fill my mind with whatever happens to be the contents of a room or a railway carriage as one fills a fountain-pen in an inkpot" (p. 221). The comparison is precise. Through Bernard's sensibility, things become words, and words, rather than merely pointing to things, become things themselves: "The fact is that I have little aptitude for reflection. I require the concrete in everything. It is only so that I lay hands on the world. A good phrase, however, seems to me to have an independent existence" (p. 222). In attempting to be *about* the world, the word often finds itself a part of the world, possessing an "independent existence." This dual quality of language—the quality of being both signifier and signified, leads to uncertainty when the reality of language contends with the reality of the self.[30]

In the passage in which Bernard attempts to write a love letter in the manner of Byron, we are led to feel that language is acting as an agent of character transformation. If the letter falls flat, it is because Bernard is unable to get into the role that language sets for him. Its failure is due less to Bernard's pretending to be someone he is not than to his failure to pretend to be someone he is not. Writing always involves an act of impersonation; the question becomes a matter of how well the role is played.

In *A Writer's Diary* Virginia Woolf clarifies what she means by this act of impersonation: "The test of a book (to a writer) is if it makes a space in which, quite naturally, you can say what you want to say. As this morning I could say what Rhoda said. This proves that the book itself is alive: because it has not crushed the thing I wanted to say, but allowed me to slip it in, without any compression or alteration."[31] The act of writing is here seen as a compromise between an alien form (the book, which is not the self but is made by the self only to abandon the self to make its own space) and "what I want to say" (the self as yet undefined by words—"what I want to say" is unsaid. Once said, put into language, it is no longer "what I want to say.") The book itself can create a condition in which it is possible for the writer to appear as someone she is not. The book becomes an instrument for facilitating a "natural" impersonation. But notice that the final test comes when the writer compares the language of the created self to the "real" self and finds that they match: ". . . I could say what Rhoda said." Obviously this matching process is something that can only occur for the writer and should not be confused with the act of identification between reader and character, which is one kind of response, as we have seen, that is characteristic of realistic fictions. It is less a matter of identifying one's self with what *has been said*—as in reading—but rather a simultaneous matching of the spoken and the unspoken self. Writers are like readers, however, in that they too find themselves in relation to an alien object, the book, which has the capacity to "crush" the unspoken self.

If we can assume that this matching occurs on every level of *The Waves*, that Virginia Woolf is able to be each of her characters in turn, then the question of point of view in the novel can be seen in a clearer light. *The Waves* is dramatic in the sense that *the* author doesn't appear. But neither does she disappear behind her creation. If *The Waves* were adapted for the stage, each part would be played by one person, the author. But the difficulty in describing this kind of presentation is that one is forced to use the notion of "one person" or "the author" in opposition to the created characters when one actually wants to say that this person, this author, is as nonexistent as the characters themselves. Matching of the "real" self with the created self can only occur when both are seen to exist on a fictional plane. The text of *The Waves* is not *about* the act of self-creation through language but rather it *is* such an act.

Language is a means of self-creation; therefore, to create a self is to adopt a certain attitude toward language, and this is precisely what each of Woolf's characters does. All of her characters, with varying degrees of self-consciousness, speak of language and its relation to reality. By impersonating each character in turn, Woolf is able to present a comprehensive view of possible theories of language.

For Neville, as for Bernard, language offers a means of escape from the disorder of the world: "Each tense means differently. There is an order in the world" (p. 188). That he is in need of some form of escape is evidenced by his hypersensitive response to even the most innocuous intrusions of the world through perception. In the medley of voices that opens the novel, Neville characterizes himself as one offended by the touch of cold stones, the sound of scraping "fish scales with a jagged

knife on a wooden board," the booming sound of a bee (pp. 181–82).
Upon arriving in London to begin his study at the university, he notes his
terror at leaving the enclosed security of the train: "I will sit still one
moment before I emerge into that chaos, that tumult. . . . The huge
uproar is in my ears. It sounds and resounds under this glass roof like
the surge of the sea. We are cast down on the platform with our hand-
bags. We are whirled asunder. My sense of self almost perishes; my
contempt. I become drawn in, tossed down, thrown sky-high" (p. 224).
Unlike Bernard, however, Neville feels that the escape from the world
into language must be complete. There must be a total disjunction
between language and experience if words are to offer the solace Neville
requires. For Neville, the appeal of language lies in its clarity, its order,
and its *deadness*. The library is a retreat where he will "explore the
exactitude of the Latin language, and step firmly upon the well-laid
sentences, and pronounce the explicit the sonorous hexameters of Virgil;
of Lucretius; and chant with a passion that is never obscure or formless
the loves of Catullus" (p. 196). The reference to Catullus, whose loves
were often obscure and formless, is surely ironic. Neville seems to be
training himself to mimic those Latinists in Yeats's poem "The Scholars"
who

> Edit and annotate the lines
> That young men, tossing on their beds,
> Rhymed out in love's despair
> To flatter beauty's ignorant ear.
>
> All shuffle there; all cough in ink;
> All wear the carpet with their shoes;
> All think what other people think;
> All know the man their neighbor knows.
> Lord, what would they say
> Did their Catullus walk that way?

Neville is fully conscious of his own limitations, however, and if he
chooses to escape into a dead language, he secretly admires those, like
Percival, who seem to lie in direct relation to nature without mediation of
language. Despising the ordinary world, he longs to be a part of that
world: "It would be better to breed horses and live in one of those red
villas than to run in and out of the skulls of Sophocles and Euripides like
a maggot" (p. 223). Like Bernard and Louis, he is a failed poet, but his
failure lies in part in his inability to give himself over to words: "Words
and words and words, how they gallop—how they lash their long manes
and tails, but for some fault in me I cannot give myself over to their

backs; I cannot fly with them, scattering women and string bags. There is some flaw in me—some fatal hesitancy, which, if I pass it over, turns to foam and falsity" (p. 232). This flaw, this hesitancy, arises from Neville's need of perfection, a perfection that for him is embodied in the moment, enjoyed by the senses, and impervious to our attempts to capture it in language: "Nothing should be named lest by so doing we change it. Let it exist, this bank, this beauty, and I, for one instant, steeped in pleasure" (p. 231). Rather than try to make language reflect life, Neville finally decides to see life as a kind of poetry. The division between life and poetry remains, but it is the written word that is rejected in favor of the poetry of earth. Life itself "is poetry if we do not write it" (p. 312), and all the world becomes a stage on which things are said "as if they were written" (p. 313). Neville admits that "one cannot read this poem without effort. The page is often corrupt and mud-stained" (p. 313). To admit this is to surrender, finally, to the disorder of life, which then is seen to make its own order.

Neville becomes a reader of nature, giving up his artistic pretensions. His contrary is Louis, who, instead of lying open to the preexistent order of nature, seeks to impose his own order, "to fix in words, to forge in a ring of steel" (p. 201) the flux of experience. Closer to the language of ordinary discourse than either Bernard or Neville, "half in love with the typewriter and the telephone" (p. 291), those instruments of his will, Louis reads poetry in a cheap restaurant, his book propped against a bottle of Worcestershire sauce, and dreams, like Neville, of reducing and ordering experience with a poem. But because of his extravagant, almost solipsistic notion of himself, he sees order as something contained only in his own universal consciousness: "I have signed my name . . . already twenty times. I, and again I, and again I. Clear, firm, unequivocal, there it stands. Clear-cut and unequivocal am I too" (p. 291). Even the signing of a business letter imposes order on the world without, which is always for Louis something to be subdued. But although in his work Louis has gained power, has strung the globe with his lines, they are not lines of poetry, and meaning still eludes him. He keeps his attic filled with books of poetry and still attempts to make "one poem on a page, and then die" (p. 316). But how, he asks, "can I reduce these dazzling, these dancing apparitions to one line capable of linking all in one?" (p. 328). It is finally not enough to feel that one's own self is the world, when that self itself is beyond his understanding.

Susan is "tied down to single words" (p. 185): each thing has only one name and that name is like the thing itself. During the grammar lesson she looks at the white marks on the blackboard as if they are simply what they appear to be—"white words like stones one picks up by the seashore" (p. 188). "Tied down" and "stones" both suggest that language has weight, is a burden that holds the speaker to the earth.

Susan thinks she can treat the symbols of things as if they were the things themselves. She will construct images of the things she hates and bury them (p. 204). She will destroy time by tearing up pages on the calendar so that the days no longer exist (p. 211). If all the other characters in the novel attempt to transform the world into language, Susan would change words into stones, into things in the world.

Because others refuse to use words in this way, Susan seeks either silence or a silence broken only by "the cries of love, hate, rage and pain," which are the only sounds she understands (p. 266). Planted in earth, like one of her trees (pp. 308–9), Susan resists all flights, especially those of Bernard, who travels on words: "But you [Bernard] wander off; you slip away; you rise up higher, with words and words in phrases" (p. 185). Threatened by the disorder that lies just beneath the surface of the placid, green world in which she resides, by the disorder that language not only describes but helps to create, Susan would attack the shifting forms of language, "quenching the silver-grey flickering moth-wing quiver of words with the green spurt of my clear eyes" (p. 325). (Seldom is the disjunction between character and language as striking as in this passage, where Susan's use of language is in direct opposition to the person she is supposed to be.)

Like Susan, Jinny is a naive realist: "All is real; all is firm without shadow or illusion" (p. 6). But what she sees is not life in blocks, unchanging, but life as flow, as change. She is a leaf in a hedge, quivering (p. 212). Language, an instrument for getting beyond this present moment, is an alien form, except insofar as it records the impressions of the body at the moment of experience: "I cannot follow any word through its changes. I cannot follow any thought from present to past . . . I do not dream" (p. 203). Hers is a language of gesture, a pantomime where only bodies communicate (p. 245), where dreaming is replaced by bodies: "I can imagine nothing beyond the circle cast by my body" (p. 264).

Unlike Susan, Jinny wishes to talk, to tell stories, but since language always comes *after* the experience, we must speak quickly: "One must be quick and add facts deftly, like toys to a tree, fixing them with a twist of the fingers" (p. 296). But no matter how quickly we try to grasp life, to understand it by speaking it, because it is constantly changing, it eludes our words. We can choose either to make phrases that are no longer faithful to the moment of experience or to follow the moment, surrendering our desire to comprehend. Jinny is aware of this choice, makes it without hesitation:

But we who live in the body see with the body's imagination things in outline. I see rocks in bright sunshine. I cannot take these facts into some cave and, shading my eyes, grade their yellows, blues, umbers into one substance. I cannot remain seated for long. I must jump up and go. The coach may start from Piccadilly. I drop all these facts—diamonds, withered hands, china pots and the rest of it, as a monkey drops nuts from its naked paws. I cannot tell you if life is this or that. I am going to push out into the heterogeneous crowd. I am going to be buffeted; to be flung up, and flung down, among men, like a ship on the sea. (Pp. 297–98)

An exuberant capitulation to life, Jinny's choice—her decision to impersonate the "little dog that trots down the road after the regimental band" (p. 329)—is an ultimate solution that each of the other characters, in one way or another, avoids.

The antithesis of Jinny's acceptance of the moment is found in Rhoda's rejection of both life and the meditation on life, of both sunlight and cave. All Rhoda shares with Jinny is the inability to use language as a means of transcending the moment. Wanting a world immune to change, Rhoda retreats into a timeless world of make-believe. What she imagines is a desert, a barren place where the chaos of existence has been transformed through a radical reduction of elements so that only essences remain.

There is no place in this world for language or art, which must of necessity present the experience of shifting forms. Words can only approximate the thing-in-itself, and discourse is founded on simile: " 'Like' and 'like' and 'like'—but what is the thing that lies beneath the semblance of the thing?" (p. 288). Like Susan and Jinny, Rhoda grounds her dissatisfaction with language in its inability to convey truth, but while truth for Susan lies in an unchanging physical world, for Jinny in a changing physical world, Rhoda seeks a changeless Platonic reality, where "there is a square; there is an oblong. The players take the square and place it upon the oblong. They place it very accurately; they make a perfect dwelling-place. Very little is left outside. The structure is now visible; what is inchoate is here stated; we are not so various or so mean; we have made oblongs and stood them upon squares. This is our triumph; this is our consolation" (p. 288). The use of geometric figures to convey a perfectly contained reality beyond the senses is used earlier by Rhoda as a child when she draws a figure and "the world is looped in it, and I myself am outside the loop" (p. 189). Her anguish derives from her sense of being outside this eternal world, lost in the world of change. In her visions of the square set accurately upon the oblong, people become players, that is, abstracted from life in a self-contained game with a set of unchanging rules. The game, however, is more than a distraction from the changing world. It is also a "dwelling-place." the player may live inside the game, and take with him almost all that constitutes experience ("Very little remains outside.") and transform it into a coherent whole. This eternal world may be a human construct, something *made*, a game, but it is not subject to the dissipations, the fluctuations of a linguistic construct.

Geometrical figures may be superior to words. There are moments when the mind's constructs seem to embrace all of life, "when the walls of the mind grow thin; when nothing is unabsorbed, and I could fancy that we might blow so vast a bubble that the sun might set and rise in it and we might take the blue of midday and the black of midnight and be cast off and escape from the here and now" (p. 331). But these moments of escape are sharply contrasted to the hours in which human life refuses to resolve itself into geometric figures, to the hours in which we must go through what Rhoda calls "the antics of the individual" (331). In such an hour suicide appears to Rhoda as an answer.

Neville suspects that Bernard may be the cause of the fiction that the other characters—including Neville himself—view as "life": "We are all phrases in Bernard's story, things he writes down in his notebook under A or under B. He tells our story with extraordinary understanding, except of what we most feel" (p. 223). And it is true that Bernard occupies a central position in the narrative, since it is he alone who perseveres in the attempt to bring a language to the actions of the other "characters." It is he who performs as *histor* in the last section of the novel (pp. 341–83), converting the dramatic interplay of voices into one voice that recapitulates the entire story in narrative form. His "summing up" is both an attempt to find a "plot" for his own life and for the lives of his friends and a meditation on the limits of language. As such, it bears a marked similarity to the investigations of Marlow and Quentin Compson. Unlike Conrad or Faulkner, however, Woolf presents this investigation as a single sustained monologue. In this respect, Bernard's summing up resembles nothing so much as the agonized recitations of Molloy, Moran, Malone, and the Unnameable in Samuel Beckett's trilogy—recitations that, through the purity of their exclusion of external action, focus entirely upon the process of composition itself.

Bernard, unlike Beckett's solitary scribblers, tells his final story to a stranger in a restaurant over dinner. This "audience" is given no solidity, however, and is only mentioned directly at the beginning and end of the narrative. And yet a stranger would have difficulty making any sense of the story that Bernard tells. Only the reader of *The Waves* will recognize the storyteller's allusions to earlier parts of the novel and to the interludes. This stranger, then, is a stranger only in the sense that at this point he enters the fiction itself, whereas earlier he stood apart as the reader stands apart. It is essential that he enter the fictional plane of the narrative, since all the other characters have been banished from the stage, turned into the words in Bernard's notebook. Thus the final section realizes the condition of the discourse that has only been suggested throughout the work: the only "real" people involved are the reader and the writer.

Bernard's summing up takes two forms—pictures and accompanying marginalia. The pictures are, for the most part, constituted by a reframing of earlier scenes and actions; very little new material is added. The marginalia represent Bernard's comments on these pictures, or rather his comments on the narrative itself, comments that are mainly negative: "but what is the use of painfully elaborating these consecutive sentences when what one needs in nothing consecutive but a bark, a groan?" (p. 350). Considered as an interrogation both of the preceding stories and of the fictionalizing process in general, this commentary provides the reflexive core of the novel. It not only "explains" the preceding sections of the novel, "decreating" them in the process, but also takes the reader to a kind of narrative impasse. Like all of the works I have been considering, *The Waves* has pretensions of being the last novel.

Bernard has survived, and his observations have been allowed to provide the conclusion to the novel, "because it is the panorama of life, seen not from the roof, but from the third story window that delights me, not what one woman says to one man, even if that man is myself" (p. 344). He exists, as it were, in a space that excludes the antithetical excesses of withdrawal and immersion. His "view"—unlike Rhoda's or Louis's—allows him to experience physical reality, and yet—unlike Susan and Neville and Jinny—he remains free, slightly above street level, to reflect upon his own life and the lives of others. Although he has access to the particularity of experience, this is not what interests him. It is rather the process of imposing order through language that is his task and, it would seem at the beginning of his monologue, his salvation.

As a writer, he is able to "pretend that life is a solid substance, shaped like a globe, which we turn about in our fingers" (p. 350). The pictorial portion of his monologue is structured around just such a pretense, but as he reviews the preceding narrative, the "marginalia," which suspect that "this extreme precision, this orderly and military progress" is a lie, begin to intrude: "The crystal, the globe of life as one calls it, far from being hard and cold to the touch, has walls of thinnest air. If I press them all will burst. Whatever sentence I extract whole and entire from this cauldron is only a string of six little fish that let themselves be caught while billions of others leap and sizzle, making the cauldron bubble like boiling silver, and slip through my fingers" (p. 354). (One way of *demonstrating* the multivalence of language while discussing it is to mix metaphors in the discussion. One way of focusing on the physicality of sentences is to animate them, turn them into strings of six little fishes.) Writers who still have a view of the street recognize the disparity between the unity of their work and the multiplicity of what they want to capture. If they want to be realists—and Bernard does so— they are forced either constantly to question the accuracy of the portraits or to lie.

Faced with Percival's death and his own inability to voice his pain; faced with his failure to understand his friends' stories, Bernard begins to suspect that "life is not susceptible perhaps to the treatment we give it when we try to tell it" (p. 362). If all stories are lies, how do writers then justify their work? In terms of the help it gives the individual in his struggle to survive? But Bernard undercuts this "advantage" of the writer: "Better burn one's life out like Louis, desiring perfection; or like Rhoda leave us, flying past us, to the desert; or choose one out of millions and only one like Neville; better be like Susan and love and hate the heat of the sun or the frost-bitten grass; or be like Jinny, honest, an animal" (p. 361). Like Mann's Tonio Kröger, who finally refuses to conceal his "*bourgeois* love of the human, the living and usual,"[32] Bernard longs to leave his post of observation and participate in the life around him. Most of all he wishes to *be*, since he cannot capture with words that which is his opposite—Percival (p. 284).

Percival, "being naturally truthful, . . . did not see the point of these exaggerations, and was borne on by a natural sense of the fitting, was indeed a great master of the art of living": such is Bernard's view of his dead friend. It corresponds to the views held by most of his friends. For Neville, Percival represents that natural mode of understanding which comprehends Shakespeare or Catullus without being able to read. He understands, but "not the words. But what are words?" For Neville and Bernard, words have come between the reader and the things they stand for (p. 207). Louis, although he resents Percival, recognizes his need of him, "for it is Percival who inspires poetry" (p. 202). But the object of such poetry recognizes the gap between himself and the words that he inspires. What Bernard calls life, a globe, is for Jinny best represented by Percival himself: "Let us hold it for one moment . . . love, hatred, by whatever name we call it, this globe whose walls are made of Percival, of youth and beauty, and something so deep sunk within us that we shall perhaps never make this moment out of one man again" (p. 276).

Percival's function in the novel is comparable, perhaps, to Caddy's in

The Sound and the Fury or Sutpen's in *Absalom, Absalom!* Each of these characters escapes the formulations of the narrators. Each is *lost,* and the losing of Percival, in narrative terms, is the loss of a subject. Not only are there no stories for Bernard; there are no heroes either.

And yet the novel ends with an image of the hero, or rather the writer transformed into his own hero: "Death is the enemy. It is death against whom I ride with my spear couched and my hair flying back like a young man's, like Percival's, when he galloped in India" (p. 383). Unable to resurrect the subject, writers can only become their own heroes, even if, in their present condition, their images and tasks seem chiefly Quixotic.

No stories, no heroes, and finally, no language. Beckett's notion that we have nothing to paint, nothing to paint *with,* receives early formulation by Bernard's quest for a "little language":

What is the phrase for the moon? And the phrase for love? By what name are we to call death? I do not know. I need a little language such as lovers use, words of one syllable such as children speak when they come into the room and find their mother sewing and pick up some scrap of bright wool, a feather, or a shred of chintz. I need a howl; a cry. When the storm crosses the marsh and sweeps over me where I lie in the ditch unregarded I need no words. Nothing neat. Nothing that comes down with all its feet on the floor. None of those resonances and lovely echoes that break and chime from nerve to nerve in our breasts making wild music, false phrases. I have done with phrases. (Pp. 381–82)

Bernard is an old man approaching death when he speaks these words, an old man who sounds curiously like Molloy or Malone. He sounds very unlike the popular picture of Virginia Woolf as a stylist who specializes in the phrase that "comes down with all its feet on the floor." Implicit in the passage is a self-criticism of Woolf's earlier novels, of her sensibility, of her prose style.

When they are children, Bernard and Susan escape into a world of make-believe, the world of Elvedon, where they see a lady who sits between two long windows, writing, and the gardeners who sweep the lawn with giant brooms (p. 186). These images recur throughout the book as they recur throughout Bernard's life. Emblems of production and destruction, they haunt him in the final chapter: ". . . the gardeners swept the lawns with giant brooms. The lady sat writing. Transfixed, stopped dead, I thought, 'I cannot interfere with a single stroke of those brooms they sweep and sweep. Nor with the fixity of that woman writing. It is strange that one cannot stop gardeners sweeping nor dislodge a woman. There they have remained all my life. It is as if one had woken in Stonehenge surrounded by a circle of great stones, these enemies, these presences" (p. 343). The lady writing and the gardeners are mirrored in Bernard himself writing and Mrs. Moffat, who will always come and sweep it up (p. 305). But more than an image of the endless process of composition and revision, the lady is also Virginia Woolf as a presence in her own book. Bernard cannot stop her writing, although she can stop his. Like those voices in Beckett who seem to control the narrators, the lady writing is an open acknowledgment of the presence of a self that is neither wholly fictional nor wholly real but a "presence," attempting to catch itself in the act of self-creation. An impossible task but one that insures, by its very impossibility, the continuance of the effort.

NOTES

1. Virginia Woolf, *The Second Common Reader* (New York: Harcourt, Brace, Jovanovich, 1953), p. 235.

2. Ibid., p. 236.

3. Ibid., p. 235.

4. Josephine O'Brien Schaefer, *The Three-Fold Nature of Reality in the Novels of Virginia Woolf* (The Hague: Mouton and Co., 1965), p. 12.

5. Frank D. McConnell, " 'Death among the Apple Trees': *The Waves* and the World of Things," in *Virginia Woolf: A Collection of Essays*, ed. Claire Sprague (Englewood Cliffs, N.J.: Prentice-Hall, 1971), p. 126.

6. Virginia Woolf, *Jacob's Room / The Waves* (New York: Harcourt, Brace and World, 1959), p. 179. Subsequent references to this edition will be given in the text.

7. Joan Bennett, *Virginia Woolf: Her Art as a Novelist* (Cambridge: Cambridge University Press, 1964), pp. 106–7.

8. Virginia Woolf, *A Writer's Diary* (New York: Harcourt, Brace, Jovanovich, 1953), p. 165.

9. Jean Guiget, *Virginia Woolf and Her Works*, trans. Jean Stewart (New York: Harcourt, Brace and World, 1965), p. 281.

10. James Joyce, *A Portrait of the Artist as a Young Man* (New York: Viking Press, 1968), p. 7.

11. Guiguet, *Virginia Woolf and Her Works*, p. 284.

12. Virginia Woolf, *The Captain's Deathbed and Other Essays* (New York: Harcourt, Brace and World, 1950), p. 110.

13. Ibid.

14. David Daiches, *Virginia Woolf* (New York: New Directions, 1953), p. 105.

15. Ibid., p. 107.

16. Woolf, *The Captain's Deathbed and Other Essays*, p. 103.

17. Daiches, *Virginia Woolf*, p. 108.

18. The quantitative analysis of a prose style—perhaps performed with the aid of computers—is certainly an aid to critics who wish to verify their impressions. It can even cause us to recognize our blindness to certain features of a style. Nevertheless, if such an analysis is given an absolute priority, we run the risk of distorting our *experience* of the work. An examination of a painting under a microscope will no doubt reveal things about the painting, but in most instances, these discoveries will have nothing to do with the work as experienced under normal conditions.

19. Susan Gorsky, "The Central Shadow: Characterization in *The Waves*," *Modern Fiction Studies* 18 (Autumn 1972): 450.

20. James Naremore, *The World without a Self: Virginia Woolf and the Novel* (New Haven and London: Yale University Press, 1973), p. 173.

21. James Hafley, *The Glass Roof: Virginia Woolf as Novelist* (New York: Russell and Russell, 1963), p. 108

22. Guiguet, *Virginia Woolf and Her Works*, p. 285.

23. See J. W. Graham, "Point of View in *The Waves*: Some Services of the Style," *University of Toronto Quarterly* 39 (April 1970): 193–211, for confirmation of this effect through an examination of the use of the pure present tense.

24. Geoffrey Hartman, *Beyond Formalism* (New Haven, Conn.: Yale University Press, 1970), p. 75.

25. Woolf, *A Writer's Diary*, p. 140.

26. Ibid.

27. Ibid., p. 143.

28. Ibid., p. 136.

29. Eugenio Donato has given a precise description of this duplicity: "The relationship that the order of the signifier maintains to the order of the signified, of words to their semantic content, or more simply stated, of words to things, is a paradoxical one, for it is a relationship that has to be defined simultaneously by two propositions which are contradictory: the word *is* the thing the word is identical to that which it represents, and the space between the two is continuous. Yet, words are different from things, words do not merely represent things; the two orders are discontinuous, their relationship is one of difference." "The Two Languages of Criticism," in *The Structuralist Controversy: The Languages of Criticism and the Sciences of Man*, ed. Richard Macksey and Eugenio Donato (Baltimore and London: Johns Hopkins Press, 1970), p. 94.

30. Woolf, *A Writer's Diary*, p. 153.

31. Thomas Mann, *Stories of Three Decades*, trans. H. T. Lowe-Porter (New York: Modern Library, 1936), p. 132.

5

Joyce into Beckett:
Prolegomena to Any Future Fictions

For Stephen art was neither a copy nor an imitation of nature: the artistic process was a natural process.

—James Joyce, *Stephen Hero*

I might easily have written this story in the traditional manner. Every novelist knows the recipe. It is not very difficult to follow a simple, chronological scheme which the critics will understand. But I, after all, am trying to tell the story of this Chapelizod family in a new way. Time and the river and the mountain are the real heroes of my book. Yet the elements are exactly what every novelist might use: man and woman, birth, childhood, night, sleep, marriage, prayer, death. There is nothing paradoxical about all this. Only I am trying to build many planes of narrative with a single esthetic purpose. Did you ever read Laurence Sterne?

—James Joyce, in a letter

Che sara sara che fu, there's more than Homer knows how to spew.
—Samuel Beckett, "Home Olga"

> who may tell the tale
> of the old man?
> weigh absence in a scale?
> mete want with a span?
> the sum assess of the world's woes?
> nothingness
> in words enclose?

—Samuel Beckett, addendum to *Watt*

118

For the most part, the type of novel I have been describing should be seen as the product of a post-Joycean development in attitudes toward language and literature. Before Joyce other writers—in the twentieth century, most notably Proust and Conrad—had exploited some of the resources of reflexivity in their fiction. But it was Joyce, especially in parts of *Ulysses* and in *Finnegans Wake*, who was to provide the most striking alternative to the mimetic tradition in the novel. Without wishing to detract from the originality of their individual achievements, I would find it difficult to discount the influence of Joyce's work on such diverse novelists as Woolf, Faulkner, Dos Passos, Nabokov, and Malcolm Lowry, and this is only to mention those writers for whom Joyce's value lies primarily in his attack upon the traditional forms of the novel. A far larger number of later writers have appropriated a Joyce whose major achievement is seen as a development, a refinement of the techniques of literary realism. The fact that Joyce's writings provide so many different things for so many different writers makes him an exemplary figure for the literary historian. By describing the separate strands of Joyce's achievement, the historian may be better able to determine the relationship between, on the one hand, modernism and the mimetic tradition, and, on the other, modernism and what today must be labeled postmodernism.

While it is primarily Joyce's work in the twenties and thirties that constitutes a radical break with tradition, his earlier work also shows an impatience with the notion of language as a mere means of expressing nonlinguistic phenomena. Frank O'Connor has written of Joyce's tendency in *Dubliners* to use words "not to describe an experience, but so far as possible to duplicate it. Not even perhaps to duplicate it so much as to replace it by a combination of images."[1] It is in his "replacement of the experience by a verbal arrangement"[2] rather than in his naturalism that Joyce's influence can be more clearly seen, since the lessons of formal realism can be learned elsewhere with less effort and confusion. One of the most effective means that Joyce employs to rivet our attention to his verbal arrangements (as opposed to those "things" which the words purport to describe) is the practice of making words and texts themselves the "things" described. When Lily, the maid in "The Dead," tells Gabriel that "the men that is now is only all palaver,"[3] she is voicing an assumption about the language of fiction that Joyce himself shares.

Throughout *Dubliners*, the characters and the author look at words as words as well as transparencies meant to reveal an imagined world beyond the page. The opening paragraph of the book is important not only because it introduces the theme of paralysis but also because in it the narrator, like the young Stephen Dedalus, is most interested in the sound of words. *Paralysis*, like *Araby* in the third story, is first of all a word, and *Dubliners* is first of all an arrangement of words. When attention is drawn to a word or phrase in its nonsignifying aspect, other words or phrases in the book tend to lose, by contagion, some of their ability to signify.

The songs and poems that are planted through the collection fulfill the same function as passages that deal directly with the sound and appearance of words. Quite often the songs may serve to illuminate some important aspect of the story considered as representation—as in "Silent, O Moyle," "I Dreamt That I Dwelt," Polly's Song in "The Boarding House," or "The Lass of Augrim" in "The Dead," but taken together along with other "texts" in the book, they also serve to remind readers that they are reading. The poems—in "A Little Cloud" and "Ivy Day in the Committee Room"—coming at the close of these stories, seem to dominate the action that surrounds them. Or rather, they become a part of the main action. The last line of "Ivy Day in the Committee Room"— "Mr. Crofton said that it was a very fine piece of writing"— serves to place the entire story in a verbal category.

Other recitations can be interpreted as texts as well. Gabriel's story of his grandfather's horse and King Billy is presented as a sort of set performance. The elderly homosexual in "An Encounter"—who makes his relation to the narrator felt by describing them both as "bookworms"—speaks as if he were "repeating something which he had learned by heart or that magnetised by some words of his own speech, his mind was slowly circling round and round the same orbit" (p. 26). Experience itself is formalized to the point where the wordiness of words becomes most important.

The library of cheap Westerns in "An Encounter," the books left behind by the priest in "Araby," Little Chandler's books of poetry, Duffy's library in "A Painful Case," the business letters that Farrington tries to write in "Counterparts," Gabriel Conroy's reviews and his youthful letter to Gretta all lie behind the action of the stories. The written word is never far from the experience of many of the characters, and it is often used to put those very experiences into question. The text-within-a-text effect, which invariably compromises the outer text by placing it in relation to other words rather than to nonverbal reality, alienates the reader by reminding him of the actual ontological status of the fiction he is reading. It subordinates life to words, or rather, it sees life as language, as does Farther Purdon in the sermon at the close of "Grace," the story originally intended to be the last in the collection. The priest exhorts each of his listeners to "open his books, the books of his spiritual life, and see if they tallied accurately with conscience" (p. 174).

Joyce's word-consciousness, which of course receives greater development in the later works, involves more than a desire to place "the proper words in the proper order," although this particular formulation of his intentions is useful as a means of discovering the implications of that word-consciousness. "Proper" here cannot refer to any felicitous matching of word and thing, even if such matching were possible, since there are no "things" in fiction. Following Joyce's example, later writers have often sought to remove or at least to render problematical any representation of life in their fictions. The later novels of Virginia Woolf and William Faulkner—particularly *The Waves* and *Absalom, Absalom!*— tend to move away from what has been called a Joycean concern with representing states of consciousness and to question, as Joyce questions, the possibility of representation. Often this interrogation is carried out through a fictionalization of the reading of a text, as when, in the opening story of Samuel Beckett's collection *More Pricks Than Kicks*, his hero Belacqua is engaged in reading a passage from the *Paradiso* (to the detriment of his status as "real" character). American writers like John Barth and William H. Gass have carried this concern farther still by seeking to make language itself the chief character in their fictions. The title character and narrator of Gass's allegory, *Willie Masters' Lonesome Wife*, is a Molly made of words. While it would be a mistake to suppose that *Dubliners* is a primary source for these developments, it is equally important to note that Joyce's earliest, most realistic fictions contain reflexive elements that will be further developed in the later works.

This is even more apparent in *A Portrait of the Artist as a Young Man*, which is an explicit attempt to turn the novel around so that it directs its gaze at the novelist himself. In addition to pursuing his interest in the self-referential qualities of language, Joyce here seeks to examine some of the uses of memory and the imagination, and such an examination has become almost obligatory in other novels in the reflexive mode.

Joyce's extensive use of autobiographical materials points not so much to a failure of the imagination as to a blurring of the boundaries between fiction and nonfiction, between imagination and memory. A curious process of leveling sets in, (analogous, by the way, to what happens when words as transparencies come in contact with words as words) whereby what *did* happen, what *could* have happened, and what *might* yet happen all coalesce on a single fictional plane. Stephen's memories, no less than his imaginings, acquire fictionality by virtue of their absorption by language. And his dream of the green rose becomes as real as his memory of the song of wild roses when both may be said to exist only in the mind: "Lavender and cream and pink roses were beautiful to think of. Perhaps a wild rose might be like those colours and he remembered the song about the wild rose blossoms on a little green place. But you could not have a green rose. But perhaps someplace in the world you could" (pp. 12–13).

Later, when he goes to Cork with his father, Stephen introduces the problem of his faulty memory, which may be read as the problem facing the novelist using autobiographical materials: "The memory of his childhood suddenly grew dim. He tried to call forth some of its vivid moments but could not. He recalled only names" (p. 92). In other words, the experience itself has already been replaced by a verbal abstraction. In the sparse summary that follows this passage, he gives a few remembered facts of his life as if they belonged to another. From this point on in the novel, Stephen's thoughts are increasingly devoted to what *might* happen:

> It would be a gloomy secret night. After early nightfall the yellow lamps would light up, here and there, the squalid quarter of the brothels. He would follow a devious course up and down the streets, circling always nearer and nearer in a tremor of fear and joy, until his feet led him suddenly round a dark corner. The whores would just be coming out of their houses for the night, yawning lazily after their sleep and settling the hairpins in their clusters of hair. He would pass by them calmly waiting for a sudden movement of his own will in a sudden call to his sinloving soul from their soft perfumed flesh. (P. 102)

While the description is no doubt based on previous experiences, it is presented as a prefiguration. At the same time, although created by the imagination, this future is given an inevitability, and by its circumstantiality, it receives the texture of a real event.

Imagination is also used to capture an unremembered past, and often it is *language* that sets the imagination in motion: "A vision of their life, which his father's words had been powerless to evoke, sprang up before him out of the word cut in the desk. A broadshouldered student with a moustache was cutting the letters with a jacknife, seriously. Other students stood or sat near him laughing at his handiwork. One jogged his elbow. The big student turned on him frowning. He was dressed in loose grey clothes and had tan boots" (Pp. 89–90). The tan boots, although in keeping with the circumstantiality of the entire revery, are crucial. The accumulation of detail has reached the point where it rivals that of memory or direct experience itself.

The technique of "composition of place" occurs throughout the novel and not merely in the sermon, and such composition calls for acts of imagination rather than of memory. Perhaps Joyce's novel is autobiographical to the extent that it offers an autocritical account of the novelist's own method of composition, in which case the importance of other autobiographical materials is much less than is usually supposed.

This attitude toward "facts"—fictional and autobiographical—lends itself easily to what Robert Musil calls "a sense of possibility" or "the capacity to think how everything could 'just as easily' be, and to attach no more importance to what is than to what is not."[4] Such an attitude obviously runs counter to any mimetic theory of art, regardless of whether the "thing" represented is past or present, external or internal. What has happened or is happening lays no special claim on the artist's activity. If *A Portrait of the Artist as a Young Man* remains within the tradition of realistic fiction, it nevertheless offers some justification for the games with reality Joyce will begin to play halfway through *Ulysses*.

I would like to be able to locate the precise point in the history of the novel that marks the turning point, that signals a new age of self-consciousness in texts and novelists, that most clearly establishes the commencement of that situation described by Olga Bernal in her work on Samuel Beckett: "If the literature of the past described reality (or believed it did), that of today realizes that what it describes is not reality, but the very language of which it is captive as soon as it begins to speak. And no doubt this is the first time in the history of literature that language no longer situates itself opposite the world but opposite itself."[5] Obviously, such a revolutionary shift in perspective cannot be precisely situated in time, but several dates suggest themselves. Virginia Woolf said human nature changed in 1910. Perhaps, in a similar fashion, the nature of prose fiction changed toward the end of 1918. It was at this time that Joyce began work on the "Wandering Rocks" episode of *Ulysses*.[6]

Much recent criticism of *Ulysses* has been directed toward coming to an understanding of the shift in Joyce's aesthetic that occurs somewhere in the middle sections of that novel. It is an aesthetic that governs most of the second half of *Ulysses* as well as all of *Finnegans Wake*. Although he marks this shift as occurring later, L. A. Murillo has described it well: ". . . Joyce after 1922 turned from an art of representing a dramatic situation between characters to one in which the tensions arising from an oppositeness of meanings were confined almost entirely to the surface structure of words and their relationships."[7] I would suggest that we do not have to wait for the first installment of *Work in Progress* for the drama of words but that it might be encountered in the June–July 1919 issues of *Little Review*, which presented the "Wandering Rocks" episode to the public for the first time.[8]

What happens to *Ulysses* at this point is simply that the narrative is taken out of the hands of the characters and given over to "the arranger."[9] It is given back to Bloom, briefly, in the second half of "Nausicaa"; Molly takes partial possession of it in "Penelope," but things are never quite the same as they were before, in the first nine sections of the book.

Judgments as to the work's value have invariably been conditioned by the critic's response to this shift. According to S. L. Goldberg, for whom a novel's worth lies in "its imaginative illumination of the moral—and ultimately, spiritual—experience of representative human beings,"[10] *Ulysses* fails in much of the second half because its language is no longer put in the service of a representation of reality. For Goldberg most of the later sections suffer from a development that is "intellectual rather than imaginative."[11] Goldberg does go on to note, however, that this development is perhaps "the necessary price for the attempt Joyce makes to shift our attention from the represented reality to the shaping activity of the artist."[12]

Why does Joyce wish to shift our attention to this activity? The answer is at least partially given in "Scylla and Charybdis," the last chapter to be written in the realistic mode,[13] in Stephen's presentation and defense of his theory of *Hamlet*.

What is most immediately apparent about the theory is its absurdity and its distance from Joyce's often-voiced claims for a classical, impersonal art. According to the theory that Stephen proposes, *Hamlet* is a dramatic re-creation of Shakespeare's betrayal by Anne Hathaway, his cuckolding by his own brothers. Life and art are intermingled in a fashion that offends the modern's sense of the autonomy of the text. George Russell (AE) would seem to voice the modern reader's objections to the theory—"this prying into the life of a great man": "I mean, we have the plays, I mean when we read the poetry of *King Lear* what is it to us how the poet lived? As for living, our servants can do that for us, Villiers de l'Isle has said. Peeping and prying into greenroom gossip of the day, the poet's drinking, the poet's debts. We have *King Lear* and it is immortal" (p. 189). Russell's view would seem, in spite of its Platonic overtones, to be compatible with Joyce's own, which stresses the *impersonal* nature of artistic creation. As one critic has noted, Joyce seems to view *style* primarily as "a means to objectivity and impersonality in works inspired, and impelled to their strange elaboration, by a powerful self-exorcism."[14] The presentation of an outlandish example of biographical criticism—and the apparent approval, on Joyce's part, of such criticism—seems incompatible with the notion of art as a means of "self-exorcism."

Of course, it could be argued that the theory is not to be taken seriously, that it merely provides us with an illustration of Stephen's ingenuity and playfulness. When John Eglinton asks the critic if he believes his own theory, Stephen promptly replies that he does not (p. 214).

Or it could be argued that the theory is not to be valued for its own sake but for the light it throws on the father-son motif that runs through the novel: "Who is the father of any son that any son should love him or he any son?" (p. 207). This question of the nature of true paternity, the theme that links Stephen to Bloom even before they have met in the novel, can be simply read as a foreshadowing of the action and the development of the characters.

Both of these readings are valid but partial: I propose to offer another partial reading, but one that should have a kind of priority in that it discovers in the *Hamlet* theory an aesthetic that underlies most of the second half of *Ulysses* and therefore determines *how* we are to read that part of the novel. Stephen's theory in "Scylla and Charybdis," like his earlier theory in *Portrait*, provides rules for reading, a way of incorporating the author's intentions into the text.

Stephen begins his argument with a story, or, more properly, the composition of place. In answering the questions he has posed—What is a ghost? Who is King Hamlet?—Stephen creates a scene:

> —The play begins. A player comes on under the shadow made up in the castoff mail of a court buck, a wellset man with a bass voice. It is the ghost, the king, a king and no king, and the player is Shakespeare who has studied Hamlet all the years of his life which were not vanity in order to play the part of the spectre. He speaks the words to Burbage, the young player who stands before him beyond the rack of cerecloth, calling him by a name:
> Hamlet, I am thy father's spirit bidding him list. To a son he speaks, the son of his soul, the prince, young Hamlet and to the son of his body, Hamnet Shakespeare, who has died in Stratford that his namesake may live for ever. (P. 188)

What Stephen has traced here are the possible stages of the relationship between the artist and his work or between life and art. At one extreme, there is a man, William Shakespeare, of Stratford-on-the-Avon; at the other, Hamlet's father, who at one level exists on a more "fictive" level than Hamlet himself, since he appears in the play as a ghost, and at another level is identified with that man who fathered both Hamlet and *Hamlet*.

Between these two extremes lie other stages in the relationship. There is also Shakespeare the writer, not to be totally confused with the man; there is Shakespeare the actor, who, not content to create the play *out* of his own person, must be in the play *in* his own person. It is Shakespeare the actor who should concern us most, for it is in this particular role that Joyce attempts to cast himself for the remainder of his life's work. Whatever other reasons Joyce might have had for dealing with Shakespeare and *Hamlet*—and a few of those have already been suggested by other critics—the most essential is explained by the story, which places the playwright as an actor in his own play, and not merely as an actor but as an actor who is to represent a figure who is not *really* there, who is a ghost.

Of all the forms of representational art, drama can present the closest approximation of reality. Or perhaps, in a sense, we are not dealing with a representation at all, since the characters are real, they are *there*, and what happens happens *now*. There does not seem to be any way, apart from the convention of presenting drama on some sort of stage, to distinguish life from the play, and this business of a stage seems far more contingent than any of the defining properties of the other representational arts. (Note the ease with which certain contemporary forms of guerrilla theater dispense with the notion of a "stage.")

Illusion in drama is of a different order from that in the other arts in that it is closer to the meaning of illusion in real life. Like all illusion, it is based on appearance, but because its mode of appearance can match perfectly the mode of appearance in real life, we say that the actions and the characters are simply not what they seem to be, which is exactly the way we would describe illusion in ordinary life.

Drama is also unlike the other representational arts in that the events that occur on the stage are usually not understood as mirroring some prior event. The action of the play *is* what it represents in a way in which a written description of a house, in a novel, is not the house, and the representation of a bowl of fruit in a painting is not a bowl of fruit.

Yet even if we deny this and say that there is some prior event to which the drama refers, we are forced to conclude that this event and its representation exist on the same ontological plane. In drama, a man scratching his head is represented by a man scratching his head. In a novel, a man scratching his head is represented by words on a page. In the drama the existential gap between signifier and signified is reduced to a minimum.

Perhaps the modern novelist's predilection for the dramatic—or in Jamesian terms, "the scenic"—derives in part not merely from the desire for a heightened realism, nor from the desire to efface the narrator (Joyce), but also from the discovery that the drama provides the most suitable illustration of the identity, at one level, of real and fictional worlds, an identity that is often a *theme* of the novel itself.

To act a part in one's own play is to transform one's self into a fictional character while at the same time retaining one's presence in the real world. Any actor, as he performs, exists simultaneously in both real and fictive worlds, but the actor who writes his own part "realizes" his double creation in a special way: Not only is his imagination given presence but also his reality. He walks, as a living man, through his own dream.

It would seem that in the last months of 1918, while writing "Scylla and Charybdis" and perhaps planning "The Wandering Rocks" and "Sirens" episodes, Joyce decided to enter his book in a decisive way. Although it could be said that the historical Joyce and historical Dublin were never far from the page Joyce wrote and that Joyce never "imagined" anything but wrote only of himself as he was or thought that he was, it is nevertheless true that the imagined Joyce and Joyce imagining had remained, to this point, relatively separate entities. While writing *about* the young man who would later write, he had not sought to dramatize his present self in the act of writing. A portrait of the writer had yet to become a portrait of the writing.

It is appropriate that the theory of artistic *practice* that we find in "Scylla and Charybdis" should itself take the form of practical criticism rather than the highly abstract form in which Stephen presents the aesthetic theory in *Portrait*. The technic of "Scylla and Charybdis" is dialectic, itself a method of presentation that pushes the speaker or writer into the foreground. It is surely at this point that Joyce the writer becomes something like what Goldberg calls a fourth character in the novel.[15] And it is this presence that best accounts for the shift from representation to the practice of writing.

Arnold Goldman recognizes that the differences between the later episodes of *Ulysses* and *Finnegans Wake* are mainly matters of technique rather than aesthetic purpose. In writing of "Cyclops," he notes that all that distinguishes this episode from *Finnegans Wake* "is the sporadic appearance of the 'actual' scene in the pub. As in the *Wake*, the incidient encyclopedism promotes a sense of the randomness and arbitrariness of any one particular 'interpretation' of the action or direction of the narrative."[16] And Goldman goes on to admit that even the realism of the pub scene may be considered as just one more verbal display, containing no more representative value than any other.[17]

Hugh Kenner, writing of *Ulysses*, tries to describe the nature of the reader's relation to the text: "Things are not talked about, they happen in the prose. Appropriate exegesis does not consist in transposing the allegorical to the propositional, but in a detailed apprehension of the rich concrete particularity of what has been placed before our eyes."[18] While my own reading of Stephen's *Hamlet* theory may appear allegorical, I would say that it is not to the extent that Joyce is able to project himself into the text as Shakespeare projects himself into his play. To read Hamlet's father's ghost = Shakespeare when Shakespeare is playing the part of the ghost is not to read allegorically. To read Stephen's theory = Joyce's theory when Joyce replaces Stephen's reality with his own is not to read allegorically. In both cases, things are just what they appear to be: Intrusions of the self into self-created fictions.

It is this property of the text—its opacity, its resistence to referential understanding—that constitutes Joyce's most important contribution toward the development of reflexive fiction. If Joyce offers us, in *Ulysses*, the culmination of the naturalistic novel, he also undermines that novel and provides a model for the problematic narratives of postmodernism, most notably those of Samuel Beckett.

There are many Joyces, but for Beckett there is mainly only one, the one whose "writing is not *about* something; *it is that something itself*."[19] Beckett's statement is probably the most famous and the most extreme judgement on *Work in Progress* to appear in that slender collection of essays, *Our Exagmination Round His Factification for Incamination of Work in Progress*, published in 1929. It is important because it makes clear that Joyce's new work cannot be read or judged as other novels, even *Ulysses*, are read and judged, as representations of reality. *Finnegans Wake* supposedly refers to nothing; it simply *is*.

For the young reader (Beckett is 23 and not yet a novelist), there can no longer be any reading about something but only reading. And for the writer he is to become, there will no longer be writing about something but only writing. Novels were always like this, of course, although they pretended that they were not, and Beckett's statement applies equally to every work of fiction. The difference lies in the open acknowledgment that novels and the people and events in them are only made of words. This is a great discovery, especially if you are a gifted writer and can make words take the place of whatever it was that novels formerly pretended to be made of. If you can make language do anything you want, so much the better. Amanuensis to Joyce, Beckett came late. His despair—there is nothing to write and nothing to write with—proceeds as much from his reading of Joyce as from his reading of Descartes. It is a despair conditioned less by a sense of personal inadequacy than by an honest appraisal of his own position in the history of the novel. Whatever else Beckett may borrow from Joyce, he seems to offer an alternative to the cyclical theory of history that provides the structural framework of *Finnegans Wake*. Entropic fictions do not allow for Viconian renewals, and the progression of Beckett's trilogy toward an ultimate end, toward an exhaustion of all possibilities may be taken as indicative of Beckett's development as a writer as well as the plot of all of his fictions.

Significantly, Beckett's only film script is entitled *Film*. By turning the medium in on itself, by examining the nature of visual perception, *Film* is above all an exercise in the construction of a paradigm. Similarly, *Watt* examines its own what-ness and could be appropriately subtitled *Novel*. In a sense *Watt* is the first in a series of "last novels," which are best seen as responses to Joyce's decision to stop pretending to write *about* something. Beckett will extend the possibilities for considering the text as text, and he will examine, critically/creatively, the implications of the self-referential art work. From this critique, he will evolve a post-Joycean aesthetic, and this aesthetic will give rise to a series of fictions that shatter the traditional frame surrounding the work of art. An examination of Beckett's English fiction should provide an introduction to the ways in which the author has become uniquely post-Joycean.

In *Ulysses* Joyce's mixture of various elements—the Homeric and the modern, the different prose styles, the whole concept of using different "technics" for each chapter—constitutes an intended affront to the sense of unity sought by the realistic novel. In contrasting Shakespeare's use of various sources to the modern's sense of unity, John Eglinton provides an ironic self-reference to the book that contains him: "That was Will's way, John Eglinton defended. We should not now combine a Norse saga with an excerpt from a novel by George Meredith" (p. 211), which of course is precisely what Joyce *would* do. When unity of style or tone is broken, the reader is made more aware of the manipulation of the material and becomes thereby more conscious of the presence, *in* the work, of a manipulator or "arranger."

Beckett's first published work of fiction, *More Pricks Than Kicks*, exhibits a stylistic disunity comparable to that found in *Ulysses*. This disunity is almost always explained by describing the volume as a collection of stories, even though its hero, Belacqua, appears throughout the book and the "stories" are arranged in chronological order. Events in earlier sections are referred to in later sections, and an individual story is perhaps even less self-contained than is a story from, say, *Dubliners*, in which the serial arrangement suggests a narrative structure which lies somewhere between a random collection of stories and a novel. Perhaps *More Pricks Than Kicks* is best viewed as a picaresque novel, since Belacqua is described as a "sort of cretinous Tom Jones."

One critic has recently suggested that each chapter of this work, like the chapters of *Ulysses*, employs a different technic, the only difference being that Joyce's intentions are positive while Beckett's are negative: Joyce varies his method in order to exercise his own virtuosity and gift for mimicry, while Beckett is primarily engaged in discrediting as many methods as possible.[21] This judgment seems extreme, since only one chapter of Beckett's work, "The Smeraldina's Billet Doux," is in a form radically different from that of the rest of the work. But the central contrast between Joyce's positive motives and Beckett's more negative ones is instructive. It is but one example of Beckett's critical orientation toward the innovations suggested by Joyce.

The mixture of forms in *Murphy*, Beckett's second fiction, is more subtle and perhaps less effective. The variety of elements found in the first novel shared a common rejection of the illusionism of realistic fiction. In *Murphy*, while parodies and various style shifts are still in evidence, the essential mixture is composed of only two, seemingly incompatible elements. These two elements are best described by the novel itself: "All the puppets in this book whinge sooner or later, except Murphy, who is not a puppet" (p. 122). In this book Beckett tries to bring together characters who appear to exist on radically different fictional planes. Not only does Murphy himself possess the kind of reality we generally associate with that of the hero of the realistic novel, but Celia, the heroine, shifts planes in the course of the novel. In chapter 2 she is an assortment of statistics, but by the end of the novel she, perhaps more than any other of Beckett's creations, elicits a kind of reader response that is more in keeping with the rhetoric of the traditional novel than with the techniques of alienation we associate with the reflexive novel.

Hugh Kenner has defended this particular mixture of mimetic and nonmimetic modes on the gounds that it helps to clarify Beckett's critical position toward traditional realism: "If it is possible to regard Celia as a mistake, diminishing as she does the coherent comic vision with pathos strayed as if from a different order of fiction, it is also possible to regard her as a hostage, gladly given, to ensure that the comic vision will be seen for what it is, an act of judgment, not a lack of competence. So a careful pastel might establish that cartoon figures within the same composition are stylizations and not scribbles."[22] We can go farther and suggest that Celia is not just a foil for the caricatures, but that they serve as a standard for gauging our sense of her reality and, by extension, our sense of a reality of which all fictional characters partake, for after all, if Celia seems real and yet is made of words no less than are the caricatures that people the comic vision, then talk of various fictional planes may be just another form of illusionism. Finally, the function of Celia may be compared to the function of the opening chapters of *Ulysses*, where Joyce allows us to become involved in characters in a more or less traditional way before embarking on the more extreme experiments in distancing in the later chapters. Like Joyce, Beckett may have conceived of the possibility of having it both ways, of receiving some of the benefits of realistic fiction while at the same time attacking the fundamental attitudes of such fiction.

In *Watt* Beckett moves away from the extreme formal discontinuity of the earlier works. While he has not yet adopted the monotonality of the later first-person fictions, he has, in effect, anticipated it by linking his narrative to the obsessional consciousness of his hero. It is as if the author recognized, at least for the course of the novel, the futility of using shifting forms to express the monumental sameness of things. Against the redundancy of experience, formal variations seem a lie (not that Beckett is against lying), and like Arsene in the novel, Beckett accepts this sameness: "And if I could begin it all over again, knowing what I know now, the result would be the same. And if I could begin again a third time, knowing what I would know then, the result would be the same. And if I could begin it all over again a hundred times, knowing each time a little more than the time before, the result would always be the same, and the hundredth life as the first, and the hundred lives as one. A cat's flux" (p. 47). Although the subject of the passage is "life," here as elsewhere in Beckett's later works, "life" is a figure for "writing," where existence is seen as an act of composition and text and world become one.

Beckett's movement away from mixed forms (and this is not meant to imply that he ever repeats himself from work to work) may also have been anticipated by Joyce. While Anthony Burgess certainly exaggerates when he claims that "in *Ulysses* there are many kinds of language, while in the *Wake* there is really only one,"[23] it is in a sense true that Joyce's last work is constructed from a single formal principle. We can speak of *the* style of *Finnegans Wake* and *Watt* in a way in which we cannot speak of *the* style of *Ulysses* or even of *More Pricks Than Kicks*.

The last three words of Beckett's first published story, "Dante and the Lobster," represent an authorial intrusion of some significance as we come to an understanding of Beckett's narrative techniques in his first three novels: "Well, thought Belacqua, it's a quick death, God help us all. [paragraph break] It is not" (p. 22). In context, those words sound godlike, and indeed in a later story the narrator will simply use words to make time pass: "Let us call it Winter, that the dusk may fall now and a moon rise" (p. 20). The voice sounds familiar but not one we find in Joyce—uninvolved in the action, omniscient, occasionally chatty: "We know something of Belacqua, but Ruby Tough is a stranger to these pages. Anxious that those who read this incredible adventure shall not pooh-pooh it as unintelligible, we avail ourselves now of this lull, what time Belacqua is on his way, Mrs. Tough broods in the kitchen and Ruby dreams over her gloria, to enlarge a little on the latter lady" (p. 87). The artificial is stressed: Ruby only comes and goes on these pages, and time is clearly fictional. Like My Father and Uncle Toby in *Tristram Shandy*, who are left on the stairs as Tristram pursues other matters, Belacqua, Mrs. Tough, and Ruby must wait until the narrative comes back to them.

And yet in the third story of this volume, the narrator reveals himself as a friend of the hero: "I know all this because [Belacqua] told me. We were Pylades and Orestes for a period" (p. 37) until, that is, the narrator discovered that "Belacqua was not serious" (p. 38). The problems of verification that always exist when the narrator exists on the same fictional plane as the other characters are not completely removed when the next story returns to the omniscient mode.

This confusion in point of view is later continued in *Watt*, where the narrator, named Sam, appears in his own person in Part III as a fellow inmate in what seems to be an asylum for the insane, where Watt now resides following his stay at Mr. Knott's house. The narrator tells us that Watt is his sole source of information concerning the events that have been and will be related. And yet, having introduced the problem of verification, Beckett proceeds to undercut it. Both teller (Watt) and listener (Sam) are probably insane; Watt's memory is imperfect; his speech is inverted; and the narrator tells us things that he could not have learned from Watt or from anyone else. The major reason for introducing a first-person narrator then seems to have been to throw the whole notion of a mimesis into doubt and reduce everything in the novel to an overt fabrication.

In Joyce, mixed points of view and unreliable narrators like the one in "Cyclops" do not so much undermine our sense of reality behind the words as force us to reconstruct that reality from the fragments and distortions we are given. In Beckett, however, there is often nothing to reconstruct. The drama stops with the words on the page.

Strangely enough, there is little or nothing in Beckett's English fiction to correspond to Joyce's use of the interior monologue in *Ulysses*. This seems strange, perhaps, since one of Beckett's major themes is the quest for the peace of the inner world. Both Belacqua and Murphy are "seedy solipsists" who wish above all things to withdraw from "the big blooming buzzing confusion" of physical reality. Although this withdrawal is occasionally possible for the characters, there is no attempt to *present* an inner world. For an account of this world in *Murphy*, we are referred to chapter 6, where instead of Murphy thinking, we have an extremely analytical account, from the outside, of Murphy's mind: "It is most unfortunate, but the point of this story has been reached where a justification of the expression 'Murphy's mind' has to be attempted. Happily we need not concern ourselves with this apparatus as it really was—that would be an impertinence—but solely with what it felt and pictured itself to be. Murphy's mind is after all the gravamen of these informations. A short section to itself at this stage will relieve us from the necessity of apologizing for it further" (p. 107). Why does Beckett reject a narrative tool that seems particularly appropriate to his subject matter? Because instead of being primarily an excuse for experiments in language, interior monologue is often taken seriously as a mimetic device. Virginia Woolf's revolutionary essay on "Mr. Bennett and Mrs. Brown" is not that revolutionary if all she means to say is that novelists should stop representing furniture and bodies and start representing minds. Rather, she seems to be suggesting that Mrs. Brown cannot be represented at all, that Mrs. Brown is precisely what does not and cannot get into a novel.

Beckett understands this, as does Joyce, and as early as *Ulysses*. S. L. Goldberg has noted that the common practice of attacking or defending the stream-of-consciousness technique in terms of its "psychological realism" fails to account for the different uses of the technique by individual writers.[24] While the sections of *Ulysses* that employ a more or less constant stream-of-consciousness narrative—the first six chapters, "Lestrygonians," "Scylla and Charybdis," the second half of "Nausicaa," and "Penelope"—constitute the realistic base of the novel, it may also be said that the thoughts of the characters take on a non-mimetic role when an image from one consciousness reappears in another. The "coincidence" serves to reinforce our notion of the shaping imagination *behind* the characters.

In a similiar manner, the breakdown of ordinary syntax calls attention to the passages of stream-of-consciousness not as representations of minds so much as conscious manipulations of segments of language. The experience of reading "Penelope" does not support the notion that it is a "natural" flow. On the contrary, the reader is forced to provide the stops himself, an activity that can only accentuate the artificiality of the writing.

Later, in *Finnegans Wake*, Joyce uses the dream only as a justification for wordplay. Perhaps to ask who is the dreamer is to perpetuate a misconception about the nature of the work, to seek something beyond the work itself, even if it be only an imaginary or imagined consciousness.

Like Joyce, Beckett most often parodies a *kind* of writing rather than a specific author, although his treatment of the ending of Joyce's "The

Dead" is a striking example of precise mimicry: "and the rain fell in a uniform and untroubled manner. It fell upon the bay, the littoral, the mountains and the plains, and notably upon the Central Bog it fell with a rather desolate uniformity" ("A Wet Night," p. 83). And like Joyce, he uses parodies to distance the action and to question traditional modes of representation. Parody also implies a kind of virtuoso performance, playing up the quality of writing itself as an *act*. Joyce writes: "Speech, speech. But act. Act Speech" (*Ulysses,* p. 211). Parody is one way of focusing attention on the act of composition and away from the action of characters. To the extent that parody involves an attack on the material parodied, it serves as a means of severing one's self from a literary tradition. Even when no attack is implied, as in the parody of "The Dead," it suggests that a thing once done cannot be repeated without irony.

In his earlier work Beckett uses parody to attack certain conventional modes of writing and to put forward the notion of the writer as performer without commitment. While retaining the idea of performance, the later work, beginning with *Watt*, seeks to go beyond parody as a means of dramatizing the act of writing.

The portrait of Alba Perdue in "A Wet Night" is a typical example of Beckett's early use of broad parody: "But now she cometh that all this may disdain, Alba, dauntless daughter of desires. Entering just on the turn of the hush, advancing like a midinette to pay her ironical respects to the Beldam, she fired the thorns under every pot. Turning her scarlet back on the crass crackling of the Parabimbi she mounted the estrade and there, silent and still before the elements of refreshment, in profile to the assistance, cast her gravitational nets" (p. 68). The elevated style is hardly a serious opponent, and the writer's purpose seems little more than comic. More serious, perhaps, is the opening paragraph of "Walking Out," where the mock sentimental style represents a form of expression still found in popular fiction:

> Belacqua regretted the horses of the good old days, for they would have given to the landscape something that the legions of sheep and lambs could not give. These latter were springing into the world every minute, the grass was spangled with scarlet afterbirths, the larks were singing, the hedges were breaking, the sun was shining, the sky was Mary's cloak, the daisies were there, everything was in order. Only the cuckoo was wanting. It was one of those Spring evenings when it is a matter of some difficulty to keep God out of one's meditations. (P. 101)

In *Murphy* the openly fictional characters who pursue Murphy are given an openly fictional language: " 'Oh if you have,' cried Miss Couni-han, 'if you have news of my love, speak, speak I adjure you!' She was an omnivorous reader" (p. 119).

In *Watt*, although Beckett continues to employ parody as a means of attacking conventional fiction, several new elements have been in-troduced. For one thing, the entire work may be taken as a parody of Kafka's *The Castle* as written by a machine. Or as a dream-parody of the ultimate naturalistic novel, which leaves out nothing. Also, the entire novel resembles the work of some British analytical philosophers. In any case, parody is no longer an occasional device but the very substance of the work itself, which deals exclusively with a "text" and not with "things as they really are."

"It was morning and Belacqua was stuck in the first canti of the moon. He was so bogged down that he could move neither backward nor for-ward" ("Dante and the Lobster," p. 9). These are the opening sentences of Beckett's first work of fiction. It is not a work of science fiction, and we know that Dante's Belacqua is still waiting to leave Antepurgatory. So the question is Where is Belacqua?

> Blissful Beatrice was there, Dante also, and she explained the spots on the moon to him. She shewed him in the first place where he was at fault, then she put her own explanation. She had it from God, there-fore he could rely on its being accurate in every particular. All he had to do was to follow her step by step. Part one, the refutation, was plain sailing. She made her point clearly, she said what she had to say without fuss or loss of time. But part two, the demonstration, was so dense that Belacqua could not make head or tale of it. The disproof, the reproof, that was patent. But then came the proof, a rapid short-hand of the real facts, and Belacqua was bogged indeed. (P. 9)

He is in a book. Or rather, two books—Dante's and Beckett's. To open Beckett's first novel and to read about someone reading seems to imply an interest in the act of reading to correspond to an interest in the act of writing.

Unlike Joyce's, Beckett's narrators do not eschew addressing readers directly in the eighteenth- or nineteenth-century manner—"gentle skim-mer" he is often called. The narrator, sensing that the reader may be unfamiliar with the vocabulary of the characters, comes to his assist-ance:

"And the rosiner," said Mrs. Tough, "will you have that in the lave too?"

Reader, a rosiner is a drop of the hard. . . .

"I'll have a gloria," she said.

Reader, a gloria is coffee laced with brandy. (Pp. 86–87)

And when Belacqua's French thoughts enter the text, we are given an explanation: "Pardon these French expressions, but the creature dreams in French" (p. 82).

In *Murphy*, characters sometimes serve as reader-surrogates, as when Celia's grandfather responds to the story his granddaughter tells with the same impatience that might be expected of the reader (p. 15). Murphy is described as a strict nonreader, which places him in a different category from all the other characters, who persist in responding to experience as if it were a book. Consider Celia's response to Murphy's speech: "She felt, as she felt so often with Murphy, spattered with words that went dead as soon as they sounded; each word obliterated, before it had time to make sense, by the word that came next. . . . It was like difficult music heard for the first time" (p. 40). This curious response seems inappropriate to Murphy's use of language, but it prefigures the reader's response to the language of the later novels.

In *Watt* Beckett often gives his reader something approximating the experience of pure reading, that is, the simple physical sensation of eyes moving across a page, since there is, in the repeated formulae of certain passages, little besides that physical movement to think about. (Unless, of course, we think of the tedium involved in *writing* such sentences, a tedium that resembles nothing so much as that of a schoolboy who is required to write the same sentence over and over.[25] Perhaps the "pensum" that is later mentioned in the trilogy refers precisely to the deadening effect created by contemplating this act of composition.) Like the counting of the banana trees in Robbe-Grillet's *Jealousy* or the catalogues in *Ulysses*, *Watt* tempts us, at our own risk, to skim. If *Ulysses* is almost unreadable in parts because Joyce insists on putting everything in it, *Watt* encourages us to skim a meager amount of material that is exhaustively reworked as the narrative approaches an almost total stasis.

It is possible to read *Watt* as an allegory of the act of interpretation in which the text to be interpreted is Watt's world (or Knott's), but since that world is a text, we can remove the notion of allegory (no A = B, since B is missing). *Finnegans Wake* is also *about* reading *Finnegans Wake*, and there are other, more recent novels, that seem to fit this mode, most notably Witold Gombrowitz's *Cosmos*, John Fowles's *The Magus*, and some of the fictions of Julio Cortázar.

In his interview with Georges Duthuit, Beckett outlines the situation in which the contemporary painter—and by extension, writer—finds himself. The painter is helpless to paint, because "there is nothing to paint and nothing to paint with."[26] *Why* there is nothing to paint or to write *about* has been considered. The question of why there is nothing to paint *with* or nothing to write *with* deserves special consideration.

Writing in the wake of the *Wake*, Beckett is faced with essentially three choices: (1) he may return to a pre-Joycean respect for ordinary usage; (2) he may imitate the master, and invent his own language; (3) he may offer a critique of Joyce's multilingual punning and in the process of offering such a critique develop a language that may be identified as his own. Beckett rejected the first alternative, which would involve pretending that Joyce had never written, an act of the imagination Beckett never performed. He did, for a while, in the early thirties, write as if he would be content to impersonate Joyce, as his "Text" clearly shows.[27] That short passage in Wake language is more than parody or homage: It represents a sincere attempt by a young writer to imitate the kind of language he most admires. The early poetry, too, is characterized by a Joycean diction and allusiveness. As late as Murphy, Beckett has a character declare that "in the beginning was the pun" (p. 65), when the author's own sentiments must have been to see the pun as an end rather than a beginning. Whatever the other sources of Beckett's feeling that there was nothing left to write *with*, surely he must have felt that *Work in Progress* was using up a particular kind of language.

One way in which Beckett sought to "answer" Joyce was by occasionally advancing his narrative without recourse to words, as in the chess notation in *Murphy*, the frog croaks in *Watt*, and the general movement toward numbers in *Watt*. Later he would write in French, an extremely impoverished French that perhaps would be as far removed as possible from Joyce's dense-textured prose.

Like Joyce, Beckett always forced his reader to look at the word rather than through it. The comic dialogue in "Fingal," which arises from the confusion over "motte" and "moth," is similar to the malapropisms of Joyce's "The Sisters." In addition to his penchant in the early fiction for the unusual word, Beckett often places ordinary words in strange lights, making them seem as if they were placed within quotation marks: "The effect was to send what is called a glow of warmth what is called coursing through his veins" ("A Wet Night," p. 74).

Beckett's first exercise in a distinctly anti-Joycean language, *Watt*, focuses on the limitations of ordinary language. By implication he seems to be saying that if meaning eludes us when we deal in only the most prosaic language, then Joyce has taken too much for granted in attempting to convey meaning through the dense style. It seems clear that the inversions that Watt uses to recount his experiences to Sam are intended as reflections on the dense style in general and on Joyce in particular: "These were sounds that at first, though we walked glued together, were so much Irish to me" (p. 169).

More typical of the kind of reflection on language that we find in *Watt* is the naming of the pot episode. Here Beckett insists on that enormous gap which is not to be bridged by any art: "Looking at a pot, for example, or thinking of a pot, at one of Mr Knott's pot, of one of Mr Knott's pots, it was in vain that Watt said, Pot, pot. Well, perhaps not quite in vain, but very nearly. For it was not a pot, the more he looked, the more he reflected, the more he felt sure of that, that it was not a pot at all. It resembled a pot, it was almost a pot, but it was not a pot of which one could say, Pot, pot, and be comforted" (p. 81). Extreme nominalism does not invoke silence but rather clarifies the opposition between signifier and signified. Rather than a "literature of silence," Beckett gives us something like a literature of literature, series of works, beginning with *Watt*, that take for granted that tendency of language to refer only to itself.

Beckett's systematic attack on the traditional elements of fiction proceeds at all levels. On the level of plot, it might be instructive to consider his handling of the Joycean epiphany. Considered as a narrative device, the epiphany provides a climax which, according to the standards of most nineteenth-century fiction, may seem somewhat anti-climactic, since it involves common objects and ordinary experiences. In Joyce's hands, however, the epiphany is often a naturalistic means of providing significance to represented events. It should not be forgotten that Joyce is many writers, and that if his experimentalism provided an impetus to nonnaturalistic writing, other aspects of his work may be viewed as continuations and extensions of the nineteenth-century search for a method to reveal things as they are. The epiphany and the sort of understatement it implies has provided twentieth-century naturalists with a model for making something happen while avoiding the theatrical.

Joyce's use of the anti-epiphany in *A Portrait of the Artist as a Young Man* indicates that the author does not share his hero's uncritical attitude toward the theory itself, and in *Ulysses* even Stephen has come to look on his earlier enthusiasm with some irony: "Remember your epiphanies on green oval leaves, deeply deep, copies to be sent if you died to all the great libraries of the world, including Alexandria?"

(p. 40). And yet both Joyce and his hero still believe in the possibility of the "revelation of the whatness of a thing," in the moment in which "the soul of the commonest object . . . seems to us radiant,"[28] a possibility that becomes actualized at the end of the Circe episode and perhaps elsewhere in *Ulysses*. If Bloom's encounter with Gertie MacDowell in "Nausicaa" is a self-parody of the conclusion of chapter 4 in *Portrait*, Joyce never implies a rejection of the idea of an epiphany.

Joyce's problem is to raise the ordinary to the level of interest. If an epiphany fails, the results are bathetic. Beckett seems to work consciously for this kind of failure. For instance, consider the closing section of "A Wet Night," a passage that contains the word *epiphany*, the parody of "The Dead," and an allusion to *Finnegans Wake*. Sitting on a curb after a long evening notably lacking in significant incident, Belacqua has his moment of insight: "What was that? He shook off his glasses and stooped his head to see. That was his hands. Now who would have thought of that! He began to try would they work, clenching them and unclenching, keeping them moving for the wonder of his weak eyes. Finally he opened them in unison, finger by finger together, till there they were, wide open, face upward, rancid, an inch from his squint, which however slowly righted itself as he began to lose interest in them as a spectacle" (pp. 83–84). In a later story, "Love and Lethe," the two lovers, Belacqua and Ruby Tough, make a suicide pact but have difficulties—similar to those experienced by Didi and Gogo—in fulfilling their intentions. As the tension in the story lessens—the narrator complains that "the gas seems to be escaping somewhere" (p. 98)—the lovers conclude not with suicide but by coming "together in inevitable nuptial" (p. 99). Both passages are instances of the sabotaged epiphany, the intentional dissipation of any possible tension created through plot.

In *Murphy* Beckett frustrates the reader's desire for significant event or discovery by interrupting the "real" story of Murphy and Celia. Chapters alternate between the hero and the farcical pursuit of him by Neary, Miss Counihan, Wylie, and Cooper. Those stories in the novel which do seem to lend themselves to dramatic portrayal—such as the death of "the old boy"—have to be undercut by emphasis on their fictiveness: "The story that Miss Carridge had to tell was very pathetic and tedious. It brightened up a little with her reconstruction of the death scene, cupidity lending wings to her imagination" (p. 144). The story that Miss Carridge then tells is punctuated by the assurance that it is constructed of "lies. All lies."

Watt is an unsuccessful search for an epiphany, for the scholastic *quidditas*, the whatness of the thing. But for Watt not only does the object refuse to reveal its whatness: it refuses to reveal anything at all. The figure Watt sees on the road to the station in the last chapter may be a man or a woman or a priest or a nun or one of those dressed up as one of the others: "For Watt's concern, deep as it appeared, was not after all with what the figure was in reality, but with what the figure appeared to be, in reality. For since when were Watt's concerns with what things were, in reality?" (p. 227). But finally even the appearances of things prove elusive and Watt is left only with his questions.

Beckett also attacks what is perhaps the central axiom of the naturalistic novel—the notion that particulars, individuating circumstances, unique characters matter. He could have learned that particulars don't matter from his reading of *Finnegans Wake*, where everybody is everybody else and one fall is all falls. He might have learned it from *Ulysses* too, although he would have been obliged to read that novel in a very limited way in order to do so. He would have had to disregard the fact that whatever universalizing features the work contains, it also presents us with what is perhaps the most particularized rendering of character, action, and setting in the history of the novel: "Is it possible," Joyce writes to Josephine Murray in Dublin, "for an ordinary person to climb over the area railings of no 7 Eccles Street, either from the path or the steps, lower himself from the lowest part of the railings till his feet are within 2 feet or 3 feet of the ground and drop unhurt." Try to imagine Beckett sending anyone out to do research for *Watt* and you will have some idea of how Beckett approaches Joyce's naturalism.

When it is said that Joyce and Beckett are antithetical writers, what is usually meant is simply that Joyce seems to put everything into his work, while Beckett seems to leave everything out. It is important, however, to see the relation between these two processes and to recognize that Beckett's movement toward abstraction is best understood as a response to the Joycean plenum.

If characters are made of words, does the omission of a descriptive detail constitute an omission in the fictional world? Must a character's legs, for example, be described before he is allowed to walk? Realism often seems to imply this, and Beckett makes a half hearted attempt to give one of his characters all her parts when he provides his reader with a statistical description of Celia, but in context his omissions draw attention to the fact that mere words always fall short in the task of building a person. As early as *More Pricks Than Kicks*, he has recognized a certain futility in the description of physical appearances:

In face and figure Lucy was entrancing, her entire person was quite perfect. For example, she was as dark as jet and of a paleness that never altered, and her thickshort hair went back like a pennon from her fanlight forehead. But it would be a waste of time to itemise her. Truly there was no fault or flaw in the young woman. Yet we feel we must say before we let her be, her poor body that must wither, that her nether limbs, from where they began even unto where they ended, would have done credit to a Signorelli page. Let us put it this way, that through her riding-breeches they came through. What more can be said of a woman's legs, thighs included? Or is all this merely ridiculous? (Pp. 105–6)

Beckett here manages to undermine his description in the very act of delivering it. The effect is to render Lucy intangible and to emphasize the arbitrary quality of any form of selection.

In *Murphy* the characters are constantly telling each other stories, stories—the narrator intrudes to tell us—that have been "expurgated, accelerated, improved and reduced" (p. 12). Even so, Mr. Kelly has to interrupt Celia's account of how she met Murphy: "But I beseech you, be less beastly circumstantial" (p. 13). "How do you know all this?" he later asks. "All these demented particulars" (p. 13). Sentences in the novel that promise to be filled with "information" are allowed to dwindle off unfinished, and "etc." is permitted to do much of the work of providing detail. The narrator's impatience with the circumstantial, like Mr. Kelly's, anticipates Malone's disgust, in *Malone Dies*, at "writing out" stories.

Watt would seem to mark a break in Beckett's tendency toward abstraction. The reader is bombarded with particulars, what Neary in *Murphy* calls "the big blooming buzzing confusion" (p. 4). But in fact, the movement toward an all-inclusive vision, the attempt to record all trivial experiences in all of their permutations, serves only to emphasize the sameness of things.

Insofar as Beckett's plays employ a similar use of abstraction, they may be seen to represent extensions of Brecht's alienation effect. But the effect of abstraction—in the novels perhaps even more than in the plays, which are compelled to particularize to some extent—is to distance the reader from the characters and to force him to take a critical position with regard to the representation. It is, if you like, an example of "dehumanization in the arts," a charge that has often been brought against not only Beckett but Joyce as well, particularly with reference to the "Ithaca" episode of *Ulysses*, not to mention *Finnegans Wake*. I would suggest that what is lost in terms of "a sense of life" for the characters in these works is more than made up for by placing the writer in the foreground. Hugh Kenner is correct when he enjoins us to see both Joyce and Beckett "as their own greatest inventions."[29] Both writers become, in the course of their careers, less and less willing to share the spotlight with any imaginary figures. Beckett differs from Joyce in this insofar as he is able to suggest that even the self of the writer may be ultimately fictional, a consideration that leads directly to the contrast between both writers' relationship to their creations.

Joyce belongs to the Romantic tradition, which posits the omnipotence of the imagination: The poet creates worlds as real as the one in which we live. Or more real. In spite of the fact that Beckett centers his work around the artist and the act of composition in a way in which Joyce does not, at least in works prior to *Finnegans Wake*, his view of the imagination is distinctly non-Romantic: "But to elicit something from nothing requires a certain skill and Watt was not always successful in his efforts to do so" (*W*, p. 77). This understatement should not be read merely as a description of Watt's impotence but also as a direct rejection of the semi-magical pretensions surrounding the works of Joyce, Proust, and, in Beckett's own generation, Nabokov. With the possible exception of William Faulkner, no other major modern writer denies so vehemently as Beckett the possibility of creation *ex nihilo*. And no other writer has practiced so assiduously what Michael Robinson and Richard Coe have called "the art of failure."[30]

It is only with the French fiction that Beckett begins to deal directly with the writer and the act of composition, but the early works too are peopled with artist-figures. In *More Pricks Than Kicks*, there is Walter Draffin, to whom Beckett ascribes the authorship of his own unsuccessful first draft of *More Pricks*, *Dream of Fair to Middling Women*. Belacqua's friend Hairy Quinn is pictured as one of "the coming writers," although his general inarticulateness, his inability to construct a sentence with subject, predicate, and object without a pencil and a piece of paper throws doubt on our willingness to believe in his possibilities of success in his chosen field (p. 124). Even Belacqua is a word man, as he walks through the streets of Dublin, "exalted, fashioning intricate festoons of words" (p. 72). And in *Watt*, both Watt and Sam are involved in the task of artistic reconstruction. What all of these figures share is a general inability to get the job done. The author allows himself to be swept into the current of failure at the end of *Watt*, where a note accompanying the "Addenda" to the novel reads: "the following precious and illuminating material should be carefully studied. Only fatigue and disgust prevented its incorporation" (p. 247). The comment is perhaps only half-serious, just as the notion of an "art of failure" is in part a figure of speech. Nevertheless, we are a long way from the notion that the novelist is God. Beckett has isolated one particular aspect of his art to contrast it with that of Joyce: "The more Joyce knew the more he could. He's tending toward omniscience and omnipotence as an artist. I'm working with impotence, ignorance."[31] One of the consequences of this art is that it tends to place the writer not "within or behind or beyond or above his handiwork" but *in* it, in a way that questions the whole tradition of impersonality from Flaubert to Eliot and Joyce.

In the story "Yellow" Belacqua is reminded, by an "angel of the Lord," of a very funny story,

> really very funny indeed, it always made Belacqua laugh till he cried, about the parson who was invited to take a small part in an amateur production. All he had to do was to snatch at his heart when the revolver went off, cry "By God! I'm shot!" and drop dead. The parson said certainly, he would be most happy, if they would have no objection to his drawing the line at "By God!" on such a secular occasion. He would replace it, if they had no objection, by "Mercy!" or "Upon my word!" or something of that kind. "Oh my! I'm shot!" how would that be?
>
> But the production was so amateur that the revolver went off indeed and the man of God was transfixed.
>
> "Oh!" he cried "Oh . . . ! . . . BY CHRIST! I *am* SHOT!" (P. 172)

A comic digression, yes, but the story should also be read as a comment on the shifting relationship between art and life.

Certain ontological questions are raised by a text that refers to itself. Whatever image of life the text possesses cannot be derived from a representational relation to the world. It must issue from a severing of this relation and a subsequent establishing of the text *in* the world. Once the text becomes a thing *in* the world and not something *about* the world, it can reestablish relations with other objects but on a different level than that between objects in the world and the work of art as representation. For one thing, the self-referential work of art is no longer framed, any more than other objects in the world are framed. It requires a real bullet to remove the frame from the parson's performance. In *Watt* Beckett carries his techniques of alienation to a new extreme; but paradoxically, the effect of diminishing the value of the work as representation, by insisting on its artificiality, has been to present the reader with something like a real bullet: a book that doesn't pretend to be what it is not, a book that presents itself as book.

To pretend that a book is a *natural* object, however, and not some-thing written, is just another strategy of illusionism. To admit that a book is just a book is also to recognize it as the end product of an act of writing. The significance of the addenda to *Watt* is that they break the frame of the novel by introducing the world of the scratch pad, the wastebasket, the man alone in a room writing. Finally, the addenda may be a lie: Beckett may have arranged the material there as carefully as in the rest of the novel. But how would we know? And how would it help to know?

Beckett's early fiction, and to a greater extent the works in French, compel the reader to surrender his notion of the self-contained work of art, an idea that, paradoxically, is tied to the concept of mimesis. When a work of art begins to point to itself, it tends to lose its special status in a world of things. It is not so much that Beckett rejects either fiction or reality; rather, his interests and his sense of the modern lead him to examine the problematic relationship between the two. Lawrence E. Harvey has described the nature of this examination: "All art, of course, both engages the reader in its own world and implicates non-fictional reality, but the pure or self-contained tendency that is one of the two poles of art minimizes the art-life relationship, while Beckett shakes the reader mercilessly back and forth between fiction and reality."[32]

While our typical picture of Joyce places him at the "pure or self-contained" pole of art, perhaps a reading of Beckett clarifies certain elements in the Joyce canon. Certainly a reading of Joyce helps us to understand Beckett's work, but moving in the opposite direction may prove equally helpful. Beckett's own sustained effort to place the writer in the work may help us to view *Finnegans Wake* in new ways and to recognize that that work too calls for the presence of a reality that is not merely the illusion of reality.

NOTES

1. Frank O'Connor, "Work in Progress," in *Dubliners: Text, Criticism, and Notes*, ed. Robert Scholes and A. Walton Litz (New York: Viking Press, 1967), p. 306.

2. Ibid., p. 307.

3. James Joyce, "The Dead," in *Dubliners: Text, Criticism, and Notes*, p. 178. Other works by Joyce cited: *A Portrait of the Artist as a Young Man: Text, Criticism, and Notes*, ed. Chester G. Anderson (New York: Viking Press, 1968); *Ulysses* (New York: Modern Library, 1961). Subsequent references will be given in the text.

4. Robert Musil, *The Man without Qualities*, trans. Eithne Wilkins and Ernst Kaiser (New York: Capricorn Books, 1965), p. 12.

5. Quoted by Raymond Federman in "Beckettian Paradox," *Samuel Beckett Now*, ed. Melvin J. Friedman (Chicago: University of Chicago Press, 1970), p. 115.

6. The fullest account of the composition of *Ulysses* is Michael L. Groden's "The Growth of James

Joyce's *Ulysses*," dissertation, Princeton University, 1975. Groden's examination of the manuscripts and printed text substantiates the claim that Joyce altered his objectives following the completion of the first nine episodes.

7. L. A. Murillo, *The Cyclical Night: Irony in James Joyce and Jorge Luis Borges* (Cambridge, Mass.: Harvard University Press, 1968), p. 61.

8. Michael Groden notes in "Growth of James Joyce's *Ulysses*" that most of the striking "alienation techniques" of the first nine episodes did not appear in the original versions presented in *Little Review* (March 1918–May 1919) but were added later, during and after Joyce's work on the second half of the book. Still, the first of the book remains relatively free of the experimentation with reflexive forms. Groden speculates that Joyce intended *Ulysses* to be "a record of all the stages he passed through and not merely the product of the last one" (p. 311). The emphasis on product rather than process is a characteristic of mimetic fiction. By emphasizing process, the reflexive writer *foregrounds* the writing.

9. The concept of the "arranger" comes from David Hayman's *Ulysses: The Mechanics of Meaning* (Englewood Cliffs, N.J.: Prentice-Hall, 1970), p. 70: "I use the term 'arranger' to designate a figure who can be identified neither with the author nor with any of his narrators, but who exercises an increasing degree of control over his increasingly challenging materials."

10. S. L. Goldberg, *The Classical Temper: A Study of James Joyce's Ulysses* (London: Chatto and Windus, 1963), p. 30.

11. Ibid., p. 284.

12. Ibid., p. 288.

13. Michael Groden notes that the playfulness of Stephen's mood, the use of musical notation, free verse, and dramatic dialogue all change the appearance of the page and anticipate some of the innovations of the later chapters. "Growth of James Joyce's *Ulysses*," p. 34.

14. Murillo, *Man Without Qualities*, p. 54.

15. Goldberg, *Classical Temper*, p. 263.

16. Arnold Goldman, *The Joyce Paradox* (Evanston, Ill.: Northwestern University Press, 1966), pp. 92–93.

17. Ibid., p. 94

18. Hugh Kenner, *Dublin's Joyce* (Bloomington: University of Indiana Press, 1966), p. 153.

19. Samuel Beckett, "Dante . . . Bruno. Vico . . . Joyce," in *Our Exagmination Round His Factification for Incamination of Work in Progress* (London: Faber and Faber, 1936), p. 14.

20. Samuel Beckett, *More Pricks Than Kicks* (New York: Grove Press, 1972), p. 103. Other works by Beckett cited: *Murphy* (New York: Grove Press, 1957); *Watt* (New York: Grove Press, 1959). Subsequent references will be given in the text.

21. H. Porter Abbot, *The Fiction of Samuel Beckett: Form and Effect* (Berkeley and Los Angeles: University of California Press, 1973), p. 28.

22. Hugh Kenner, *A Reader's Guide to Samuel Beckett* (New York: Farrar, Straus and Giroux, 1973), p. 69.

23. Anthony Burgess, *Joysprick: The Language of James Joyce* (London: André Deutsch, 1973), p. 10.

24. Goldberg, *Classical Temper*, p. 235.

25. See Hugh Kenner, *Samuel Beckett* (Berkeley and Los Angeles: University of California Press, 1968), p. 23.

26. Quoted in Martin Esslin, *Samuel Beckett: A Collection of Critical Essays* (Englewood Cliffs, N.J.: Prentice-Hall, 1965), p. 19.

27. From *New Review* (April 1932).

28. James Joyce, *Stephen Hero* (New York: New Directions, 1963), p. 213.

29. Hugh Kenner, *Flaubert, Joyce and Beckett: The Stoic Comedians* (Boston: Beacon Press, 1962), p. xix.

30. Richard Coe, *Samuel Beckett* (New York: Grove Press, 1970), pp. 1–19; Michael Robinson, *The Long Sonata of the Dead* (New York: Grove Press, 1969), pp. 33–61.

31. Quoted by Bell Gale Chevigny in her introduction to *Twentieth-Century Interpretations of "Endgame,"* ed. Bell Gale Chevigny (Englewood Cliffs, N.J.: Prentice-Hall, 1969), p. 9.

32. Lawrence E. Harvey, *Samuel Beckett: Poet and Critic* (Princeton, N.J.: Princeton University Press, 1970), p. 7.

6

Nabokov and the Self's Effacement

where Molloy could not be, nor Moran either for that matter, there
Moran could bend over Molloy.

—Samuel Beckett, *Molloy*

But above and beyond there's still one name left over,
    And that is the name that you never will guess;
The name that no human research can discover—
    But THE CAT HIMSELF KNOWS, and will never confess.
When you notice a cat in profound meditation,
    The reason, I tell you, is always the same:
His mind is engaged in a rapt contemplation
    Of the thought, of the thought, of the thought of his name:
        His ineffable effable
        Effanineffable
Deep and inscrutable singular name.

—T. S. Eliot, in "The Naming
of Cats," *Old Possum's Book
of Practical Cats*

The reflexive mode tends toward infinite regress, a series of Chinese
boxes or diminishing mirror-images. Writing about writing, it naturally
takes the next step and writes about writing about writing. Its critique
includes not only a "baring of the devices" of traditional mimesis but
also an examination of its own devices. It wishes to demystify fiction, to
describe the mimetic fallacy, but it also creates its own myths of creation
that must undergo self-scrutiny.

One of the central contentions of the preceeding chapters has been
that the reflexive novel does not avoid "reality," that it is merely more
honest than traditional fiction with regard to the kind of "reality" to
which it has access. Rather than representing or even inventing

"worlds," the reflexive novel looks at what it *means* to represent, to invent. It focuses on the process of creation, but in doing so it invariably seems to reduce this process to a product, to a book that is more like other books than not. To establish a difference, to push forward the notion of the book as process, as activity, it has seemed necessary to posit an actor—one who writes and who, in writing, subsumes all the functions previously ascribed to his inventions. He becomes all characters, and the plot of his story is just the movement of his writing. Fictional houses and trees, marriages and murders are all replaced by a reality of a different order: the writer becomes his own hero, and his presence is said to fill the vacuum created when the work of fiction no longer pretends to be *about* something but to be that something itself.

And yet, "that something itself" can hardly be anything but words, which, once written, have no need of the writer. The reflexive novel must finally reject its own creation myth, which is grounded in the illusion of authorial presence—an illusion that is no less predicated on a falsification of the writing process than are the illusions of mimetic fiction. This illusion of presence, which was once formulated by Yeats's inability to tell the dancer from the dance, is based—like those of mimetic fiction—on a refusal to recognize the limits of language. Insofar as it is a heroic, quixotic refusal, however, it serves, even in its falsity, to carry forward the program of impersonating the absent hero.

Samuel Beckett's trilogy *(Molloy, Malone Dies, The Unnamable)* is a sustained effort to give substance to the self through a process of reduction. The movement of the trilogy, taken as a single work, is toward the author himself, that final mask which lies underneath all the masks that his words make. The reader, however, never meets this maker face-to-face. The last recorded stage of the journey toward Samuel Beckett, that which is presented by the I-narrator of *The Unnamable*, pretends to assemble all of Beckett's previous incarnations in order to distinguish them from the present speaker, who impersonates the true self. But the "real" Beckett still resides somewhere beyond or beneath the page: "To tell the truth I believe they are all here, at least from Murphy on, I believe we are all here, but so far I have only seen Malone. Another hypothesis, they were here, but are here no longer. I shall examine it after my fashion. Are there other pits, deeper down? To which one accedes by mine? Stupid obsession with depth. Are there other places set aside for us and this one where I am, with Malone, merely their narthex?"[1] The "I" has already answered his question affirmatively by shifting from the third person plural to the first person plural in the first line of the passage. The "I" ceases to serve as the self once it resides with the fictional Malone. As Moran observes in the first volume of the trilogy—"where Molloy could not be, nor Moran either for that matter, there Moran could bend over Molloy."[2] Certain conjunctions, certain juxtapositions of disparate "objects" are only possible when the rules of reality are abrogated.

In the screenplay of *Lolita,* which Nabokov submitted to director-writer Stanley Kubrick but which was not followed by the finished film, the novelist has written a small part for himself, that of a butterfly hunter named Vladimir Nabokov.[3] When critic Alfred Appel, Jr., suggested to the novelist that Alfred Hitchcock's on-screen appearances provided the precedent for this maneuver, Nabokov replied that, in fact, he had had in mind Shakespeare performing as the ghost in *Hamlet.*[4] One might also wonder if Nabokov remembered Joyce's use of that ghost in *Ulysses,* especially since the Russian writer had, in an earlier novel (*Bend Sinister,* 1947, chap. 7), dramatized a theory of *Hamlet* even more whimsical than Stephen's. Whatever the case, both Joyce and Nabokov, as well as Beckett and a host of other postmodern writers, have attempted to leave their signatures *within* their works as well as on the covers. But perhaps *signature,* as written word, creates the difficulty: it is not the self, any more than the celluloid image of Alfred Hitchcock is Alfred Hitchcock, although the writer might envy the director's ability to *seem* to appear in person in his own work.

Lionel Trilling has noted the contradictions in the great modernists' avowals of impersonality: "For all their intentions of impersonality, they figure in our minds exactly as persons, as personalities, of a large exemplary kind, asking, each one of them, what his own self is and whether or not he is being true to it, drawing us to the emulation of their self-scrutiny."[5] Trilling here is speaking primarily of Joyce and Eliot; there can be no question but that the great postmodernist writers— Beckett, Nabokov, and Jorge Luis Borges—have examined their predecessors' notions of impersonality and found them untrue to the facts of literary composition, but perhaps for reasons not immediately apparent.

For Eliot, the artist's act of self-effacement is a choice, a decision to remove the self from the work and thereby purify that work of elements that do not properly belong to it. For Borges, there is no question of removing the self from the work. It was, of necessity, never there. His story "Borges and Myself" describes a totally unsuccessful attempt on the part of the self to enter literature.

It's to the other man, to Borges, that things happen. I walk along the streets of Buenos Aires, stopping now and then—perhaps out of habit—to look at the arch of an old entranceway or a grillwork gate; of Borges I get news through the mail and glimpse his name among a committee of professors or in a dictionary of biography. I have a taste for hourglasses, maps, eighteenth century topography, the roots of words, the smell of coffee, and Stevenson's prose; the other man shares these likes, but in a showy way that turns them into stagy mannerisms. It would be an exaggeration to say that we are on bad terms; I live, I let myself live, so that Borges can weave his tales and poems, and those tales and poems are my justification. It is not hard for me to admit that he has managed to write a few worthwhile pages, but these pages cannot save me, perhaps because what is good no longer belongs to anyone—not even the other man—but rather to speech or tradition. In any case, I am fated to become lost once and for all, and only some moment of myself will survive in the other man. Little by little, I have been surrendering everything to him, even though I have evidence of his stubborn habit of falsification and exaggerating. Spinoza held that all things keep on trying to be them-selves; a stone wants to be a stone and the tiger, a tiger. I shall remain in Borges, not in myself (if it is so that I am someone), but I recognize myself less in his books than in those of others or than in the laborious tuning of a guitar. Years ago, I tried ridding myself of him and I went from myths of the outlying slums of the city to games with time and infinity, but those games are now part of Borges and I will have to turn to other things. And so, my life is a running away, and I lose every-thing and everything is left to oblivion or to the other man.

Which of us is writing this page I don't know.[6]

An attempt at what I have called "breaking the frame" that surrounds the work of art, "Borges and Myself" is an extension of Borges's practice of mentioning himself or his friends by name in the stories he writes, his obsession with the mingling of real and fictional worlds. Borges himself describes this tale as a variation on the Jekyll-and-Hyde theme in which the two protagonists are the spectator and the spectacle,[7] but this expla-nation does not go far enough in exposing the intricacies of the story and its impact on the reader. "Borges" in the story is the name for the various personae that the "I" constructs and attempts to inhabit—the man of letters, the "personality" of the writer, the character who appears to others, both in print and in ordinary exchanges with other "persons." The "I" of the story is the real Borges, who in fact has no name, can have no name, since the name he would have belongs to that other "Borges."

Words are as ill-equipped for the task of expressing the self as they are for the project of representing the world. And yet "Borges and Myself" takes on the quality of a privileged communication, as if, for once, the voice of the self were allowed to slip through, as if the rules of discourse were momentarily abrogated and consciousness were allowed to present itself without mediation. At least, this is the impression entertained by readers until they reach the last line of the tale: "Which of us is writing this page I don't know." But we suddenly know, as does "Borges." What the "I" knows we cannot say, since that "I"—always "he" to us—cannot be known to us. We and "Borges" know that it was always "Borges" speaking, that there are no privileged moments, that for us there can only be one real Borges and his name is "Borges."

What Borges stresses in the story is the self's eternal separation from its many manifestations as "Borges." Even the words—most especially the words, perhaps—the "I" has allowed "Borges" to write are not possessed by the "I" who imagines or the "Borges" who writes but belong solely to Literature, which finally has no respect for persons. In a sense, all works of literature, as products, invest their producers with a kind of anonymity, since upon completion they reside apart from their creators, who continue to write or die, forgotten or remembered quite apart from the mere fact that their work exists. Michel Foucault has numbered what he calls the "author-principle," a method for attributing the unity of a work to the alleged unity of a founding subject, among those constraints which seek to "elide the reality of discourse."[8] The reader performs this elision in order that he may not recognize the utter indifference of language toward the thoughts, feelings, and intentions of the person who uses it:

> What! All those words piled up one after another, all those marks made on all that paper and presented to innumerable pairs of eyes, all that concern to make them survive beyond the gesture that articulated them, so much piety expended in preserving them and inscribing them in men's memories—all that and nothing remaining of the poor hand that traced them, of the anxiety that sought appeasement in them, of that completed life that has nothing but them to survive in? Is not discourse, in its more profound determination, a "trace"? And is its murmur not the place of insubstantial immortalities? Must we admit that the time of discourse is not the time of consciousness extrapolated to the dimensions of history, or the time of history present in the form of consciousness? Must I suppose that in my discourse I can have no survival? And that in speaking I am not banishing my death, but actually establishing it; or rather that I am abolishing all interiority in that exterior that is so indifferent to my life, and so *neutral,* that it makes no distinction between my life and my death?[9]

Foucault's formulation should be seen as a precise and eloquent description of the peculiar pathos of Borges' story, a pathos that derives not merely from the self's discovery that it cannot speak with its own voice but also from the reader's discovery that his or her consciousness is as unspeakable as the writer's. Foucault's questions—although rhetorical—attempt to approximate the terror of one who recognizes his total separation from all that we recognize as real.

We cannot sing of the self, and we cannot tell the truth. It would seem to follow that all autobiographies are actually biographies and that all biographies are fictions. Although "Vladimir Nabokov" retains the traditional distinctions—he has written a real biography *(Nicolai Gogol)* and a fictional one *(The Real Life of Sebastian Knight)*, a real autobiography *(Speak, Memory)* and a fictional one *(Look at the Harlequins!)*; although he seems in many ways—in his public literary quarrels, in the prefaces to his Russian novels, in his hide-and-seek games of exposure within the novels themselves—the most self-aggrandizing of contemporary novelist-performers, he, too, persistently addresses himself to the question of whether or not it is possible for the self to leave a "trace." The question, if not the answer, is seldom evaded in his works and often is central to both his fiction and nonfiction.

Consider the closing lines of *The Real Life of Sebastian Knight*, where the narrator-biographer expresses his own confusion concerning "which of us is writing this page": "And then the masquerade draws to a close. The bald little prompter shuts his book, as the light fades gently. The end, the end . . .—but the hero remains, for, try as I may, I cannot get out of my part: Sebastian's mask clings to my face, the likeness will not be washed off. I am Sebastian, or Sebastian is I, or perhaps we are both someone whom neither of us knows."[10] Readers of Nabokov will immediately recognize and accept that third option, that "someone whom neither of us knows" but whom the reader knows as a Russian author composing his first novel in English. This author, "Vladimir Nabokov," lies at the center of all of his works, but *The Real Life of Sebastian Knight* represents his first sustained attempt to deal directly with the problem of authorial selfhood, to create in novel form a paradigmatic exposition of the ways in which an author does and does not get into his own work. Like Borges, Nabokov attempts to leap from one world to another, to become a presence in his own fiction. For both writers, writing is seen as an attempt to save the self by making it visible in the work, but both writers are also acutely aware of the promise of failure inherent in such an effort. Nabokov's posturing, his playing the role of the "anthropomorphic deity impersonated by me,"[11] should not detract from evasions that allow him to purchase his omnipotence. Gods and puppet-masters sometimes acquire their power by sacrificing their presence in the theology of reflexive fiction. That "someone" who is known by neither Sebastian nor the I-narrator is also not known by the reader, except insofar as Nabokov is able to intimate a terror that the reader shares. By participating in this terror, the reader is perhaps able to go halfway to meet a self as insubstantial as his own.

Noting that the "life of the artist and the life of a device in the consciousness of the artist" is a constant theme in Nabokov's fiction, the poet-critic Vladislav Khodasevich, writing of Sirin (Nabokov's Russian pseudonym) in 1937, perceives certain advantages in treating the artist obliquely by disguising him as a chess-player *(The Defense)* or a murderer *(Despair)*, and certain difficulties, difficulties that Nabokov would later accept, in allowing the artist-writer to appear as himself: "Had he represented his heroes directly as writers, Sirin would have had, in depicting their creative work, to place a novel inside a story or a story inside a story, which would excessively complicate the plot and necessitate on the part of the reader a certain knowledge of the writer's craft."[12] (We may wonder why Khodasevich assumes that readers don't already have "a certain knowledge of the writer's craft," as if that craft were not part of the *substance* of every novel.) Of course this is precisely what Nabokov does in his later work in English, particularly in *The Real Life of Sebastian Knight* and *Look at the Harlequins!*, where much attention is given to the imaginary (in the sense of *unwritten*) fictions of the writer-heroes. If Nabokov's covert subject matter has always been the making of fiction, these two novels bring that activity into the foreground, with all the complications and involutions that Khodasevich predicts. More directly than any of the other works I have considered, these belong clearly to the tradition of the *Künstlerroman*. They are portraits of the artist *as* artist, which means that they stress the actual creative aspect of the writer's life as opposed to his other involvements in the world.

Maurice Beebe sees as a characteristic of the protagonist in the novel of the artist a certain duality—"the Divided Self of the artist-man wavering between the Ivory Tower and the Sacred Fount, between the 'holy' or esthetic demands of his mission as artist and his natural desire as a human being to participate in the life around him."[13] This duality is not unrelated to the one posited by "Borges and Myself" and *The Real Life of Sebastian Knight*, in spite of the fact that in those works the Ivory Tower seems more like a prison and the dualism of the artist-figure is just one aspect of a division that cuts more deeply than the character's psyche. Nabokov, in particular, presents us with a self that is more doubled than divided: locked within his own consciousness, the writer is unable to project even a fragment of himself. Instead, he stresses the total "otherness" of his creation by a process of doubling.

Since Beebe also sees the *Doppelgänger* motif common to much modern fiction as a means of objectifying the divided self of the artist, it is necessary to insist on this distinction between dividing and doubling. In this respect it is interesting to note that, although almost every major work by Nabokov seems to employ the idea of the double, Nabokov himself has denied that there are any "real" doubles in his work.[14] What Nabokov seems to be rejecting is the notion of the double as an objectification of a division in the artist-figure himself, and *not* the process of doubling as an objectification of the separation of what Foucault calls the interiority that is the self and the exteriority that is composed of words. Doubling, in other words, need not be considered as a psychological process but may be viewed as a literary technique that serves to foreground the ontological separation of self and other. In this view the idea of the divided self presupposes some essential unity of subject and object, and it is this unity and the *similarities* that exist between two characters that are most important. The process of doubling, however, becomes a way of asserting disunity and *differences*. If Hermann, the narrator-murderer of *Despair*, fails to execute the perfect crime, it is mainly because he cannot see that his "double" is totally *other*. Failing in both crime and art, he does not understand that "what the artist perceives is primarily, the *differences* between things. It is the vulgar who notice their resemblance."[15]

The process of doubling in Nabokov is not restricted to characterization. Other, seemingly disparate, aspects of his work can best be seen as extensions of this technique. At the level of recurring images, reflections—in water, in mirrors, in palindromes—rank as one of the most important. And what is the *meaning* of Nabokov's favorite sexual pairing, incest, but that it expresses a kind of doubling? There are textual doubles as well: Consider the repeated use of works-within-works that comment upon the larger frame; consider the role of commentary, most spectacularly employed in *Pale Fire*, as a doubling of an original text. Within the Nabokovian *oeuvre* there are entire novels that appear as "doubles" of other novels, revisions that self-consciously rework older material—*Lolita* for *Laughter in the Dark*, *Pale Fire* for the novellas *Ultima Thule* and *Solus Rex*, *Bend Sinister* for *Invitation to a Beheading*, *Look at the Harlequins!* for *The Real Life of Sebastian Knight*.

Perhaps the most intense form of doubling comes with the translation of Nabokov's Russian novels into English and in one case *(Lolita)* of English into Russian. Earlier, I suggested that Nabokov, Borges, and Beckett should be considered as the true successors of the great modernists, and it is interesting to note the role that linguistic doubling, in the form of translation, plays in the work of all three. Roland Christ's observation that a Borges translation, performed under the guidance of the author, creates a *new* work, is equally applicable to the translations of Nabokov and Beckett.[16] Also relevant in this regard is Nabokov's theory of translation and his controversial translation of *Eugene Onegin*.[17] In both the theory and practice of translation, Nabokov stresses the importance of necessary difference.

There is yet another form of doubling in Nabokov's work, one that comes closer to the problems of the self's relation to its fictions, and that is the mirroring of events from the author's life in his novels. (Of course, this too may be seen as simply a variation of textual mirroring, since, for the most part, what we know of the author's "life" is to be found in his autobiography, *Speak, Memory*.) Like Joyce, Nabokov makes extensive use of actual experience, but unlike Joyce he is usually systematic in his distortions. When Nabokov departs from the facts, he does so dialectically, so that the distortion is presented *for its own sake* or rather so that it may come to exist in an opposing relationship with the fact. When the narrator of *Look at the Harlequins!* goes out of his way to proclaim his ignorance of Lepidoptera, he does so just in order to establish a dissimilarity to the butterfly specialist Nabokov, in order to tease out the presence of the real person who writes the page. Another way of expressing the difference between the handling of autobiographical material in Joyce and in Nabokov is to say that Joyce wrote of his life because he was obsessed by it: nothing seemed to have meaning to him unless it could be directly subsumed under some episode of his life story. Nabokov, on the other hand, uses his life as a foil, as an agent for establishing differences. Immune to obsession, at least to those of the confessional variety, he treats his life as an unspoken but ubiquitous counter in the play of his fictions.[18]

As in *Chance*, *Absalom, Absalom!*, and to some extent, depending upon the meaning assigned to Percival, *The Waves*, *The Real Life of Sebastian Knight* centers around an investigation of the private life of an absent character. But Sebastian Knight's absence takes on a sinister meaning once it begins to figure as an emblem of the author's absence from his work. V's biography of Sebastian, which is above all an attempt to resurrect the dead, is also an attempt to affirm the existence of all authors in the pages they have written. But like Faulkner and Beckett, Nabokov cultivates failure.

One way of guarding against failure would be to establish an identity between V and Sebastian: if V can turn biography into autobiography, then so might Nabokov. And, in fact, V and Sebastian do seem to become one person as V reconstructs, in his biography and in his own life, Sebastian's soul, his "manner of being." As reader and writer, V may project himself into the main character so thoroughly that, in some quasi-mystical fashion, he merges with the object of his research.

Or V's final declaration that he *is* Sebastian Knight may be taken literally and as a final uncovering of a hoax. V then may be seen as a fictional character that the real Sebastian creates as a mask to present autobiography as biography, albeit a curiously reticent autobiography. In this way Sebastian would be able to circumvent a persistent defect of the autobiographical form: how to write an ending when life goes on? Sebastian can do this only by turning himself into a fictional character who can be prematurely killed off. If the rest of Sebastian's story is true, his fictional death becomes a prefiguration of the death by heart attack that will come, someday, beyond the limits of the novel.

Many details in the novel seem to support this reading: Sebastian's next work was to be an autobiography; in his encounter with Goodman, V has trouble establishing his own existence; the remarkable instances of nature copying art can be explained if Sebastian is made the sole author, his life the only "book." V's improbable affinities with Sebastian become the affinities of the self with the self. And finally, Sebastian's fate of being "blissfully condemned to the solitary confinement of his own self" seems to disavow the possibility of the existence of the perfect reader that V purports to be. In general, all the fundamental mysteries of the novel are dissolved when the work is accepted as a novel by the inventive Sebastian Knight.

Such a reading of the novel, however, fails to consider the intrusion of a self that is neither V nor Sebastian: "I am Sebastian, or Sebastian is I, or perhaps we are both someone whom neither of us knows" (*RLSK*, p. 205). This "someone" is introduced earlier in the novel when V asks, "Who is speaking of Sebastian Knight? That voice in the mist rang out in the dimmest passage of my mind. It was but an echo of some possible truth, some timely reminder: don't be too certain of learning the past from the lips of the present. . . . Remember that what you are told is really three-fold: shaped by the teller, reshaped by the listener, concealed from both by the dead man in the tale" (*RLSK*, p. 52). The dead man is of course Sebastian Knight, "rotting peacefully in the cemetery of St. Daumier," but also "laughingly alive in five volumes" (p. 52). But he is also he who is *not* present, and V's assertion that his half-brother somehow lives in his books is partially discredited by his own failure to bring Sebastian back to life in his biography. The threefold form of expression is an indication of that which is always beyond communication.

Although V is allowed to believe that he possesses a special inner knowledge of Sebastian, the analogies he provides for the special relationship suggest his failure: "Once I happened to see twin brothers, tennis champions, matched against one another; their strokes were totally different, and one of the two was far, far better than the other; but the general rhythm of their motions as they swept all over the court was exactly the same, so that had it been possible to draft both systems two identical designs would have appeared" (*RLSK*, p. 34). What V's analogy neglects, and what subsequently destroys his impersonation of his half-brother, is the fact that the tennis game provides a mirror image rather than a duplication. The writer, by an extension of the image, may be mirrored in his work, but that mirror image should always be distinguished from the writer himself. It is significant that there is another portrait of Sebastian Knight in V's biography—the painting done by Roy Carswell. But Carswell, like V, presents us with a mirror image: "These eyes and the face itself are painted in such a manner as to convey the impression that they are mirrored narcissus-like in clear water" (*RLSK*, p. 119). The doubling process of mirroring contains a necessary distortion in that it inverts the original rather than reproducing it.

Of course, the mirror image also serves another, related purpose: it functions as an image of self-consciousness and of the ultimately solipsistic attitude of the self. In his most autobiographical work, *Lost Property*, Sebastian Knight declares that "all things belong to the same order of things, for such is the oneness of human perception, the oneness of individuality, the oneness of matter, whatever that may be. The only real number is one, the rest are mere repetition" (*RLSK*, p. 105). It would be a mistake to view this passage uncritically as a denial of the gap between the self and the order of things.[19] It is rather the statement of an ideal, a yearning of the self toward a perfection of the life and the work and a perfect combining of the two. V himself makes this clear when he discusses Sebastian's attitude toward writing, which is seen as an attempt at "bridging the abyss lying between expression and thought" (*RLSK*, pp. 83–84). Clare, Sebastian's typist-lover, understands "that the words she typed . . . were not so much the conveyors of their natural sense, but the curves and gaps and zigzags showing Sebastian's groping along a certain ideal line of expression" (p. 84). The sense of oneness that Sebastian feels is made possible only by sacrificing the desire to express, which is always accompanied by a groping for words that do not match the self's desires.

V tells the reader that "the keynote of Sebastian's life was solitude and the kindlier fate tried to make him feel at home by counterfeiting admirably the things he though he wanted, the more he was aware of his inability to fit into the picture,—into any picture" (*RLSK*, p. 44). If this describes Sebastian's "real" life, then any picturing of that life is a necessary fiction.

To what kind of fictions will such an artist commit himself? If writing does not reflect the world or mirror the self but only is what it is, then writing about writing seems to be all that is left. For Sebastian Knight, as for Vladimir Nabokov, such writing falls naturally into the category of parody. According to one of Nabokov's most successful critics, Alfred Appel, "by definition, parody and self-parody suspend the possibility of a fully 'realistic' fiction, since their referents are either other literary works or themselves, and not the world of objective reality which the 'realist' or the 'impressionist' tries to reproduce. Only an authorial sensibility, outside the book, can be said to have ordered the texture of parody; the dizzying, multiform perspectives it achieves are beyond the capacities of any 'point of view' within the book."[20] Appel, curiously, uses parody as a means of establishing the existence of "an authorial sensibility, outside the book," although it seems more likely to assume that parody represents a sophisticated form of self-effacement. While it is true that, in order to distinguish between parody and mere imitation of other texts, it is necessary to posit an attitude on the part of the writer toward his text, it is also true that this parodist, perhaps to a greater extent than either the "realist" or "impressionist," voluntarily places himself under the severe constraints of an order of things—in this case, words—that is antithetical to the order of the self.

Coexistent with and supportive of the notion of a unique, autonomous, and expressive self is the romantic and postromantic belief in the value of originality. What gives a work of art value is its sincerity—or better, its authenticity.[21] René Girard also associates this aesthetic with what he calls the symbolist subjectivity, which "casts an uninterested glance on the world. It never discovers there anything as precious as itself."[22] This solipsistic, romantic attitude reminds Girard of Proust's theories if not his practice, and it is interesting to note that Sebastian's writing habits are distinctly Proustian (*RLSK*, p. 48). The following passage, too, seems inspired by Proust. From Knight's last, most successful book, *The Doubtful Asphodel*, it describes a man who learns that he is

like a traveller realizing that the wild country he surveys is not an accidental assembly of natural phenomena, but the page in a book where these mountains and forests, fields and rivers are disposed in such a way as to form a coherent sentence; the vowel of a lake fusing with the consonant of a sibilant slope; the windings of a road writing its message in a round hand. . . . Thus the traveller spells the landscape and its sense is disclosed, and likewise, the intricate pattern of human life turns out to be monogrammatic, now quite clear to the inner eye disentangling the interwoven letters. (*RLSK*, p. 179)

The Proustian elements of the passage consist largely of the positing of an "inner eye," an interpreting self. The world is transformed into a book in the eyes of the imagination. The artist, with his "parthenogenetic imagination,"[23] has created as well as discovered a world. After completing *Success*, Sebastian Knight is disclosed lying spread-eagle on the floor of his study: "'No, Leslie,' says Sebastian from the floor, 'I'm not dead. I have finished building a world, and this is my Sabbath rest'" (*RLSK*, p. 90).

Against Sebastian's pretensions, against this deification of the artist-self and the imagination is what Girard calls "novelistic genius," which "begins with the collapse of the autonomous self."[24] Through a close examination of four exemplary novelists—Cervantes, Stendhal, Dostoyevsky, and Proust—Girard examines the *triangular* nature of desire, whereby our desires are not seen as originating within the self but rather created in us by a mediator: we want what we want because others want it. It is the function of the novel to reveal the true sources of desire and to discredit the myth of "spontaneous desire."

It seems legitimate to use Girard's notion of mediation to discuss the role parody plays in Nabokov's work, since it offers a way of analyzing the retreat of the author before the presence of literature. It captures again that sense of "exhaustion" which characterizes Nabokov's work as well as that of other writers in the reflexive mode. Confronted with the achievements of the past, the modern writer can either acknowledge his poverty and, in the manner of Nabokov or Beckett or Borges, draw his strength from parody and retreat, or he can continue to practice an art that denies its own modernity:

The romantic *vaniteux* always wants to convince himself that his desire is written into the nature of things, or, which amounts to the same thing, that it is the emanation of a serene subjectivity, the creation *ex nihilo* of a quasi-divine ego. Desire is no longer rooted in the object perhaps, but it is rooted in the subject; it is certainly not rooted in the Other. The objective and subjective fallacies are one and the same; both originate in the image which we all have of our own desires. Subjectivisms and objectivisms, romanticisms and realisms, individualisms and scientisms, idealisms and positivisms appear to be in opposition but are secretly in agreement to conceal the presence of the mediator. All these dogmas are the aesthetic or philosophic translation of world views peculiar to internal mediation. They all depend directly or indirectly on the lie of spontaneous desire. They all defend the same illusion of autonomy to which modern man is passionately devoted.[25]

If we read Girard's "Other" or "mediator" as *that which has already been written,* then parody is not so much an attack on tradition as an expression of a necessary lack of originality: everything we write should be placed within quotation marks, since to write is to plagiarize the past. Furthermore, the self, like the literature it gives rise to, belongs not to itself but to an "Other."

V tells his reader that Sebastian

> was ever hunting out things which had once been fresh and bright but which were now worn to a thread . . . dead things shamming life, painted and repainted. . . . The decayed idea might be in itself quite innocent and it may be argued that there is not much sin in continually exploiting this or that thoroughly worn subject or style if it still pleases and amuses. But for Sebastian Knight the merest trifle, as, say, the adopted method of the detective story, becomes a bloated and malodorous corpse. (*RLSK*, p. 91)

The appeal of the "decayed idea," "the bloated and malodorous corpse," is that it openly acknowledges the condition of literature in general, and the writer who adopts such forms no longer attempts to conceal his poverty. The meaning of the various coincidences in *The Real Life of Sebastian Knight* in which V's life seems to mimic Sebastian's fiction becomes clear: of course life imitates art, since we are incapable of generating either new ideas or new experiences. Not a romantic celebration of the victory of art over life, Nabokov's novel is rather a monody to the imagination.

Nabokov's *Look at the Harlequins!* echoes more directly than any of the author's previous novels the facts of "Vladimir Nabokov's" public life. Unlike the other novels, which use the similarities between the author and his characters in only a limited way, this last work is constructed upon the notion of the biographical fallacy. Its "implied reader" is one who knows the facts of the author's life as well as all of his other novels, Russian and English. It is safe to say that the object of the "representation" is not reality but Nabokov's *oeuvre,* which provides the context for the "action" of the novel. Like *The Real Life of Sebastian*

Knight—which it renames *See Under Real* and which is its own twin—this novel also explores the relation of self to language by contrasting the real to the fictitious and attempting to dissolve distinctions between the two, but unlike the earlier novel *Look at the Harlequins!* does not invent novels for its protagonist to write but rather borrows from Nabokov's *oeuvre*. To be sure, something is lost in this borrowing, like that which is lost in a translation: there is a diminishment, a slackening of creative force (not in Nabokov's novel but in the novels of his protagonist), even a debasement. There is, above all, what I have called a retreat before the strength of the works of the past, an enactment of that sense of exhaustion, of exhausted possibilities—only here Nabokov is using contrasts with his own earlier work as a means of self-effacement.

W. Jackson Bate, in *The Burden of the Past and the English Poet*, has argued that "the remorseless deepening of self-consciousness, before the rich and intimidating legacy of the past, has become the greatest single problem that modern art . . . has had to face."[26] Harold Bloom's theory of poetry goes farther and states that the modern poet has turned this problem—what Bloom calls "the anxiety of influence, each poet's fear that no proper work remains for him to perform"—into the "covert subject" of his poetry.[27] While neither Bate nor Bloom seeks to apply his ideas to prose fiction, it seems obvious that the modern novelist faces similar problems. For John Barth, in his essay "The Literature of Exhaustion," the postmodern novelist, when faced with the inhibiting power of tradition, must make his own embarrassment before this tradition function as the source of inspiration, writing—paradoxically—of his inability to write.[28] The variation that Nabokov offers on this theme in *Look at the Harlequins!* is that instead of turning outward to consider the accomplishments of his precursors, he turns inward to refashion his own novels in parodic form. In effect, he joins the ranks of younger writers like Barth and places himself in competition with himself, revising and denying his earlier work, becoming his own precursor—the enemy, him whom he writes *against*.

Vadim, the author-narrator of this fictional autobiography, is constantly haunted by "a dream feeling that my life was the non-identical twin, a parody, an inferior variant of another man's life, somewhere on this or another earth. A demon, I felt, was forcing me to impersonate that other man, that other writer who was and would always be incomparably greater, healthier, and crueler than your obedient servant" (*LATH*, p. 89). Like Beckett, Nabokov endows his creation with a partial awareness of his fictional nature, but Vadim is not allowed to see that the "demon" who commands the impersonation is identical with the impersonated author. Or is that other author distinct from the "demon" and as fictional as Vadim? That other author is "Vladimir Nabokov," but by entering the fictional plane he too is fictionalized. The self's attempt to enter the frame alive and intact has failed: Instead of putting the "real" self into his fiction, Nabokov has merely succeeded in turning himself— for purposes of narrative irony—into a character. Just as Vadim is a "parody, an inferior variant" of "Vladimir," so too is "Vladimir" a nonidentical twin of the imprisoned self.

This novel is consistently constructed around doubling games, which seek to establish an identity between author and character only to block those proposed mergings and, by extension, to emphasize the gap between the text and the writing self. Vadim visits a bookseller who mistakes the author's *Camera Lucida* for "Vladimir's" *Camera Obscura*, his *Tamara* for the "real" Nabokov's *Mary*. (These mistakes are appropriately seen as "slips of the tongue," since the essential issue here is not the difference between two authors but the difference between what is uttered or written and that self which, in speaking, loses itself.) Vadim's distress upon hearing these "slips of the tongue" causes him to consider how he might become totally independent, his own man:

> Should I ignore the coincidence and its implications? Should I, on the contrary, repattern my entire life? Should I abandon my art, choose another line of achievement, take up chess seriously, or become, say, a lepidopterist, or spend a dozen years as an obscure scholar making a Russian translation of *Paradise Lost* that would cause hacks to shy and asses to kick? But only the writing of fiction, the endless re-creation of my fluid self could keep me more or less sane. All I did finally was drop my pen name, the rather cloying and somehow misleading "V. Irisin." (*LATH*, p. 97)

The allusions to chess and lepidoptery and the transformations of Nabokov's English translation of *Eugene Onegin* exemplify a technique the author employs throughout this novel. "V. Irisin" for Nabokov's "V. Sirin" is comparable to "Vivian Darkbloom" and all those other jumbled doubles in Nabokov's fiction. But the notion that the writing of fiction is to be seen as "the endless re-creation of my fluid self" offers an explanation for what might appear as a blatant form of self-aggrandizement. When Vadim says that he is "the kind of snob who assumes that bad readers are by nature aware of an author's origins but who hopes that good readers will be more interested in his books than in his stemma" (*LATH*, p. 111), he is actually voicing something that lies very close to Nabokov's own perspective, although it seems to be contradicted by the practice of author-impersonation. But perhaps this notion of impersonation is misleading, since it presupposes some fixed, unitary self that serves as a model for testing the accuracy of different "impersonations." And it is significant that reference to this stable self is made possible only through the use of a *name*.

After his mental breakdown, Vadim becomes an amnesiac: "Without a name I remained unreal in regained consciousness. Poor Vivian, poor Vadim Vadimovich, was but a figment of somebody's imagination" (*LATH*, p. 249). Of course, writing is a matter of naming and a fictional character is only a name and a group of adjectives that cluster around that name.[29] Without a name—that is, without the words of fiction— there is no fiction, fiction here being *opposed* to the unreal, that which exists only in the imagination. Vadim's "real life" is a life conferred through naming. Opposed to the notion of a stable, nonlinguistic self, we have the notion of a fluid self that is the *product* of writing and not antecedent to it. The problem posed by Borges, Beckett, and Nabokov— how to connect the text to the self—is resolved by sacrificing the notion of interiority, by seeing the self as a fiction.

And yet, characteristically, Nabokov will refuse this expensive solution.

And yet "the I of the book / cannot die in the book" (*LATH*, p. 239), as Vadim says in versifying that old rule of autobiography. Just as the "I" of the autobiography must survive the last page in order to write it, so the "I" of any text must point beyond that "death" which is conceived of as the last page of the text. For Nabokov, death is above all a means of establishing limits—between life and death, fiction and reality, text and self. The real meaning of the biographical form of *The Real Life of Sebastian Knight* as opposed to the autobiographical form of *Look at the Harlequins!* is that in the latter work Nabokov wishes to be forced to acknowledge an "I" that is not made of words.

To speak of death is to focus on the nature of time and its irreversibility. Vadim's parody of Nabokov's notion of time, as found in *Ada*, is presented through his confusion of the notions of time and space. Vadim's inability to turn back in space is a result of his confusing direction with duration (*LATH*, p. 252). And yet there is a realm in which a turning back in space can effect a turning back of the hands of a clock; in which time, so irreversible in life, is as flexible as our movements in space. In the realm of written narrative, space and time are so related that to turn back to an "earlier" page—an act that is always part of the reader's prerogative—is to capture an earlier time. The spatial and temporal aspects of written narrative—for the reader as well as for the writer—achieve a balance and harmony that theoretical attempts to give priority to one or the other merely distort.[30]

Because readers can always turn back to an earlier time in the novel, the equation between death and the last page is misleading. But just as "the I of the book/cannot die in the book," so too do readers not find their own deaths in the book. I said that readers can always turn back the page, but this "always" suffers the same restriction that is placed on all of our *always*. The minutes we live are not written down, are not texts. We are led to a recognition of an unwritten self by our awareness of our own impending death, which, like the author's, occurs beyond the page.

Nabokov published an English translation of a story first written around 1926, which, according to the author, "shares certain shades of thought" with Sartre's *La Nausée*. "Terror" ("Uzhas") attempts to describe what for the narrator is the "supreme terror," that sense of the absolute estrangement of the self from the world. I say "attempts" because the story itself is preoccupied with the disparity between the experience and the words that the narrator uses to describe the experience: "I wish the part of my story to which I am coming now," says the narrator as he approaches the end of his tale, "could be set in italics; no not even italics would do: I need some new, unique kind of type" (*TD*, p. 118). This request for a special type, one that would adequately express the self's reality, only serves to reaffirm the artificiality of expression through conventional means, even though it does not explicitly recognize that there is *no* way of escaping the limits of language.

By way of introduction, the narrator first describes three kinds of experience, which approach but do not match the "supreme terror." Significantly, the first experience involves a mirror. After working at his desk for a large part of the night, the narrator would sometimes get up and happen to catch a glimpse of his image in a mirror: "And the more keenly I examined my face—those unblinking, alien eyes, that sheen of tiny hairs along the jaw, that shade along the nose—and the more insistently I told myself 'This is I, this is so-and-so,' the less clear it became *why* this should be 'I', the harder I found it to make the face in the mirror merge with that 'I' whose identity I failed to grasp" (*TD*, pp. 113–14). The narrator's inability to recognize his image or to join it with his notion of "I" seems directly related to the activity he had been engaged in prior to his looking into the mirror. What that work was we are not told, but later we learn that the narrator is a poet. We may assume that he was writing and that this writing, itself an act of impersonation, contributed to the self's estrangement from its double, its image in the mirror.

The second type of experience involves the sudden recognition of one's own mortality. Typically, Nabokov's narrator distances the experience by bracketing it with a theater metaphor. This experience is compared to what happens "in a huge theatre if the lights suddenly go out, and someone shrilly screams in the swift-winged darkness, and the other voices join in, resulting in a blind tempest, with the black thunder of panic growing—until suddenly the lights come on again, and the performance of the play is blandly resumed" (*TD*, p. 114). In terms of convention, language, and ordered forms, the artificial clarity of the play is replaced by obscurity, chaos, and screams. One's awareness of others and one's relationship with them go out with the lights. One is left with an unbodied self and its unintelligible shrieks. Later in his story the narrator clarifies the relation between the inability to recognize the self and the fear of death: "You see, we find comfort in telling ourselves that the world could not exist without us, that it exists only inasmuch as we ourselves exist, inasmuch as we can represent it to ourselves. Death, infinite space, galaxies, all this is frightening, exactly because it transcends the limits of our perception" (*TD*, p. 118). The thought of death, like my unidentified image in the mirror, terrorizes me because it puts before me a reality of which I can have no part, forces me to think of this, and to recognize that this thinking is excluded from participation in the realm of those things which it thinks about.

The third experience, which moves even closer to the "supreme terror," involves the perception of a loved one as completely *other*. Feeling again "what a clumsy instrument human speech is" (p. 115), the narrator tries to describe a quiet domestic scene with his mistress. As she darns a sock and the narrator writes, he is suddenly "terrified by there being another person in the room with me; I am terrified by the notion of *another person*. No wonder lunatics don't recognize relatives" (*TD*, p. 115). Here the experience of the other is all the more terrifying in that it has transformed the object of love into an object of terror. In Nabokov love is sometimes presented as the single means by which the self escapes its isolation, but here the narrator is deprived of that saving means of expression.

The narrator finally arrives at the ultimate experience of terror: "Supreme terror, special terror—I am groping for the exact term but my store of ready-made words, which in vain I keep trying on, does not contain even one that will fit" (*TD*, p. 115). Yeats would rather go naked, though he never did: words always conceal. The narrator walks out into a world that is bereft of meaning, that is, that no longer possesses the meanings ascribed to it by humanity: "All this had evaporated, leaving nothing but an absurd shell the same way an absurd sound is left after one has repeated sufficiently long the commonest word without heeding its meaning: house, howss, whowss" (*TD*, p. 119). The comparison is appropriate, since the experience deals with the loss of meaning and meaning is a function of language. When words become only absurd sounds, we are reminded that that is really all they are in themselves. The signifier has lost contact with the signified.

The narrator then recalls a similar experience of terror from childhood and how it was domesticated:

> In vain did I try to master my terror by recalling how once in my childhood, on waking up, I raised my still sleepy eyes while pressing the back of my neck to my low pillow and saw, leaning toward me over the bed head, an incomprehensible face, noseless, with a hussar's black mustache just below its octopus eyes, and with teeth set in its forehead. I sat up with a shriek and immediately the mustache became eyebrows and the entire face was transformed into that of my mother which I had glimpsed at first in an unwonted upside-down aspect. (*TD*, p. 119)

It should be noted that this represents a variation on the mirror image. Truth, reality, is merely given a turn—not, as in the case of the mirror, from left to right but from top to bottom. The child fails to recognize the familiar face of his mother because his mind has not made a corresponding turn. In like manner, the narrator is unable to see the world in familiar terms until his mind makes the proper adjustment, which occurs only when he is informed by telegram that the woman he loves is dying.

Traveling to her bedside, he notes that it no longer occurred to him to analyze the meaning of being and nonbeing, that those thoughts no longer terrified him. It is as if the knowledge of death reduces his experience to a common condition. Not that his insight concerning his separation from the world is lost, but rather that this discovery becomes naturalized, becomes the terms under which he now must live.

Standing by his dying mistress's bedside, the narrator then chronicles the death of his double, that creature who had pretended to exist in a world of other beings: "She did not recognize my living presence, but by the slight smile that raised once or twice the corners of her lips, I knew that she saw me in her quiet delirium, in her dying fancy—so that there were two of me standing before her: I myself, whom she did not see, and my double, who was invisible to me. And then I remained alone: my double died with her" (*TD*, p. 121). With the woman's death, the narrator's contact with the world is broken, and he is left alone —that is, he is left as that self which cannot speak.

Cannot? Does not the story, as written, with its hesitations, its under-

standing of the inadequacies of language intimate at least a problematical presence, a true voice, which is, paradoxically, most clearly heard
while it insists on its own lack of substance? This reading of Nabokov,
like the one of Borges's story, is largely inspired by the uneasiness that
this paradox creates. The voice of the self that I am trying to locate is
called a "trace" by the French philosopher Jacques Derrida:

> The trace is not a presence but is rather the simulacrum of a presence
> that dislocates, displaces, and refers beyond itself. The trace has,
> properly speaking, no place, for effacement belongs to the very struc-
> ture of the trace. Effacement must always be able to overtake the
> trace; otherwise it would not be a trace but an indestructable and
> monumental substance. In addition, and from the start, effacement
> constitutes it as a trace, effacement establishes the trace in a change
> of place and makes it disappear in its appearing.[31]

For writers who wish to do more than merely tell another story, who
wish to make writing itself stand out as the problematical activity that it
is, this statement provides a means of establishing their own uncertain-
ties. The self may be a fiction, but it is one that is remarkably resistant to
demystification. If it cannot say "I doubt that I am, therefore I am," it
can recognize its own death as an estrangement of a different order from
that which is offered by the limits of language. Borges, like Nabokov,
recognizes that there is another terror, which supplants that terror with
which we behold our lack of presence. The discovery that the self is a
fiction is perhaps a necessary prelude to the discovery—not to be "expressed"—that it is not:

> And yet, and yet. . . . Denying temporal succession, denying the self,
> denying the astronomical universe, are apparent desperations and
> secret consolations. Our destiny . . . is not frightful by being unreal; it
> is frightful because it is irreversible and iron-clad. Time is the sub-
> stance I am made of. Time is a river which sweeps me along, but I am
> the river; it is a tiger which destroys me, but I am the tiger; it is a fire
> which consumes me, but I am the fire. The world, unfortunately, is
> real; I, unfortunately, am Borges.[32]

NOTES

1. Samuel Beckett, *The Unnamable* (New York: Grove Press, 1958), p. 6.
2. Samuel Beckett, *Molloy* (New York: Grove Press, 1955), p. 152.
3. Vladimir Nabokov, *Lolita: A Screenplay* (New York: McGraw-Hill, 1974), pp. 127–28.
4. Alfred Appel, *Nabokov's Dark Cinema* (New York: Oxford University Press, 1974), p. 251.

5. Lionel Trilling, *Sincerity and Authenticity* (Cambridge, Mass.: Harvard University Press, 1972), pp. 7–8.

6. Jorge Luis Borges, *The Aleph and Other Stories*, trans. Norman Thomas di Giovanni (New York: Bantam Books, 1971), pp. 98–99.

7. Ibid., p. 201.

8. Michel Foucault, *The Archaeology of Knowledge*, trans. A. M. Sheridan Smith (New York: Pantheon Books, 1972), p. 228.

9. Ibid., p. 210.

10. Vladimir Nabokov, *The Real Life of Sebastian Knight* (Norfolk, Conn.: New Directions, 1941, 1959), p. 205. Subsequent references to this and the following works by Nabokov will be given in the text: *Look at the Harlequins!* (New York: McGraw Hill, 1974); *Tyrants Destroyed and Other Stories* (New York: McGraw-Hill, 1975).

11. Vladimir Nabokov, *Bend Sinister* (New York: Time-Life Books, 1964), p. xviii.

12. Vladislav Khodasevich, "On Sirin," trans. Michael H. Walker, *Tri-Quarterly* 17 (Winter 1970): 100.

13. Maurice Beebe, *Ivory Towers and Sacred Founts* (New York: New York University Press, 1964), p. 18.

14. In an interview with Alfred Appel in *Nabokov: The Man and the Work*, ed. L. S. Dembo (Madison: University of Wisconsin Press, 1967), p. 37.

15. Vladimir Nabokov, *Despair* (New York: G. P. Putnam, 1966, p. 51.

16. Ronald Christ, "Borges Justified: Notes and Texts Toward Stations of a Theme," in *Prose for Borges*, ed. Charles Newman and Mary Kinzie (Evanston, Ill.: Northwestern University Press, 1974), pp. 68–69.

17. One critic suggests that Nabokov's controversial "pony" of *Eugene Onegin* is the least important aspect of his four-volume work for Bollingen. The Pushkin text is seen as necessary only to provide a pretext for the commentary, which constitutes Nabokov's major contribution. See Larry Gregg, "Slava Snabokovu," in *A Book of Things about Vladimir Nabokov*, ed. Carl R. Proffer (Ann Arbor, Mich.: Ardis, Inc., 1974), pp. 104–21.

18. Nabokov's inclusion of several sections from his autobiography, *Speak, Memory*, in the collection of short fiction, *Nabokov's Dozen*, perhaps suggests that the author does not accept conventional distinctions between fiction and fact.

19. Julia Bader's *Crystal Land; Artifice in Nabokov's English Novels* (Berkeley and Los Angeles: University of California Press, 1972) places too much emphasis on Nabokov's monism, which may exist as an ideal but which is never successfully envisioned by any of the author's characters.

20. Alfred Appel, *"Lolita:* The Springboard of Parody," in *Nabokov: The Man and His Work*, p. 23.

21. See Trilling, *Sincerity and Authenticity*.

22. René Girard, *Deceit, Desire, and the Novel: Self and Other in Literary Structure*, trans. Yvonne Freccero (Baltimore, Md.: Johns Hopkins Press, 1966), p. 28.

23. Ibid., p. 17.

24. Ibid., p. 38.

25. Ibid., pp. 15–16

26. W. Jackson Bate, *The Burden of The Past and The English Poet*, (New York: W. W. Norton and Co., 1972), p. 4.

27. Harold Bloom, *The Anxiety of Influence* (New York: Oxford University Press, 1975), p. 148.

28. John Barth, "The Literature of Exhaustion," in *The American Novel since World War II*, ed. Marcus Klein (New York: Fawcett World Library, 1969), p. 269.

29. See Roland Barthes, *S/Z*, trans. Richard Miller (New York: Hill and Wang, 1974) pp. 190–192, on character as a collection of "semes."

30. Compare Joseph Frank, "Spatial Form in Modern Literature," in *The Widening Gyre* (Bloomington: Indiana University Press, 1968), pp. 3–62, and Frank Kermode, *The Sense of an Ending* (London: Oxford University Press, 1968).

31. Jacques Derrida, *Speech and Phenomena and Other Essays on Husserl's Theory of Signs*, trans. David B. Allison (Evanston, Ill.: Northwestern University Press, 1973), p. 156.

32. Jorge Luis Borges, "A New Refutation of Time," in *Labyrinths*, ed. Donald A. Yates and James E. Irby (New York: New Directions, 1964), pp. 233–34.

7

The Mimetic Fallacy

Paul de Man, using the painted image as his model, locates the motive for mimesis in art in the desire to bring back an absent object.[1] Although mimesis conceived of as a kind of wish fulfillment—the instant gratification of our nostalgia for a real or imagined past—accounts for the value we place on portraits of our ancestors and old love letters (even though in these cases we may not always wish for a return to the past), it hardly seems to offer an acceptable reason for looking at realistic paintings or reading novels that pretend to be histories. If our attention is directed too much toward an illusory presence, both art and the world suffer. If our attention is directed toward the signified at the expense of the signifier, then we are merely back where we began before we picked up the book—in a world in which presence can be not only an incalculable richness, but also a burden. Imitation, magically creating more worlds like the one we know, undermines its own usefulness, since we hardly need more of what we already have. Such a theory devalues both art and life.

But perhaps it is precisely this devaluation which is the conscious or unconscious motive for mimesis. Familiarity does breed contempt, and what the realist strives for above all is to promote an act of recognition on the part of the reader: yes, this is the way a tree looks to me; yes, these are the words I would use to describe this particular feeling. What the realist seeks to confirm is the universality of perception and emotion, the belief that you and I may talk together of our common experience. What this attitude conceals, however, is the mind's enormous inertia, its willingness to be simultaneously content with and contemptuous of the "known."

This act of recognition presupposes a knowledge of the world. In order to judge a work of art as a good copy we have to know what it is a copy of.

But curiously enough, we often forget how instrumental the copy is in forming our notion of the original. Good copies turn out to be nothing more than duplications of other copies, and what passes as knowledge of the world is nothing more than a familiarity with the prejudices and conventions of the dominant modes of representation. The motive for mimesis is to conceal from us the mediated, secondhand quality of our experience and to provide us with the easiest means of reassuring ourselves that we know the world.

Nelson Goodman has observed that most people in our culture would grade a painting's realism in terms of the degree to which it approaches the appearance of a color photograph. But anthropologists have found that members of primitive societies have to be taught to "read" photographs. According to Goodman, "what we regard as the most realistic pictures are merely pictures of the sort that most of us, unfortunately, are brought up on. An African or a Japanese would make a quite different choice when asked to select the pictures that most closely depict what he sees. Indeed our resistance to new or exotic ways of painting stems from our normal lethargic resistance to retraining; on the other hand the excitement lies in the acquisition of new skills."[2] Of course, art is only one of the cultural constructs that teaches us to see and then to forget that we have been taught. The general disfavor with which we now view didactic art derives in part from our unwillingness to admit that art *always* reinforces and often shapes some philosophical, religious, or political position, always teaches, and perhaps teaches most when it does so surreptitiously. By refusing to acknowledge its own conventions, realistic art persuades us to see the world in a particular way and then to block out other possible visions.

It is no accident that the popular art of the twentieth century is an imitation of nineteenth-century realism. Hugh Kenner has remarked that if the tenets of realism are carried to their logical conclusion, we would be forced to admit that the hack writer is the supreme realist, since life tends toward cliché, a redundance of language and event that reduces the need for an active participation in experience.[3] Realist art is popular because it fits easily into our normal modes of perception. Because it offers nothing new, even denies the possibility of anything new, we cling to it even as we despise it—until one day our faith in our ability to know reality is shaken, and we begin to question the ways in which that reality has been represented.

ii

Any discussion of modern literature that fails to account for its critique of the foundations of literary realism is incomplete, since such a discussion would fail to place that literature within its own age, an age that defines itself primarily in terms of its self-consciousness and through the activity of self-examination. Yet even allowing that modern literature *reflects* the interests of the age, it can also be said that it occupies a privileged position with regard to other disciplines and activities. When language loses its transparency, its ability to represent things, then literature—that use of language which, by its fictive nature, has always expressed a problematical relation to things—will be seen to offer itself as a kind of model in the process of questioning the representational qualities of language.

Michel Foucault, perhaps more than any other writer, has attempted to define modernity in terms of its reflexivity and the language of the moderns in terms of its lost transparency. For Foucault, there are compensations for this loss, the most important and the most unexpected being what he calls "the appearance of literature":

> of literature as such—for there has of course existed in the western world, since Dante, since Homer, a form of language that we now call "literature." But the word is of a recent date, as is also, in our culture, the isolation of a particular language whose peculiar mode of being is "literary." This is because at the beginning of the nineteenth century, at a time when language was burying itself within its own density as an object and allowing itself to be traversed, through and through, by knowledge, it was also reconstituting itself elsewhere, in an independent form, difficult of access, folded back upon the enigma of its own origin and existing wholly in reference to the pure act of writing. Literature is the contestation of philology (of which it is nevertheless the twin figure): it leads language back from grammar to the naked power of speech, and there it encounters the untamed, imperious being of words. From the Romantic revolt against a discourse frozen in its own ritual pomp, to the Mallarméan discovery of the word in its impotent power, it becomes clear what the function of literature was, in the nineteenth century, in relation to the modern mode of being of language. Against the background of this essential interaction, the rest is merely effect: literature becomes progressively more differentiated from the discourse of ideas, and encloses itself within a radical intransitivity . . . it breaks with the whole definition of *genres* as forms adapted to an order of representations, and becomes merely a manifestation of a language which has no other law than that of affirming—in opposition to all other forms of discourse—its own precipitous existence; and so there is nothing for it to do but to curve back in a perpetual return upon itself, as if its discourse could have no other content than the expression of its own form; it addresses itself to itself as a writing subjectivity, or seeks to re-apprehend the essence of all literature in the movement that brought it into being; and thus all

its threads converge upon the finest of points—singular, instantane-
ous, and yet absolutely universal—upon the simple act of writing. At
the moment when language, as spoken and scattered words, becomes
an object of knowledge, we see it reappearing in a strictly opposite
modality: a silent, cautious deposition of the word upon the whiteness
of a piece of paper, where it can possess neither sound nor inter-
locutor, where it has nothing to say but itself, nothing to do but shine
in the brightness of its being.[4]

Foucault's way of viewing history as a series of cataclysmic shifts in
the "episteme" of a given age—the limit of what can be thought and
said—leads him to a comparative study of the "ages of man" (although
his radical anti-humanism would reject this expression, would insist that
"man" is a nineteenth-century invention that is about to wither away) in
terms of the way in which different epochs employ language. For the
Classical Age, from the early seventeenth century until the end of the
eighteenth century, language is a transparent instrument of representation. Invisible and effaced, its function is to reveal the truth of the
classifications possible to the Classical mind. In the nineteenth century,
with the rise of philology, language loses its neutrality and becomes
itself an object of study. But this look of language at itself creates a
literature that refuses to be taken as the expression of some nonlinguistic
truth. This literature recovers a sense of its autonomy: ". . . throughout
the nineteenth century and right up to our own day—from Hölderlin to
Mallarmé and on to Antonin Artaud—literature achieved autonomous
existence, and separated itself from all other language with a deep
scission, only by forming a sort of 'counter-discourse,' and by finding its
way back from the representative or signifying function of language to
this raw being that had been forgotten since the sixteenth century."[5]
    At first glance this reading of the present status of literature seems to
posit that notion of an absolute autonomy for literature which my study of
the reflexive novel has sought to discredit. But if modern literature has
become "progressively more differentiated from the discourse of ideas"
and has enclosed itself within a "radical intransitivity," if, in other
words, it has expressed its difference from language understood in terms
of its representative or signifying functions, it has done so in order to
establish a new unity of language, a unity founded upon the inescapable
"literariness" of all language. By focusing on "the pure act of writing"
and on the question of the ontological status of language, modern reflexive literature encourages us to look at "the discourse of ideas" as simply
another manifestation—albeit in heavy masquerade—of language
affirming its own opacity.
    Such explorations are essentially exercises in demystification, under-

stood as the effort to see things as they really are. To see things as they really are is to see that *they are not*, at least in any unmediated sense. What is *given* is not the thing, but a transformation or transformations of the thing in language. Paul Ricoeur, in *Freud and Philosophy*, sees these exercises as acts of interpretation, interpretation understood as an "exercise in suspicion," which "begins by doubting whether there is such an object and whether this object could be the place of the transformation of intentionality into kerygma, manifestation, proclamation. This hermeneutic is not an explication of the object, but a tearing off of masks, an interpretation that reduces disguises."[6] Although Ricoeur's metaphor of disclosure, of exposing illusion, is one that is used by all of the novels I have examined, his subject is Freud, considered both as interpreter and as one whose own words required interpretation. Freud, along with Marx and Nietzsche, is represented as one who deals primarily with signs and language as such, who, in other words, is engaged in exploring the "literariness" of all language and in dissolving that false neutrality which is implied by the notion of a "discourse of ideas."

Foucault has spoken of nineteenth-century romanticism and Mallarmé as central to our understanding of a language that is no longer representational and signifying, but it is in the twentieth-century reflexive novel that the issue becomes crucial. Because the novel has always been grounded in some mimetic theory, even when—as in *Don Quixote* and *Tristram Shandy*—the theory itself comes under attack, it is the genre most vulnerable to the process of demystification. At the same time, since it is the form of literature that most closely imitates the form of historical writing, an exposure of *its* conventions comes closest to exposing the act of mediation as it occurs in "ordinary language." If the novel succeeds in demystifying itself, it will do so not only at its own expense but also at the expense of disciplines that can only pretend to an aloofness or indifference to the question of whether or not the novel is dead.

According to Foucault, modern literature "seeks to re-apprehend the essence of all literature in the movement that brought it into being," a movement that Foucault isolates as "the simple act of writing." That strain of the modern novel which I have been examining has studied this act by subordinating all of the elements of fiction to the reflexive impulse—that determination not merely to tell another story but to examine the process through which a story, any story, gets told. If the subject of these fictions has been "the simple act of writing," then they should provide a commentary on all fictions, even those which take that act for granted. The reflexive novel should certainly provide us with new ways to read old novels. But since "the act of writing" is performed continuously in nonliterary contexts, the reflexive novel can also help us to understand the ways in which we use everyday language and narrative to shape our perception of the world.

iii

A corollary to the idea that the reflexive novel tries to isolate and examine the act of writing is the notion that the act of reading requires special consideration. Effaced readers, like effaced writers, are a product of realism, and their roles must be demystified if we are to come to an understanding of the nature of fiction. We must begin to ask what it means "to read." If, as Wolfgang Iser contends, "the phenomenological theory of art lays full stress on the idea that, in considering a literary work of art, one must take into account not only the actual text but also, and in an equal measure, the actions involved in responding to that text,"[7] then we must all become phenomenologists of art. The difficulty here is similar to the one writers encounter when they want to examine their own activities: how does one place in the foreground an activity that seems *by its very nature* to point away from itself?

Again, we are guilty of ascribing to nature what belongs to habit. One need only recall the experience of learning to read, or watch a child going through that same experience, to realize how quickly and completely one moves away from the act itself toward some sort of product. Reflexive fiction often attempts to bring us back to the fundamentals of the reading process.

Robert Coover has written a story about a writer's wife who mistakenly takes the manuscript of her husband's latest fiction for a grocery list and almost poisons her family.[8] A cautionary tale, it shows, among other things, the danger of devouring and digesting pieces of printed matter. That reading fiction involves a kind of consumption is a notion shared by critics as dissimilar as Georges Poulet and Norman Holland. For Poulet, books enter us in order to displace us: "Reading, then, is the act in which the subjective principle which I call *I* is modified in such a way that I no longer have the right, strictly speaking, to consider it as my *I*. I am on loan to another, and this other thinks, feels, suffers, and acts within me."[9] A similar view of reading as an act of internalization is offered by Holland, for whom the pleasures of reading are related, in Freudian terms, to oral gratification.[10]

A somewhat more conventional theory holds that readers, instead of taking something into themselves, leave themselves and project outward into an imagined world. In Julio Cortázar's short story "The Continuity of Parks" the hero is a reader who projects himself so thoroughly into the novel he is reading that he literally enters that world to become the murderer's victim.[11] Again the tone is cautionary: beware of confusing real and fictional realms.

This confusion is traditionally called "the willing suspension of disbelief," an expression that perhaps takes too much for granted and conceals some of the distinctive features of the act of reading fiction. It assumes, I believe, that the tears we shed for a moving characterization are basically no different from those we shed for real people. The willing suspension of disbelief is supposedly an act we perform when we commence to read a fiction, which enables us to transform, through the duration of the reading, print into life. Reading becomes a form of make-believe, in which, like children, we become so engrossed in our play that we forget that it is play.

Unless some care is exercised, however, such an understanding of the willing suspension of disbelief can lead us to evaluate the performance of readers in terms of the degree of thoroughness to which they give themselves over to the illusion. And certainly we do not wish to describe the "ideal reader" as the country bumpkin who on the first visit to a theater rushes onstage to rescue the heroine.

It might be possible to classify novels on the basis of the types of readers they create. And readers are created, no less than are characters or authorial voices: different texts engender different implied readers just as they create different implied authors.[12] Just as the activity of writing involves a kind of role-playing, so too does reading create different roles. Part of the reader's job is to discover the nature of the role she or he has been asked to play.

The most important fact about this kind of role-playing is that it is *learned*. The instinctual response to literature counts for nothing, since reading itself is above all an unnatural activity. Of course, practice and habit work to naturalize all of our activities, but certain kinds of writing, because of the kind of reading they encourage, reinforce the naturalizing or neutralizing effects of habit. The realistic novel, for example, can be partially defined in terms of readers who are made to forget that they are reading or at the very least in terms of readers who read only in order that they may do something else—picture, imagine, or understand a reality that lies beyond the page. We can all recite lines of poetry, but few of us, when asked to recall a novel, will offer to quote directly from the novel itself. And if we do quote, the passage quoted is likely to be from dialogue, that is, from a dramatic scene in which the merely verbal is buttressed by a picturable situation. In no other art form does the medium of presentation count for so little as it does in the realistic novel, since such novels actively discourage perception of that medium.

All of what I have called the techniques of alienation in reflexive fiction make sense only in reference to the reader's response, and the response created is always one that reminds us that a novel is not a history or a dream or a play or a film or an event of any kind, but rather a string of words. To read such fiction is to be conscious of the physical properties of the printed word. One example of what this might entail will perhaps suffice. Michel Butor's *L'Emploi du temps* is written in the form of a journal.[13] The time scheme of the novel is so complex—with accounts of events mixed in time and with accounts of the writing itself—that the reader is continually forced to go back over pages he or she has just read. Attention, that is, is directed toward the text as text. Readers will invariably find themselves constructing some sort of index to the novel, as all readers of *Ulysses* have no doubt been doing over the years.

When the reader picks up a pen and begins to make a list of cross-references in the text, it may be that this activity can no longer be described as *reading*. Such a reader seems to be *writing*, and this is a transformation that lies at the center of Roland Barthes's distinction between traditional, "readerly" texts and the "writerly," which is something very like what I have called the reflexive:

> On the one hand, there is what it is possible to write, and on the other, what it is no longer possible to write: what is within the practice of the writer and what has left it: which texts I would consent to write (rewrite), to desire, to put forth as a force in this world of mine? What evaluation finds is precisely this value: what can be written (rewritten) today: the *writerly*. Why is the writerly our value? Because the goal of literary work (of literature as work) is to make the reader no longer a consumer, but a producer of the text. Our literature is characterized by the pitiless divorce which the literary institution maintains between the producer of the text and its user, between its owner and its customer, between its author and its reader. This reader is thereby plunged into a kind of idleness—he is intransitive; he is, in short, *serious:* instead of functioning himself, instead of gaining access to the magic of the signifier, to the pleasure of writing, he is left with no more than the poor freedom to either accept or reject the text: reading is nothing more than a *referendum*. Opposite the writerly text, then, is its countervalue, its negative, reactive value: what can be read, but not written: the *readerly*. We call any readerly text a classic text.[14]

On the one hand, there is the reader of the realistic, "readerly" text (elsewhere, Barthes calls it the "archaic," the "infantile" text[15]), engrossed in the illusion, passively pretending that the words of fiction point away from themselves; on the other hand, there is the reader of the "writerly," whose reading is a writing, that is, a systematizing of the words of the text and a naming of those systems or groupings: "To read, in fact, is a labor of language. To read is to find meanings, and to find meanings is to name them; but these named meanings are swept toward other names; names call to each other, reassemble, and their grouping calls for further naming: I name, I unname, I rename: so the text passes: it is a nomination in the course of becoming, a tireless approximation, a metonymic labor."[16]

The central tenet of Barthes's examination of different types of reading is the belief in the indeterminacy of meaning, in what he calls the plurality of texts. In this regard, the realistic text differs from the writerly text only in degree, since any work of language, even if it pretends otherwise, allows for a plurality of meaning. The writerly text, because it never attempts to represent a knowable world, allows or encourages or forces the reader to become writer, that is, to become involved in the text as text. This reader, in "gaining access to the magic of the signifier," becomes co-creator of a text that is not a product but a production.[17]

iv

Clearly, Barthes's *S/Z* represents a new approach, a new way of talking about literature. Taking Balzac's story "Sarrasine" as his subject, Barthes presents us with a slow-motion reading of a readerly text. More important, however, than his idiosyncratic interpretation of this story are the digressions on reading, or what he calls "decompositions of the work of reading."[18] A superb example of what Paul Ricoeur calls a hermeneutic of demystification, *S/Z* simultaneously exposes the mimetic fallacy and presents us with the groundwork for any future *reflexive* reading of a realistic text. In effect, he rewrites Balzac's story as he rereads it, and shows us how we might recover the innocent fictions of the mimetic tradition by exposing their conventions, and thereby again becoming ourselves the producers of the text we read.

Such a recovery or transformation is necessary, I believe, if literary study is to be more than a form of antiquarianism, for Barthes is correct in noting that realism has left the province of what it is possible to write, especially if we hold that writing is never innocent, that it is the most intensely self-conscious of activities. Hacks will no doubt continue to produce soporific illusions, just as some readers will continue to require such products for their easy consumption. Occasionally, humanistic critics will decry these wordy times as without substance and pine for a good story, replete with life, laughter, and tears. Let there be a place for the sentimental reader: we need to understand the past. But let us also take seriously the notion that the creation of a truly new work alters the structure of literature as it changes the way in which we read. This does not mean that it is impossible to recover the original meaning of texts, only that this original meaning is in no way privileged, and in many instances is inhibiting. It is in no sense certain that the idea of a "correct" understanding of a text is a meaningful goal for interpretation, but even if it is, even if we say, along with E. D. Hirsch, that a text means what the author meant for it to mean,[19] what we then discover to say about that text may be correct but trivial. *S/Z* succeeds not because its argument shows us how to read Balzac's story. Indeed, it does not present us with this kind of argument. It succeeds because it is interesting, because it gives an old story new life. And life, after all, is what the humanists profess to be concerned about.

I am assuming that what I think readers and critics should do is only what they must do, in good faith. Each of the novels I have studied attempts to change my perception of literature. the way I read. This is the meaning of "fiction as critique": these novels offer, in the language of fiction, a theory of fiction. Perhaps Barthes' essay is best seen as an attempt to move in the opposite yet sympathetic direction—criticism becoming fiction, which is to say criticism giving up its putative objectivity in favor of an involvement in the act of writing. I mentioned earlier the hope that the reflexive novel's self-critical stance might be adopted by other forms of writing. Perhaps the best place to begin to bridge the gap between "literature" and "the discourse of ideas" would be the domain of literary criticism. It might then be the case that literary criticism is preserved not by becoming more scientific, but by showing all the sciences how to recognize the "literariness" of their own languages.

NOTES

1. See Paul de Man, *Blindness and Insight: Essays in the Rhetoric of Contemporary Criticism* (New York: Oxford University Press, 1971), pp. 111–141.

2. Nelson Goodman, "The Way the World Is," *Review of Metaphysics* 14 (1960): 52.

3. Hugh Kenner, *Flaubert, Joyce, and Beckett: The Stoic Comedians* (Boston: Beacon Press, 1962), p. 19.

4. Michel Foucault, *The Order of Things* (New York: Vintage Books, 1973), pp. 299–300.

5. Ibid., pp. 43–44.

6. Paul Ricoeur, *Freud and Philosophy*, trans. Denis Savage (New Haven, Conn.: Yale University Press, 1970), p. 30.

7. Wolfgang Iser, *The Implied Reader* (Baltimore, Md.: Johns Hopkins Press, 1974), p. 274.

8. Robert Coover, "Beginnings," *Harper's* 244 (January 1972): 82–87.

9. Georges Poulet, "Criticism and the Experience of Interiority," in *The Structuralist Controversy: The Languages of Criticism and the Sciences of Man*, ed. Richard Macksey and Eugenio Donato (Baltimore, Md.: Johns Hopkins Press, 1972), p. 60.

10. Norman Holland, *The Dynamics of Literary Response* (New York: Oxford University Press, 1968), p. 63.

11. Julio Cortazar, *Blow-Up*, trans. Paul Blackburn (New York: Collier Books, 1968).

12. See Wolfgang Iser's *The Implied Reader: Patterns of Communication in Prose Fiction from Bunyan to Beckett* (Baltimore, Md.: Johns Hopkins Press, 1974) for examples of this type of literary inquiry.

13. Michel Butor, *Passing Time/A Change of Heart*, trans. Jean Stewart (New York: Simon and Schuster, 1969).

14. Barthes, *S/Z*, p. 4.

15. Ibid., p. 79.

16. Ibid., p. 11.

17. Ibid., p. 5.

18. Ibid., p. 12.

19. E. D. Hirsch, *Validity in Interpretation* (New Haven and London: Yale University Press, 1967), pp. 10–23.

List of Works Cited

Abbot, H. Porter. *The Fiction of Samuel Beckett: Form and Effect*. Berkeley and Los Angeles: University of California Press, 1973.

Abel, Lionel. *Metatheatre: A New View of Dramatic Form*. New York: Hill and Wang, 1963.

Adams, Richard. *Faulkner: Myth and Motion*. Princeton, N.J.: Princeton University Press, 1968.

Alter, Robert. *Partial Magic*. Berkeley: University of California Press, 1975.

Appel, Alfred. "*Lolita:* The Springboard of Parody." In *Nabokov: The Man and The Work*, edited by L. S. Dembo. Madison: University of Wisconsin Press, 1967. Pp. 106–143.

———. *Nabokov's Dark Cinema*. New York: Oxford University Press, 1974.

Aswell, Duncan. "The Puzzling Design of *Absalom, Absalom!*" *Kenyon Review* 30 (Winter 1963): 67–84.

Auerbach, Erich. *Mimesis*. Translated by Willard Trask. Princeton, N.J.: Princeton University Press, 1953.

Bader, Julia. *Crystal Land: Artifice in Nabokov's English Novels*. Berkeley: University of California Press, 1972.

Baines, Jocelyn. *Joseph Conrad: A Critical Biography*. London: Weiden and Nicolson, 1959.

Barth, John. "The Literature of Exhaustion." In *The American Novel since World War II*, edited by Marcus Klein. New York: Fawcett World Library, 1969. Pp. 267–79

Barthes, Roland. "Science versus Literature." In *Introduction to Structuralism*, edited by Michael Lane. New York: Basic Books, 1970. Pp. 410–16.

———. *S/Z*. Translated by Richard Miller. New York: Hill and Wang, 1974.

Bate, Walter Jackson. *The Burden of the Past and the English Poet*. New York: W. W. Norton, 1972.

Beckett, Samuel. "Dante . . . Bruno. Vico . . . Joyce." In *Our Exagmination Round His Factification for Incamination of Work in Progress*. London: Faber and Faber, 1936.

179

————. *Molloy*. New York: Grove Press, 1955.

————. *More Pricks Than Kicks*. New York: Grove Press, 1972.

————. *Murphy*. New York: Grove Press, 1957.

————. *The Unnamable*. New York: Grove Press, 1958.

————. *Watt*. New York: Grove Press, 1959.

Beebe, Maurice. *Ivory Towers and Sacred Founts*. New York: New York University Press, 1964.

Bennett, Joan. *Virginia Woolf: Her Art as a Novelist*. Cambridge: Cambridge University Press, 1964.

Bloom, Harold. *The Anxiety of Influence*. New York: Oxford University Press, 1975.

Booth, Wayne C. *The Rhetoric of Fiction*. Chicago: University of Chicago Press, 1961.

Borges, Jorge Luis. *The Aleph and Other Stories*. Translated by Norman Thomas di Giovanni. New York: Bantam Books, 1971.

————. *Labyrinths*. Edited by Donald A. Yates and James E. Irby. New York: New Directions, 1964.

Brecht, Bertolt. *Brecht on Theatre*. Edited and translated by John Willet. New York: Hill and Wang, 1964.

Brooks, Cleanth. *The Yoknapatawpha Country*. New Haven, Conn.: Yale University Press, 1963.

Brown, E. K. "James and Conrad." *Yale Review* 35 (Winter 1946): 265–85.

Brumm, Ursula. "Symbolism and the Novel." In *The Theory of the Novel*, edited by Philip Stevick. New York: The Free Press, 1967. Pp. 354–68.

Büdel, Oscar. "Contemporary Theatre and Aesthetic Distance." In *Brecht: A Collection of Critical Essays*, edited by Peter Demetz. Englewood Cliffs, N.J.: Prentice-Hall, 1962. Pp. 59–85.

Burgess, Anthony. *Joysprick: The Language of James Joyce*. London: André Deutsch, 1973.

Butor, Michel. *Passing Time/A Change of Heart*. Translated by Jean Stewart. New York: Simon and Schuster, 1969.

Cameron, J. M. *The Night Battle*. Baltimore, Md.: Helicon Press, 1963.

Caute, David. *The Illusion: An Essay on Politics, Theatre, and the Novel*. New York: Harper and Row, 1971.

Chevigny, Bell Gale. "Introduction." *Twentieth Century Interpretations of "Endgame,"* edited by Bell Gale Chevigny. Englewood Cliffs, N.J.: Prentice-Hall, 1969. Pp. 1–13.

Christ, Ronald. "Borges Justified: Notes and Texts Toward Stations of a Theme." In *Prose for Borges*, edited by Charles Newman and Mary Kinzie. Evanston, Ill.: Northwestern University Press, 1974. Pp. 46–81.

Cioran, E. M. *The Temptation to Exist*. Translated by Richard Howard. Chicago: Quadrangle Books, 1968.

Coe, Richard N. *Samuel Beckett*. New York: Grove Press, 1968.

Conrad, Joseph. *Chance*. New York: Norton Library, 1968.

————. *Joseph Conrad on Fiction*. Edited by Walter F. Wright. Lincoln: University of Nebraska Press, 1964.

————. *Lord Jim*. Edited by Thomas Moser. New York: W. W. Norton, 1968.

Cook, Albert. *The Meaning of Fiction*. Detroit, Mich.: Wayne State University Press, 1960.

Coover, Robert. "Beginnings." *Harper's* 244 (January 1972): 82–87.

————. *The Universal Baseball Association, Inc., J. Henry Waugh, Prop.* New York: New American Library, 1971.

Cortázar, Julio. *Blow-Up*. Translated by Paul Blackburn. New York: Collier Books, 1968.

Crankshaw, Edward. *Joseph Conrad: Some Aspects of the Art of the Novel*. London: John Lane, 1936.

Curle, Richard. *Joseph Conrad and His Characters*. London: Bowes and Bowes, 1957.

Daiches, David. *Virginia Woolf*. New York: New Directions, 1963.

Derrida, Jacques. *Speech and Phenomena and Other Essays on Husserl's Theory of Signs*. Translated by David B. Allison. Evanston, Ill.: Northwestern University Press, 1973.

Donato, Eugenio. "The Two Languages of Criticism." In *The Structuralist Controversy: The Languages of Criticism and the Sciences of Man*, edited by Richard Macksey and Eugenio Donato. Baltimore and London: Johns Hopkins Press, 1970. Pp. 89–97.

Esslin, Martin. "Introduction." *Samuel Beckett: A Collection of Critical Essays*.Englewood Cliffs, N.J.: Prentice-Hall, 1965. Pp. 1–15.

————. *The Theatre of the Absurd*. New York: Anchor Books, 1969.

Faulkner, William. *Absalom, Absalom!* Introduction by Harvey Breit. New York: Modern Library, 1951.

Federman, Raymond. "Beckettian Paradox." In *Samuel Beckett Now*, edited by Melvin J. Friedman. Chicago: University of Chicago Press, 1970. Pp. 103–17.

Forster, E. M. *Aspects of the Novel*. New York: Harcourt, Brace and World, 1927.

Foucault, Michel. *The Archaeology of Knowledge*. Translated by A. M. Sheridan Smith. New York: Pantheon Books, 1972.

————. *The Order of Things*. New York: Vintage Books, 1973.

Frank, Joseph. *The Widening Gyre*. Bloomington: Indiana University Press, 1968.

Gass, William. *Fiction and the Figures of Life*. New York: Vintage Books, 1972.

Genet, Jean. *Our Lady of the Flowers*. Translated by Bernard Frechtman. New York: Bantam Books, 1964.

Gibson, Walker. *Persona: A Style Study for Readers and Writers*. New York: Random House, 1969.

Girard, René. *Deceit, Desire and the Novel: Self and Other in Literary Structure*. Translated by Yvonne Freccero. Baltimore, Md.: Johns Hopkins Press, 1966.

Goffman, Erving. *Frame Analysis: An Essay on the Organization of Experience*. New York: Harper and Row, 1974.

————. *The Presentation of Self in Everyday Life*. Garden City, N.Y.: Doubleday, 1959.

Goldberg, S. L. *The Classical Temper: A Study of James Joyce's "Ulysses."* London: Chatto and Windus, 1963.

Golding, John. *Cubism: A History and Analysis, 1907–1914*. London: Faber and Faber, 1968.

Goldman, Arnold. *The Joyce Paradox*. Evanston, Ill.: Northwestern University Press, 1966.

Gombrich, E. H. *Art and Illusion*. New York: Pantheon Books, 1961.

Goodman, Nelson. "The Way the World Is." *Review of Metaphysics* 14 (1960): 48–56.

Gorsky, Susan. The Central Shadow: Characterization in *The Waves.*" *Modern Fiction Studies* 18 (Autumn 1972): 449–66.

Graham, J. W. "Point of View in *The Waves:* Some Services of the Style." *University of Toronto Quarterly* 39 (April 1970): 193–211.

Gras, Vernon W. "Introduction." *European Literary Theory and Practice*. Edited by Vernon W. Gras. New York: Delta Books, 1973. Pp. 1–23.

Gregg, Larry. "Slava Snabokovu." In *A Book of Things about Vladimir Nabokov*, edited by Carl R. Proffer. Ann Arbor, Mich.: Ardis, Inc., 1974. Pp. 104–21.

Groden, Michael L. "The Growth of James Joyce's Ulysses." Dissertation, Princeton University, 1975.

Guerard, Albert J. *Conrad the Novelist*. Cambridge, Mass.: Harvard University Press, 1958.

Guetti, James. *The Limits of Metaphor*. Ithaca, N.J.: Cornell University Press, 1967.

Guiguet, Jean. *Virginia Woolf and Her Works*. Translated by Jean Stewart. New York: Harcourt, Brace and World, 1965.

Hafley, James. *The Glass Roof: Virginia Woolf as Novelist*. New York: Russell and Russell, 1963.

Harkness, Bruce. "The Epigraph of Conrad's *Chance*." *Nineteenth-Century Fiction Studies* 9 (December 1954): 209–22.

Hartman, Geoffrey. *Beyond Formalism*. New Haven and London: Yale University Press, 1970.

Harvey, Lawrence E. *Samuel Beckett: Poet and Critic*. Princeton, N.J.: Princeton University Press, 1970.

Harvey, W. J. *Character and the Novel*. Ithaca, N.Y.: Cornell University Press, 1965.

Hayman, David. *Ulysses: The Mechanics of Meaning*. Englewood Cliffs, N.J.: Prentice-Hall, 1970.

Heath, Stephen. *The Nouveau Roman: A Study in the Practice of Writing*. Philadelphia: Temple University Press, 1972.

Hewitt, Douglas. *Conrad: A Reassessment*. Cambridge: Bowes and Bowes, 1952.

Hirsch E. D. Jr. *Validity in Interpretation*. New Haven and London: Yale University Press, 1967.

Holland, Norman. *The Dynamics of Literary Response*. New York: Oxford University Press, 1968.

Holthusen, Hans Egon. "Brecht's Dramatic Theory." In *Brecht: A Collection of Critical Essays* edited by Peter Demetz. Englewood Cliffs, N.J.: Prentice-Hall, 1962. Pp. 106–16.

Iser, Wolfgang. *The Implied Reader: Patterns of Communication in Prose Fiction from Bunyan to Beckett*. Baltimore, Md.: Johns Hopkins Press, 1974.

James, Henry. *The Future of the Novel*. Edited by Leon Edel. New York: Vintage Books, 1956.

Jameson, Fredric. *Marxism and Form: Twentieth Century Dialectical Theories of Literature*. Princeton, N.J.: Princeton University Press, 1971.

―――. "Three Methods in Sartre's Literary Criticism." In *Modern French Criticism*, edited by John K. Simon. Chicago: University of Chicago Press, 1972. Pp. 193–228.

―――. *The Prison-house of Language*. Princeton, N.J.: Princeton University Press, 1972.

Johnson, J. W. "Marlow and *Chance*: A Reappraisal." *Texas* Studies in *Language and Literature* 10 (Spring 1968): 91–105.

Josipovici, Gabriel. *The World and the Book*. London: Macmillan Press, 1971.

Joyce, James. *A Portrait of the Artist as a Young Man*. Edited by Chester G. Anderson. New York: Viking Press, 1968.

―――. *Dubliners: Text, Criticism and Notes*. Edited by Robert Scholes and A. Walton Litz. New York: Viking Press, 1967.

———. *Stephen Hero*. New York: New Directions, 1963.

———. *Ulysses*. New York: Modern Library, 1961.

Karl, Fredrick. *A Reader's Guide to Joseph Conrad*. New York: Noonday Press, 1960.

Kellman, Steven G. *The Self-Begetting Novel*. New York: Columbia University Press, 1980.

Kenner, Hugh. *A Reader's Guide to Samuel Beckett*. New York: Farrar, Straus, and Giroux, 1973.

———. *Dublin's Joyce*. Bloomington: University of Indiana Press, 1966.

———. *Flaubert, Joyce and Beckett: The Stoic Comedians*. Boston: Beacon Press, 1962.

———. *Samuel Beckett*. Berkeley and Los Angeles: University of California Press, 1968.

Kermode, Frank. *The Sense of an Ending*. London: Oxford University Press, 1968.

Khodasevich, Vladislav. "On Sirin." Translated by Michael Walker. *TriQuarterly* 17 (Winter 1970): 96–101.

Leavis, F. R. *The Great Tradition*. London: Chatto and Windus, 1948.

Lind, Ilse Dusoir. "Design and Meaning in *Absalom, Absalom!*" In *William Faulkner: Three Decades of Criticism*, edited by Frederick J. Hoffman and Olga Vickery. New York: Harcourt, Brace and World, 1963. Pp. 278–304.

Lodge, David. *The Novelist at the Crossroads*. Ithaca, N.Y.: Cornell University Press, 1971.

McConnell, Frank D. "'Death Among the Apple Trees': *The Waves* and the World of Things." In *Virginia Woolf: A Collection of Essays*, edited by Claire Sprague. Englewood Cliffs, N.J.: Prentice-Hall, 1971. Pp. 117–29.

Macdonald, Margaret. "The Language of Fiction." In *Contemporary Studies in Aesthetics*, edited by Francis J. Coleman. New York: McGraw-Hill, 1968.

Magny, Claude-Edmonde. *The Age of the American Novel: The Film Aesthetic of Fiction Between the Two Wars*. Translated by Eleanor Hochman. New York: Frederick Unger, 1972.

Man, Paul de. *Blindness and Insight: Essays in the Rhetoric of Contemporary Criticism*. New York: Oxford University Press, 1971.

Mann, Thomas. *Stories of Three Decades*. Translated by H. T. Lowe-Porter. New York: Modern Library, 1936.

Mayoux, Jean Jacques. "The Creation of the Real in William Faulkner." Translated by Frederick J. Hoffman. In *William Faulkner: Three Decades of Criticism*, edited by Frederick J. Hoffman and Olga Vickery. New York: Harcourt, Brace and World, 1963. Pp. 156 72.

Miller, J. Hillis. "The Critic as Host." In *Deconstruction and Criticism*, New York: Seabury Press, 1979. 217–53.

————. *Poets of Reality*. Cambridge, Mass.: Harvard University Press, 1966.

Murillo, L. A. *The Cyclical Night: Irony in James Joyce and Jorge Luis Borges*. Cambridge, Mass.: Harvard University Press, 1968.

Musil, Robert. *The Man Without Qualities*. Translated by Eithne Wilkins and Ernst Kaiser. New York: Capricorn Books, 1965.

Nabokov, Vladimir. *Bend Sinister*. New York: *Time-Life* Books, 1964.

————. *Despair*. New York: G. P. Putnam, 1966.

————. "Interview." In *Nabokov: The Man and the Work*, edited by L. S. Dembo. Madison: University of Wisconsin Press, 1967. Pp. 19–44.

————. *Lolita: A Screenplay*. New York: McGraw-Hill, 1974.

————. *Look at the Harlequins!* New York: McGraw-Hill, 1975.

————. *The Real Life of Sebastian Knight*. Norfolk, Conn.: New Directions, 1959.

————. *Tyrants Destroyed and Other Stories*. New York: McGraw-Hill, 1974.

Naremore, James. *The World Without a Self: Virginia Woolf and the Novel*. New Haven, Conn.: Yale University Press, 1973.

Nietzsche, Friedrich. *The Birth of Tragedy and The Genealogy of Morals*. Translated by Francis Golffing. Garden City, N.Y.: Anchor Books, 1956.

Nochlin, Linda. *Realism*. Baltimore, Md.: Penguin Books, 1971.

O'Brien, Josephine. *The Three-Fold Nature of Reality in the Novels of Virginia Woolf*. The Hague: Mouton and Co., 1965.

O'Connor, Frank. "Work in Progress." In *Dubliners: Text, Criticism and Notes*, edited by Robert Scholes and A. Walton Litz. New York: Viking Press, 1967. Pp. 304–15.

Peckham, Morse. *Rage for Chaos: Biology, Behavior, and the Arts*. New York: Schocken Books, 1967.

Poirier, Richard. *The Performing Self: Compositions and Decompositions in the Languages of Contemporary Life*. New York: Oxford University Press, 1971.

Poulet, Georges. "Criticism and the Experience of Interiority." In *The Structuralist Controversy: The Languages of Criticism and the Sciences of Man*, edited by Richard Macksey and Eugenio Donato. Baltimore, Md.: Johns Hopkins Press, 1972. Pp. 56–72.

Ricoeur, Paul. *Freud and Philosophy*. Translated by Denis Savage. New Haven, Conn.: Yale University Press, 1970.

Robbe-Grillet, Alain. *For a New Novel: Essays on Fiction*. Translated by Richard Howard. New York: Grove Press, 1965.

Robinson, Michael. *The Long Sonata of the Dead*. New York: Grove Press, 1969.

Roth, Philip. "Writing American Fiction." In *The American Novel since World War II*, edited by Marcus Klein. New York: Fawcett, 1969. Pp. 142–58.

Ryf, Robert S. *A New Approach to Joyce: The Portrait of the Artist as a Guidebook*. Berkeley and Los Angeles: University of California Press, 1962.

Said, Edward. "Abecedarium Culturae." In *Modern French Criticism*, edited by John K. Simon. Chicago: University of Chicago Press, 1972. Pp. 341–92.

———. *Joseph Conrad and the Fiction of Autobiography*. Cambridge, Mass.: Harvard University Press, 1966.

Sarraute, Nathalie. *The Age of Suspicion*. Translated by Marie Jolas. New York: George Braziller, 1963.

Sartre, Jean-Paul. *Saint Genet: Comedian and Martyr*. Translated by Bernard Frechtman. New York: George Braziller, 1963.

Scholes, Robert. "Metafiction." *Iowa Review* 1 (Fall 1970): 100–115.

———. *Structural Fabulation*. South Bend, Ind.: University of Notre Dame, 1975.

——— and Robert Kellogg. *The Nature of Narrative*. New York: Oxford University Press, 1966.

Shklovsky, Victor. "Art as Technique." *Russian Formalist Criticism: Four Essays*. Translated by Lee T. Lemon and Marion J. Reis. Lincoln: University of Nebraska Press, 1965. Pp. 5–24.

Slatoff, Walter J. *Quest for Failure: A Study of William Faulkner*. Ithaca, N.Y.: Cornell University Press, 1960.

Sontag, Susan. *Against Interpretation*. New York: Dell, 1969.

Spencer, Sharon. *Space, Time, and Structure in the Modern Novel*. New York: New York University Press, 1971.

Stern, J. P. *On Realism*. London and Boston: Routledge and Kegan Paul, 1973.

Stevens, Wallace. *The Palm at the End of the Mind*. Edited by Holly Stevens. New York: Vintage Books, 1972.

Sturrock, John. *The French New Novel*. New York: Oxford University Press, 1969.

Sypher, Wylie. *The Loss of Self*. New York: Random House, 1960.

———. *Rococo to Cubism in Art and Literature*. New York: Random House, 1960.

Tindall, William Y. "Apology for Marlow." In *From Jane Austen to Joseph Conrad*, edited by Robert C. Rathburn and Martin Stein, Jr. Minneapolis: University of Minnesota Press, 1958.

Trilling, Lionel. *Sincerity and Authenticity*. Cambridge, Mass.: Harvard University Press, 1972.

Vickery, Olga W. *The Novels of William Faulkner*. Baton Rouge: Louisiana State University Press, 1959.

Waggoner, Hyatt H. *William Faulkner: From Jefferson to the World*. Lexington: University of Kentucky Press, 1959.

Watt, Ian. *The Rise of the Novel*. Berkeley and Los Angeles: University of California Press, 1965.

Woolf, Virginia. *A Writer's Diary*. New York: Harcourt, Brace, and Jovanovich, 1953.

———. *The Captain's Deathbed and Other Essays*. New York: Harcourt, Brace and World, 1950.

———. *Jacob's Room/The Waves*. New York: Harcourt, Brace and World, 1959.

———. *The Second Common Reader*. New York: Harcourt, Brace and World, 1960.

Zoellner, Robert H. "Faulkner's Prose Style in *Absalom, Absalom!*" *American Literature* 30 (January 1959): 486–502.

Index